Penguin Books
My Life with Nye

My Life With Nye is the story of a remarkable marriage, ~~~~~~
also a famous political partnership. Although Jennie Lee and
Aneurin Bevan both came from mining communities, their
backgrounds were rather different: whereas Nye left school at
fourteen to work in the Welsh coalfields, and was largely
self-educated, the young Jennie enjoyed a happy and relatively
sheltered childhood in Fifeshire, with the full benefits of a good
Scottish schooling. But in 1926, when she was a student at
Edinburgh University, the General Strike closed the mines, and
her father was out of work for four months. 'It was the struggle in
the coalfields in 1926', she writes, 'that shaped the whole of my
after-life more than any other experience.'

After some years working at grass-roots level in the local
Independent Labour Party, Jennie Lee was elected to Parliament
as the Member for North Lanark in 1929, and soon made her
mark in Westminster as a combative back-bencher with a quick
wit and attractive personality. It was during this period that she
first met Aneurin Bevan. Though involved with a married MP,
Frank Wise, at the time, she recognized in Nye a fire and vision
that matched her own. When they married in 1934 they had
already fought many political battles together. Their unique
partnership lasted until Nye's tragically early death from cancer in
1960. Later, during the 1964–70 Parliament, Jennie Lee as the
Minister responsible for the Arts took a pioneering step in creating
the Open University. She became a Privy Councillor in 1966 and
was made a life peer in 1970. Her other publications include
Tomorrow is a New Day and *Russia, Our Ally*.

Jennie Lee

My Life
with Nye

Penguin Books

Penguin Books Ltd, Harmondsworth,
Middlesex, England
Penguin Books, 625 Madison Avenue,
New York, New York 10022, U.S.A.
Penguin Books Australia Ltd, Ringwood,
Victoria, Australia
Penguin Books Canada Ltd, 2801 John Street,
Markham, Ontario, Canada L3R 1B4
Penguin Books (N.Z.) Ltd, 182–190 Wairau Road,
Auckland 10, New Zealand

First published by Jonathan Cape Ltd 1980
Published in Penguin Books 1981

Made and printed in Great Britain by
Cox & Wyman Ltd, Reading
Set in Linotron 202 Plantin

Contents

Illustrations

Acknowledgements

The author and publisher are grateful to Weidenfeld and Nicolson for permission to reprint the account Israel Sieff gives of his friendship with Aneurin Bevan in his *Memoirs* (Weidenfeld and Nicolson 1970). The description of the author's mother by Benn Levy comes from his foreword to Jennie Lee's book, *This Great Journey* (MacGibbon and Kee 1963), which was originally published as *Tomorrow is a New Day* in 1939. Other quotations are taken from Aneurin Bevan's own book, *In Place of Fear* (Heinemann 1952), and Michael Foot's biography, *Aneurin Bevan 1945–1960* (Volume Two, Davis-Poynter 1973); also *Inside the Left* by Fenner Brockway (Allen and Unwin 1942), *Lord Beaverbrook* by AJP Taylor (Hamish Hamilton 1972), and *Motives of Proteus* by José Rodó (Allen and Unwin 1929). The *Guardian* kindly gave permission for the use of the last interview with Aneurin Bevan.

The following pictures are reproduced from the author's own collection: 1, 2, 3, 4, 5, 10 and 11. For permission to reproduce other pictures the author and publisher are grateful to BBC Hulton Picture Library, 8, 9; Keystone Press Agency, 16; Popperfoto, 12, 13; Press Association, 14, 17; S and G Press Agency, 7; Syndication International, 15; Lord Wise, 6.

The cartoons appear by kind permission of the *Daily Express*, pp. 205, (pocket cartoon by Osbert Lancaster), 239, 246; Illingworth and the *Daily Mail*, London, pp. 214, 232; *Punch*, p. 303; the *Sunday Express*, p. 228. The publisher has been unable to trace the copyright holder of the cartoon on p. 209.

Introduction

It is nonsense for any of us to believe we can recall the earlier years of our life with any degree of accuracy unless helped by a great deal of reliable documentation. It is my good fortune that a number of my friends kept most of my letters and that these have recently been returned to me. Also, in times of doubt and stress, I very often set out in diary form problems I was trying to solve. It is not just a matter of recalling names, dates and events. That is only the external framework. More importantly those old writings in one's own handwriting prevent any falsifying of the emotions roused by past experiences. My emotions at times were pretty violent but I have had either to state the truth or not write at all.

Aneurin Bevan was fond of quoting, 'This is my truth, now tell me yours.' I do not have his philosophical turn of mind. I am a more primitive type. Throughout, therefore, I have been careful to let him talk for himself wherever possible.

In January 1979, when I had just about finished ploughing through a chaotic mass of letters, articles, documents of various kinds, I reread *In Place of Fear*, first published in 1952, and *Tomorrow is a New Day*, published in 1939. I hardly needed to reread *In Place of Fear* for I had shared with Nye its policies and philosophies. My own early autobiography I found a useful *aide-mémoire*, more for what it does not say than for what it says.

In going back through the years what I have most wanted to do is bury for good some of the vicious nonsense written about Nye during his lifetime in order to discredit all he stood for. Once begun I found it impossible to separate the private from the public man. I had to write about both or neither. Nor could I write about Nye in a vacuum. To give a true picture of him I had also to write about our families and friends, about myself, and about the influences that shaped our lives.

When Nye came to London as a young Member of Parliament following the General Election of May 1929 he brought with him bitter memories of his early life in the Welsh coalfields. I was brought up in Scotland in an environment that was partly similar to his and partly quite different. It was my father, and still more my grandfather, who suffered all the hardships. I belonged to the generation that inherited all they had fought so hard for, above all free books and schooling right up to university level, with quite a bit of help available from public funds even in university years. I had everything going for me. Nye had to fight every step of the way. My original intention was to begin writing from 1929 onwards, when we first met. But that was not feasible. By then I was twenty-four; Nye was seven years older. To make any kind of sense I had to begin by telling something of our early formative years.

I am deeply indebted to Michael Foot for the skill and devotion that illumines his official biography of Aneurin Bevan. As he has set out in considerable detail Nye's early life in Tredegar, I leave writing about those years until we had won through to a secure personal relationship.

Nye was fond of saying, 'All history is gossip and the least reliable of all is history in the form of biography or autobiography.' One of several reasons why I have resisted until now every effort to persuade me to add to what Michael has written has been my awareness of Nye's sceptical attitude to this kind of writing.

At the moment, memoirs about the Second World War, including its causes and consequences, continue to pour from the printing presses, politicians and soldiers vying with one another as each presents his own highly personal version of events. All I can promise is that having allowed myself to be overborne by Michael and other friends who insist that there was much that should be known about Nye that only I could tell, I have not altered by so much as a comma any of the documents from which I quote. My opinions and prejudices are another matter. They mirror the world as it appeared to me through many stormy decades. I make no other claim for them than that.

1. The Old Arcade

I had been scrubbed from top to toe and was wearing my best Sunday clothes although it was a weekday. But not an ordinary weekday. My friend, Mr Eisemann, had promised to take me on holiday with him, and now the great day had arrived.

I am remembering a summer morning in 1910. I was born on 3 November 1904 so I was not yet six years old. It is curious how vivid some memories remain while others vanish entirely. My friend and I travelled from Cowdenbeath, a Fifeshire mining town, over the Forth Bridge and on to Glasgow. The journey must have been exciting but it is a complete blank in my memory. What I do vividly recall was my impatience to be on our way. I was very conscious, too, of all my finery, my white starched coat with its broad cape, my wide-brimmed straw hat adorned with flowers and ribbon, my cream parasol trimmed with white lace – hardly an appropriate outfit for a small girl setting out on a railway journey, but these were different times.

Mr Eisemann's home was an upstairs flat in a Glasgow tenement. If you know Glasgow you will not make the mistake of thinking that all tenement buildings are squalid, depressing slums. In different parts of the city they reflect widely varying standards and lifestyles. George Eliot, after visiting Glasgow for the first time, wrote to a friend describing how much she had enjoyed the comfort of 'a cosy nest in the sky'. That is how I remember the Eisemann home, and most of all the warmth of the welcome for both of us from Mrs Eisemann.

My friend was a commercial traveller who, when doing business in Cowdenbeath, stayed overnight with my parents in the Arcade Hotel. John Pollock, my grandmother's brother, owned the hotel along with the shops and theatre in the Arcade below. My grandmother managed the hotel for him but, when she became too ill to carry on, my parents were persuaded to take over the running of both hotel and theatre. They stayed on for five years after my grandmother's death. So from the age of three to eight the hotel was my home and the Arcade below my playground. These were strenuous years for my parents. Uncle John Pollock disliked spending money on essential maintenance and repairs. My mother in particular was endlessly busy cooking, cleaning and serving. But I was very contented; none of their worries reached me. And it was my good fortune that my parents were not sufficiently well off to imprison me in a nursery with a nanny as gaoler. From what I learned in later years of the unhappy childhood inflicted by many well-to-do parents on their young families, I am doubly thankful that I escaped all that.

The Arcade was my nursery. Sometimes I would follow my father around in the theatre. Or I might decide to call on Miss Maggie Corrins, whose shop sold toys, papers, sweets and cigarettes. Then there was my great-grandmother's second-hand furniture shop, also inside the Arcade. She seemed always to be sitting in her armchair by the side of a great glowing coal fire in the back-room. But she obviously did move sometimes for one of my most searing memories of her was the time we went to the theatre together. The play was a melodrama of some sort. At the moment when the murderer was creeping up behind his intended victim my great-grandmother, Jennie Pollock, rose from her seat in one of the front rows of the stalls and, pointing at the stage, called out, 'There's the blackguard, there's the blackguard.'

Even in the last years of her life she was a forceful personality. Her trade was buying and selling second-hand furniture. The goods were bought mainly in Edinburgh salerooms and brought to Cowdenbeath by train, where her numerous grandchildren had to be waiting to carry by hand objects that could not be crammed into her pony and trap. She was so enormous that she needed most of the space for herself. In all her long life my mother never forgot the shame of having to walk through Cowdenbeath High Street carrying a naked chamber pot that all the world could see. A modern child might think nothing of it, but in those far off very different days, this experience so agonized a shy, sensitive youngster that even at the age of eighty she still talked of it.

It may sound wholly irresponsible of my parents to have allowed a young daughter to wander around so many public places without proper supervision, especially as my gentle, fair-haired, blue-eyed baby brother, two and a half years younger than I, began trotting at my heels as soon as he could walk. But it was not like that at all. We were well cared for, as we had friends everywhere. Maggie Corrins told me years later how much she had enjoyed our company and our conversation, while we delighted in ducking beneath the shop counter to the delectable area behind, with its toys and sweets and a warm fire in cold weather. It was just as agreeable visiting Great-Grannie Pollock. It may be that she was growing lonely in her old age. Anyhow, we saw only her gentler side and were allowed to rummage among her treasures with no more than a mild admonition to be careful not to break anything.

The people staying in the hotel upstairs were mainly commercial travellers or touring theatre companies. My mother was a great favourite with everyone, not only for her savoury soups, steak and kidney pies, tripe and onions and a dozen other favourite dishes, but for her unfailing good temper and friendly ways. No doubt a serious snag for some thirsty travellers was that ours was a temperance hotel, but there were ways of coping with this without publicly breaking the law. The first time I saw a glass of red wine was in Florrie Ford's bedroom. I was fascinated by the rich colour of the wine and curious to try it. She good-naturedly allowed me to, and I can still remember the horrible bitter taste of that first sip.

Another of the leading ladies of the theatre had a motherly bosom and liked clutching me to it, which I definitely did not like. In the theatre in the evening, in shimmering low-cut evening dress, she thrilled her audience, young and old, with sentimental love songs.

Your eyes have told me all,
Your secret now is mine

was a great favourite. Goodness knows in what exotic ways they may have imagined her spending her leisure hours. I could have told them. She seemed to be perpetually knitting turbans for me and inevitably they were too big. I can still feel the hairy wool falling into my eyes.

A more high and mighty couple who frequently performed in the theatre and stayed in the hotel were Dr Bodie and his wife. They brought with them their adopted daughter, Dolly, who, wearing a black velvet little Lord Fauntleroy suit, sang, 'Don't Go Down the Mine, Daddy'. No doubt sentimental tears were shed by some of the audience, but it was the comic parodies that were later sung by that tough as well as tender-hearted mining community that I enjoyed most. When my mother became engaged she received a trousseau from Dr Bodie and his wife of the finest Irish linen, richly embroidered and laced with pale blue ribbon. I have good reason to remember that wedding gift, for when I was about eighteen and preparing to leave home to become a student at Edinburgh University, it was unearthed from somewhere and given to me. I could not hurt my mother by refusing to accept it, but this was the pyjama age. I would not have been seen dead in the flowing nightdress, the flounced petticoat, the camisole and knickers that my mother had 'laid away' so carefully all those years.

My father then, and throughout the whole of his life, had a passion for music. Opera, the old music-hall melodies, *Elijah*, the *Messiah*, children's songs – he delighted in them all and had a song for every mood. He did not have a good singing voice but that did not deter him. He just enjoyed singing. When the Carl Rosa or D'Oyly Carte Companies were due in our part of Scotland, my father was quick off the mark to secure every free date they could offer. We were an acceptable halfway house between Edinburgh to the south of us and Perth to the north. My father was not the only opera enthusiast. Whether it was Gilbert and Sullivan or Verdi, Mozart or Puccini, the companies that came to our mining town to play to mining audiences could depend on a full house. But I preferred Tommy Torrance, who shuffled on to the stage, dragging a toy dog behind him and singing, 'I'm happy for life, I've lost my wife, and found a rare wee dog.' Or, better still, there was the ventriloquist's doll that was very talkative and friendly, except once when I tried to pull it off its master's knee on to my own. Then it said to me, indignantly, 'Don't do that.' Another special friend was the tall, smiling Chinaman who allowed me to tug at his long pigtail as hard as I could in order to convince myself that it was real.

Looking back I now know that many of these strolling players had little or no settled home life. My mother gave them more than bed and board. She made a home from home for them. And at five or six years of age I took it for granted that their main purpose in visiting us was to join my small brother and myself in all kinds of games. Even Uncle John Pollock was kindly enough when he paid his annual visit to fish in Loch Leven and collect his rents, but he had picked up in the south the alien habit of wanting to kiss my mother and me when he arrived. That was an embarrassment. We were not a kissing breed, nor yet given to easy terms of endearment. The love given me by my parents was total, it was the air I breathed, but we did not go in for a lot of messy demonstrativeness.

After five years of hotel-keeping, my father decided he had had enough. He quarrelled violently with John Pollock. At the time I was too young to know much about it, but I sensed then and ever afterwards my father's cold contempt for, as far as I know, the only successful capitalist in our family. Part of the trouble no doubt must have been seeing my mother working so hard with so little return. When my parents left the hotel, my mother's sister Betty, Mrs William Steel, took over the management. One day when I called, Uncle John Pollock was paying his annual visit; the great man was always given a private sitting-room as well as his bedroom. My aunt, wearing her best black satin apron came into the kitchen, where I was sitting on the floor playing with my two baby cousins. 'Uncle John', she said rather breathlessly, 'wants to see you.' 'Tell Uncle John if he wants to talk to me he knows where to find me ,' I said. I had my own score to settle with our rich relative as well as thinking I would please my father by being rude to him. While we were still living in the hotel he had asked me to show him my story book. That I did and read to him about a little girl who was given a pair of silver skates. Roller skating was then a popular craze, and the Arcade hall for a short time was converted into a skating-rink. I would venture to the edge of the rink and have skates fitted on, but I never had the courage to go circling round on my own as I would have loved to do. At seven I preferred to hold on to the hand of someone older and more experienced. Uncle John promised to send me a pair of silver skates. I went off to school and boasted my head off, but the skates never came.

All the same, even before I got home I knew I had done wrong. I decided to say nothing to my mother, and before my father came home from work I had cooled off so much that I thought it just as well not to tell him either. Like Joan of Arc, I heard voices. I could hear my father saying as he had done more than once before, 'Take time to think. There is a right way and a wrong way of going about things.' My father had perfect control, perfect discipline over his children, yet he never smacked us. If we were up to something that tried our mother beyond endurance she would utter the dire threat, 'And if you do that again, I'll tell your da.' That sobered us. We could not bear to be in his black books.

The hustle and bustle of hotel life did not suit my father. He was glad to return to his old job in the pits and to the comfort of his own private fireside. He was fond of saying that the only thing he was not prepared to do underground was take his shirt off. That was an innocent enough bit of one-upmanship, as he was not suited to hard manual labour either physically or temperamentally. He was a slightly built, good-looking man with a vivid interest in public affairs, trade unionism, theological controversy and the technical side of mining. His grey Irish eyes were his most expressive feature. They would sparkle with fun and mischief when he was up to some prank, and at times say all the endearing things his stubborn Scotch tongue would not utter. One day, when he came home from work, I remember listening with pride and approval to his laughing account of the mistake made by a visiting group of geologists from Edinburgh. He had taken them around and answered all their questions, so when leaving they said they would like to say goodbye to him and thank him. They had got the impression that he was a senior pit official. In fact, although he enjoyed coaching young fellows for their mining certificates, he remained by choice a deputy, that is a safety man. In those years of crude class war between collier and coalowner you had to be on one side or the other. There could be no shilly-shallying. In some coalfields deputies were not accepted as members of the miners' union, but in Scotland they were freely admitted if they were willing to abide by union rules.

My father had no doubts about where he stood. He was back where he felt he belonged and where he wanted to be.

2. Schooldays

When we left the hotel and moved into a four-roomed rented house, there were too many new exciting things happening for me to have the slightest wish to go back to the Old Arcade. My first discovery was that we now had a garden. Behind the Arcade there was only a piece of derelict waste land with a stinking burn running throught it. Now we had a beautiful garden full of summer flowers. I thought it a good idea to pick a generous bunch to take to school for my teacher. My good-natured mother was very angry when she saw what I had done and scolded me with unusual vehemence; those white blossoms would later have given us strawberries. I liked flowers, but I liked strawberries too, and as much as anything I was grieved to have upset my kind mother.

She made 61 Foulford Street, where we now lived, very comfortable inside, but there was no back door. As the house was built on quite a steep slope, this was an idiotic omission. In the rear were a wash-house and coal cellar, with ceilings high enough to make them usable for all kinds of purposes. But Mother was for ever having to run up and down a narrow draughty close carrying coal, household refuse, clothes to be washed, and washed clothes to be carried up again. I envied and admired the house next door where Mr Brown, the jeweller, lived. They had made their wash-house into a proper bathroom, and had an inside ladder leading down to it. They owned their house; we only rented ours, so we had to improvise. Ma saw to it that when Dad came home from work he would find waiting for him in the wash-house hot towels, his changing clothes, a large Victorian tub to wash in, and lots of hot water from the boiler in the corner. On rainy days this became a favourite play-room.

My brother was now old enough to go to school. I have only the vaguest recollections of my first school, but I liked very positively the new one we now attended. Its most attractive feature was that it was near enough home for us to be able to rush there during the forenoon interval, knowing that Mother would be waiting with a large roll for each of us filled with home-made jam or Lyle's golden syrup. When I was about nine years old a confusing incident at school caught me entirely unawares. I was wearing a blue serge sailor suit that had been specially made for me. There was no difficulty in those days in finding women only too willing to eke out their husband's meagre earnings by doing spare-time dressmaking. The usual thing was for our Sunday best clothes to become in time weekday wear, but whether I was growing too fast, or whatever the reason, here I was coming to school wearing a brand-new dress. At the mid-morning break, when we tumbled thankfully out to the playground, some of my friends gathered around me, gently touching my smart sailor suit. They were wearing for the most part the cast-offs of older sisters, or whatever their mothers could find for them. Although no one showed any sign of envy or resentment, I felt embarrassed. Something seemed to be wrong somewhere.

Soon afterwards another incident occurred, and the two may have been related though I cannot be sure of that. Girls in a higher class made a habit of monopolizing a highly desirable shed in the playground, a shed open in the front. I thought we younger ones ought to be allowed to play there too, especially on rainy days. So, greatly daring, I led the way through the skipping rope of the older girls, disorganizing their game. At this point the school bell rang so we all had to hurry back to our classrooms, but at the close of the afternoon when we came out of school I found the leader of the older girls lying in wait for me. She had her gang around her. I had no one. My friends had gone off home, not knowing I had been waylaid. I was to be taught a lesson. So I was punched and pummelled, my clothes torn and, too small to fight back, all I could do was try to escape. I somehow got away at last, and with terror giving me wings I fled up the steep brae to my home, my tormentors following all the way, shouting and jeering. I was badly shaken, as much by the indignity of the whole affair as by the pain. But what was it all about? The older girl came from one of the poorest parts of the town. Had she been incensed not just by my 'cockiness', but by my fine new dress? Would she have acted quite so viciously if I had been poorer and shabbier than herself as well as younger? Or would I have got off in that case with a mild cuffing?

You can learn a lot in the playground and maybe still more in the classroom. The 'smelly' children – that is those who came to school with their clothes or themselves unwashed – were in the front rows. We brighter pupils, all clean and neat, were in the back rows, and as my father taught me my school sums and much else a year ahead of schedule, lessons did not worry me. Were we bright ones so intrinsically superior? Would we still have been 'top-of-the-class' material if we had had no one at home to guide and encourage us and see to it that we left for school warm and well-shod and with ample good food in our hungry young stomachs? How many of the 'dunces' who exhausted the patience of even the more sympathetic teachers had sight or hearing defects, and were not seeing clearly what was written on the blackboard or hearing properly what was said? Of course there were able pupils who overcame every kind of discouragement at home; and there were well-cared-for ones who were bone stupid. But there is no doubt that home influences helped or hindered us very considerably.

One day our teacher ordered us to clasp our hands above our heads and make no noise while she bent over her desk, making up her register. Anyone caught talking was warned of dire punishment to come. When she looked up I was one of the culprits, so, along with the others, was ordered to the front of the class to line up for the 'strap'. As I walked down the centre passageway from my perch in the back row I had to think and act quickly. The exit door was straight ahead of me. All I had to do was reach it, rush home, and leave my father to deal with the situation. I never for one moment doubted that he would be on my side and I knew that it was Miss Bowman, my teacher, who would have to answer to him. At the very least he would read the Riot Act to her. But I liked my teacher and I sensed she disliked having to humiliate her best pupil. I did not really want to get her into trouble, so I did not dart out of the classroom. No punishment could possibly have been milder. We were each doing our best to be considerate to the other.

Apart from an occasional, highly charged emotional incident such as this, schooldays were happy and peaceful. The small 'sweetie shop' just outside the gate was very popular. On Saturday I had twopence pocket-money. One penny went at once on the purchase of a fairy-tale. My brother bought a 'Comic Cuts'. This left another penny that gave me access to the sweetie shop on four different days: for a farthing you could pick and choose from all kinds of delights. Of course, if in an expansive mood you stood treat to a chum, your penny did not go so far. My father, like his children, was fond of sweets. So often, on a Saturday afternoon, once his meeting with ILP friends in the back-room of Mr Garvie's bookshop was over, he would cross the High Street to Low's, the grocers. From Low's he would bring home toasted marshmallows and whipped cream walnuts, saying as he plomped them on the kitchen table, 'Now, even-handed justice.' That meant all three of us having the same number of sweets. Sometimes on a Saturday afternoon, if he had no meeting to attend, I would walk with him down Cowdenbeath High Street. What I had to do was manoeuvre him into the bookshop near to the Old Arcade. I thought I was managing craftily and secretly, but of course he knew what I was about – I was longing to go inside for it had a wonderful collection of the kind of storybooks I coveted. He would go to the counter on the left to buy a newspaper or some other small purchase and I would be on hands and knees on the opposite side of the shop, for the two bottom rows of the bookshelves there were packed with children's books. Across the High Street there was a small lending library. I disliked it as much as I loved the bright bookshop with all its new books. The library had a horrible musty smell and its stock of old books was sadly in need of replacements.

My father's favourite bookshop was owned by his blind friend, Mr Garvie, but it was some years before I appreciated the kind of books he stocked. I did get round to it later on. We became good friends. I enjoyed reading to him from *A History of the Working Classes throughout the Ages* and listening to what he had to say. He provided the kind of literature the book-hungry activists of the local Labour and Trade Union Movement could find nowhere else. But my earliest memories of this remarkable, vibrantly intelligent man are not of the shop below, but of his home above. He had an ordinary piano, and also a pianola in his sitting-room. I would wind up the one, and prop my music on the other. Then off I would go, my pride being to keep perfect time. Simplified versions of the popular airs from *Tannhäuser, Il Trovatore, Aida*, 'Poet and Peasant', 'Nights of Gladness', Viennese waltzes, and lots of other tuneful pieces were drummed out with military precision. For anyone who doesn't believe me, I shall produce the certificate I received for piano playing after being taken across the Forth Bridge to Edinburgh to sit an examination. My music lessons began at a very early age. I was more fascinated by the tick-tock, tick-tock of the metronome on the top of our piano and a small packet of sweets put there to encourage me on my way than by the noises I could produce from the keyboard. I had not the slightest musical gift but my parents were good triers. They somehow managed to pay for piano lessons. The only return I ever made them was earning a bit of pocket-money by playing at the Saturday afternoon cinema performances in the Arcade Hall. Under new management, it was entirely given over to the new craze for 'pictures'. Young Mr Slora, the son of the new owner, played the violin. I played the piano. I would be about fifteen or sixteen by then; I don't think young Slora was much older. Whatever other qualifications we lacked, we were both young and strong. You needed to be to hold your own against the rowdy, restless children who crowded into the 'picture house'.

As children our weekdays were a routine affair. Off to school every morning. But Sunday had its special rituals and was every bit as pleasant as Saturday. My father was so used to rising very early in the morning that even on Sunday he was up betimes. My brother and I, when we heard him coming to wake us, would pull the bedclothes over our heads and pretend to be asleep. But it was all a game. We knew the bedclothes would be whisked off; there would be an enjoyable pillow fight, then we were ready to get up, for we knew there were good things to come. Sunday morning was the one morning we could all have breakfast together. It was not just toast or rolls and tea as during the week. Instead there might be eggs, bacon, sausages, or better still, a rich savoury Irish stew. We were allowed to dip our bread into the gravy. That was our favourite Sunday morning breakfast. On those Sundays when we had a visiting ILP speaker, my brother and I would be on our own on Sunday afternoon. But when there was no speaker to be talked to and looked after, we went off with our father to explore the countryside. Sometimes we took the tram to Lochore, then walked to the edge of Loch Leven. Sometimes we took the tram to Kelty, then we would climb Benarty Hill. From the top we could look down on Loch Leven. We saw more than a grey speck of an island in the middle of the Loch, which was all that was visible to the naked eye. Our young heads were full of the legend of Mary, Queen of Scots, who had been imprisoned on the island. We mourned for her and devoutly believed that Queen Elizabeth of England was a wicked monster, our Queen a martyred saint.

At the age of seven or eight, I loved Mary, Queen of Scots, and Bonnie Prince Charlie, and I was the sworn foe of the German upstarts who had usurped our Scottish throne.

Wha' the de'il hae we gotten for a King,
But a wee wee German lairdie.
When we went o'er to fetch him hame,
He was diggin' in his kail yaird gairdie.

We were not taught this most satisfying song in school, but picked it up from somewhere and enjoyed singing it in the playground.

A year or two later I was told in history lessons in school all about the 'divine right of kings' and why King Charles I had to have his head cut off. I could no longer idolize the Stuarts. But I had discovered Robbie Burns and learned to recite, word perfect, the whole of 'A Man's a Man for A' That'.

A king can mak' a belted knight,
A marquis, duke, and a' that,
But an honest man's abune his might,
Guid faith, ye maunna fa' that.

First thing every morning in school we sang a hymn and chanted in unison, 'Our Father, which art in Heaven, hallowed be thy name, thy Kingdom come, thy will be done on earth as it is in Heaven.' It took me some time to realize that although my mother's family, the Greigs and the Pollocks, were Protestant, and I attended the Protestant school, Grandfather Lee was a devout Catholic. Devout, but not bigoted, for although his sons, one after the other as they became old enough to think for themselves, became humanists, there was no break in kindly family relations. The father of one of my school friends was a kirk elder and on Sunday went to church wearing a tail coat and 'lum' hat. These were impressive status symbols and I longed to see my father wearing his tail coat and 'lum' hat. But although he possessed both, for some inexplicable reason, his were left hanging in his wardrobe and not worn even to funerals

When wrestling with these theological problems there was one good deed I could certainly do. I could save my young brother from harm by hearing him say his prayers every evening. Before slipping into bed he would be gently made to kneel on the cold floor and repeat after me:

This night as I lie down to sleep,
I pray the Lord my soul to keep,
And if I die before I wake,
I pray the Lord my soul to take.

It took me quite a few years to outlive this religious phase but in time I became fascinated with R. G. Ingersoll's *Lectures and Essays*, Li Hung Chang's *Scrap-book* compiled by Sir Hiram Stevens Maxim, pamphlets by Charles Darwin and Thomas Huxley – the kind of books on my father's bookshelves that earnest seekers after truth read in the early years of the century when preoccupation with theological controversy was real and deep.

My parents and grandparents lived next door to one another when I was an infant. I am sure of the date – 1905 – for Charles Lee, my father's older brother, left for America when I was still what my grandmother called 'a wee babby'. Apparently he was fond of his brother's child and would carry me from cottage to cottage. This was the memory my grandmother recalled every time I went to see her. I was her calendar. 'How old are ye noo, Jen?' she would ask; then I would be told for the hundredth time how Charlie carried me 'frae hoose to hoose'. With three other sons and seven daughters you might think that her memories of her first-born would in time have grown dim. But that did not happen. The mystery that haunted her and was never solved was that her son had written regularly and sent home a modest money gift when he could for several years, then silence. He was a keen socialist. Was he killed in some labour dispute? Had he died of some natural illness in circumstances where no one knew him, or knowing, did not take the trouble to write to his parents? I was also told again and again of how Charlie and another young collier saved up twenty-five Scotch pounds to buy a telescope. 'What were they looking for?' she would ask. She could never understand and never got over her feeling of amazement at this wanton way of spending hard-earned money. When my father followed his older brother in abandoning his father's religion, the feeling between father and son was so charged with emotion that, although living next door to one another and meeting daily, they wrote letters to one another instead of arguing directly.

By the time I was of school age I enjoyed going to our Socialist Sunday School, held on Sunday forenoon as that was the one day our elders were free to teach us. Then, in the afternoon our favourite outing was to take the tram all the way to Dunfermline. This was the one time Mother would come with us as she had friends there she liked to visit. First we would stroll through Pittencrieff Glen, where the squirrels more than earned the nuts we brought them by the delight they gave sitting up on their hind legs cracking the nuts between two paws. Then there was the band to listen to and after that off to tea with our grandparents. My father's youngest sister, Helen, who kept house for her parents, would be spreading the table cloth and preparing a sumptuous high tea as soon as we entered the door. Home-baked sponge cake with caraway seeds was one of grandmother's specialities. Even better were her cream buns generously sprinkled with sugared caraway seeds.

Occasionally when visiting Dunfermline, instead of having tea with our grandparents, we called on Mr and Mrs Jim Beveridge. Mr Beveridge had had a prosperous painter's shop in Lochgelly, but he was an ardent Guild Socialist, and sold his business in order to take charge of a local government direct-labour scheme. It was not a success, so after struggling on to the point of bankruptcy he had finally to take another job. His home was now in Dunfermline, and it was there that for the first time I saw bookshelves packed with books in foreign languages. He enjoyed reading in French, Spanish, German, and Italian, with a dictionary in constant use as he was not proficient in any of those languages. But he got along, however slowly, and found this a pleasant recreation. At home we had a copy of Robert Tressell's *The Ragged Trousered Phi-lanthropist*, but it was Jim who brought it alive for me. Just as my father knew all there was to know about the working of coal pits, he had an equally wide-ranging first-hand knowledge of the building trade. We became great friends. As I grew older I paid visits on my own, returning home hugging several of his precious books – his English ones. These I never failed to return so that I could borrow more.

In those years my father, as chairman of the local ILP, had the responsibility of finding overnight accommodation for visiting speakers. That was not easy, but he solved the problem by persuading Mother to put a bed in the corner of our parlour. The Browns next door did not have to have a bed in their parlour, but then, they were not crusaders out to save the world, as my father was. The weekend speaker was expected to talk to us children in our Socialist Sunday School, on Sunday forenoon, as well as addressing a public meeting in the evening. Some of those dedicated propagandists do not stand out clearly in my memory, but others were inspired teachers. The stories they told! Where would I ever have heard Oscar Wilde's *The Happy Prince* in an ordinary school? Or learned to sing:

We are children but one day
We'll be big, and strong and say
None shall slave and none shall slay.
Comrades all together.

We were thoroughly indoctrinated with a wealth of idealism that inspired some of us for the rest of our lives. Looking back, I can find nothing to deplore and everything to praise in all that we were taught in our Sunday School.

When we left the hotel, one of our boarders, a young man who had opened a jeweller's shop in the High Street, came with us. Mr Russell was at that time a lonely bachelor, so an easy prey. My brother and I made sure that he knew exactly what we wanted when special occasions such as Christmas or birthdays were approaching. One of my proudest possessions was the wrist-watch he gave me on my seventh birthday; the only trouble was that the glass kept getting broken. My technique was to call at his shop on the way home from school so that a new glass could be fixed without my mother knowing anything about it. He was obviously fond of his landlady's children, or he would not have played along with us in the delightful way he did. His presence and the furniture, bed linen, table linen, cutlery and the rest that Mother had brought with her from the hotel, gave us what she called 'a roughness'. A 'smoothness' would have been a more accurate word to use, but I knew what Mother meant. She did not have to scrape and save as some of our neighbours had to do for every single item they needed to furnish their homes.

In writing of things past it is hard to keep the right balance between painting a picture that is too grim or one that is too bright. I am trying as best I can to set down how my world looked and felt in those early years. Later on I came to know just how bitterly poverty ate into the bodies and souls of mining families who had no 'roughness' to help them on their way. But for a bit longer my head was in the clouds.

3. The First World War

In the early months of 1914 there was much talk of a strike
that was to be the biggest that had ever taken place in the
coalfields. Instead, before the end of the year we were at war.

When war was declared I was not yet ten years old. I remember the gusto with which we children collected old dolls
with broken or missing limbs. They were even better than
whole ones for we had discovered a fascinating new game. We
dressed up as nurses and played at 'hospitals'; the dolls were
our patients. And we marched and sang and waved flags as
every good patriot was expected to do. It is a fine exhilarating
thing to march in unison with good comrades, especially if
there is a rousing band to lead the way.

Then it all began to change. I was fast growing up and became increasingly aware that my father was not in step. He
was not cheering with the rest. He was against the war. In the
playground his kind were called cowards, traitors, conchies
(conscientious objectors). I hated it all and longed for him to
be like the fathers of the other children.

At home our visiting ILP speakers also talked against the
war. I was as fond as ever of old favourites among them such
as James Maxton, but sorely confused. We were no longer
allowed to hold meetings like decent Christians in the centre
of the town. Because of something called DORA (Defence of
the Realm Act) we had to walk miles into the country before
we could hold our meetings. I went with my father and his
friends to those meetings and listened intently to every word.
Then it all became clear. We were like the old Covenanters.
They too had to flee to the hills. They too had been persecuted. I was not sure whether thumb-screws were now used in

our prisons to break the spirit of war resisters, but I had listened at home to some horrifying accounts of men who had been thrown into cells, stripped naked, had their ordinary clothes taken away, and then been brutally kicked if they still refused to wear uniform. Although, like the Covenanters of old, we were being persecuted, we had to stand firm. We could not give in, for truth, goodness and righteousness were on our side. Never having been capable of half-measures, I was now fervently anti-war.

My grandfather, like myself, took some time before he came round to my father's point of view. In the early months, carried away by the strength of popular emotions as the first recruits marched down Dunfermline High Street, he turned to my father, who was standing on the pavement by his side, and made it quite clear that he thought the place for a young man was in the ranks, marching to war with those others. In time he came to share my father's attitude to the war and had to put up with a great deal of ill-feeling from the other local miners' leaders. The great majority of the leaders of the Labour and Trade Union Movement were as 'war mad' as their rank-and-file members. But what did it matter? They were many, we were few, but right was on our side. I could recite the whole of a long anti-war poem and still remember the opening lines:

I slaughtered a man, a brother,
In the wild, wild fight at Mons.
I see yet his eyes of terror,
Hear yet his cries and groans.
Perhaps he'd a wife, a mother . . .

Then came the unforgettable moment when for the first time I saw a grown-up man weeping. My mother's two youngest brothers had been home from the front on leave. When the time came for them to return, we were all on Cowdenbeath station platform to see them off – their brothers, sisters, uncles, aunts and we children as well. As the train moved slowly out of the station Uncle Davie leant out of the carriage window. He was weeping. He had been there before. He knew the Hell he was returning to and, although a grown man in my eyes, he was not yet out of his teens.

He was killed in action. So too was the father of my closest school-friend. Betty was a fair-haired, slender, sensitive girl. The day she came to school with a pale, tear-stained face and wearing a black pinafore over her dress, we longed to comfort her but what could any of her schoolmates say or do that was the least help? She was not the only one of my friends whose father was killed or missing. War was no longer a matter of dressing up as nurses and playing at 'hospitals'. It had become stark, cruel and terrible.

One day when I hurried home from school I saw an official envelope on the kitchen dresser. I knew it was my father's call-up papers. I was sick with fear. Would he be taken to prison? What would they do to him? When he came home from work my mother nervously handed him the unopened envelope. With hardly a glance, he threw it into the fire. But I knew that would not be the end of the matter; I continued to worry. However, at this stage in the war so many miners had joined the Army that it became essential for the others to go on with their normal work, so my worst fears for my father did not materialize.

But he had to face other dangers. The local ILP, with the redoubtable David Kirkwood from the Clyde as speaker, decided to hold a 'peace by negotiation' meeting outside a military camp in Kinross. There were both soldiers and civilians gathered around their soap-box platform. As soon as my father, who was chairing the meeting, mounted the box, a red-faced, burly figure stalked to the front and literally threw him over the heads of the crowd. As I have said, my father was lightly built. Davie Kirkwood at once jumped on the soap-box and with a voice of thunder shouted, 'If there is a better man than me among you, let him come and take this platform.' There were cheers then as well as jeers and he was allowed to speak. The soldiers listened passively; the disturbance was caused not by them but by a local butcher. I was not present at the meeting but I heard all about it round our fireside later in the evening. My friend Davie was the hero of the hour: I loved his form of 'pacifism'. Many ILP members were pacifists, in the strict sense, but others, including my father, took the same stance as a nineteen-year-old South Wales miner, Aneurin Bevan, who, when brought before the local magistrates' court for failing to respond to his call-up papers said, 'I am not and never have been a conscientious objector. I will fight, but I will choose my own enemy and my own battlefield, and I won't have you do it for me.'

In the Liberal Party as in the Labour Party, the majority followed a pro-war line. But a much harassed few campaigned for 'Peace by Negotiation'. They believed that the war could have been prevented by wise leadership, but now it was upon us the only thing to do was to bring it to an end as speedily as possible. They were not defeatists. They were not pro-German. What they advocated was a peace in which there would be neither victor nor vanquished, a peace in which both sides could emerge with dignity and set about rebuilding their shattered worlds. Dunfermline Burghs, where we lived, was contested in 1918 by William Watson, sponsored by the miners' union and very right-wing and pro-war. Arthur Ponsonby shared my father's views about the war and told him privately that when the war ended he intended to leave the Liberal Party and join the ILP. My father was once more out on a limb for, in defiance of the official pro-war Labour line, he gave his support to Ponsonby. Both were defeated, a coalition Liberal being returned.

While all this ferment was going on around me I was still under fourteen and had to get on with my school work. But it was not easy, for a new excitement had come into our lives. I knew that something of extraordinary importance had happened when I saw my father, James Lee, chairman of the local ILP, meeting Will Gray, treasurer of the local ILP, under the railway bridge across Cowdenbeath High Street, on a rainy Saturday afternoon. They were shaking hands as if they would never stop and there was the light of Heaven in my father's eyes. The first news of the Russian Revolution had reached them. Soon we had to organize 'Hands off Russia' campaigns to prevent Winston Churchill dragging us into war against Russia. We had strength enough to prevent full-scale military intervention, but were not able to prevent the attempt by the surrounding capitalist powers to strangle the Revolution at birth by an economic blockade.

By a concentrated bout of studying, the sort of lurch from one extreme to another that suited me temperamentally, I was soon once more holding my own in the classroom. I took first place and told my parents I would like to continue at school. My socialist father was too conservative to agree: he was afraid of incurring expenses he could not meet. My non-political mother was determined to let me have my way. The compromise we made with father was that I could go on for another year provided I, at the same time, went to night-school to learn typing and shorthand. The reason for this was to ensure that when my schooldays were over I need lose no time in becoming a money-earner. When the year ended, I still did not want to leave school. Somehow my mother and I overcame my father's doubts and caution. Two years later I left for Edinburgh University. I was dux of my school and, still more to the point, the Carnegie Trust agreed to pay half my university fees and Fife Education Authority awarded me a grant of £45 a year.

4. Student Days

I enjoyed my student days. Class work was routine and sometimes boring, but Edinburgh is a beautiful city. On summer evenings climbing Arthur's Seat was a favourite pastime. On Saturday forenoon we liked to parade along Princes Street and perhaps treat ourselves to tea at Crawford's, although funds did not always run to this. At that time Crawford's was a rather grand tea-shop, not cheap, but its spiced currant buns were a great attraction. At the weekend we could go further afield, sometimes spending the entire day tramping over the Pentland Hills.

It was the convention for women students to reside in one of the women's university hostels. I had two good reasons for not doing so: first, they were too expensive for me; secondly, and just as important, I did not want to be hedged in by all kinds of rules and regulations. So I found myself private lodgings for fourteen shillings a week. Before long I became close friends with Eveline. Her background was entirely different from mine. Coming from a prosperous, conservative Perthshire farming family, she was looking for something different from the atmospherics in her home. We decided to look for lodgings we could share. Going through the university's list of recommended addresses, we saw that a Miss McLaren, living on the far side of the Meadows, had a vacancy. Her rooms suited us splendidly. In addition to our bedroom we had a sitting-room with a large mahogany table in the centre. That table nearly led to our eviction.

One morning Miss McLaren came into our bedroom and said grimly she would have to ask us to leave. We were bewildered. What was the trouble? Then turning to me she said she did not mind me having one steady young man, but she was not going to allow her house to be given a bad name. I began to see daylight. The night before three men students had been with me until the early hours of the morning. We had not realized the noise we apparently had been making, but there was urgent business afoot. We were the editorial board of the *Rebel Student* and were running Bertrand Russell as our candidate for the Rectorship of the university. As we had no funds and no office, the problem was where to find privacy and space for cutting, editing and the rest. Our large mahogany table was the answer. But how could poor Miss McLaren know what we had been up to? In the end she accepted my explanation and, on a promise of good behaviour, no more late-night rowdy editorial gatherings, her eviction threat was withdrawn.

The election took place in my second year in Edinburgh. I was by then up to my eyebrows in student politics. We had our Labour Club, but did not confine our proselytizing to fellow students. Off we would go to the Mound in Princes Street or to a suitable stance in the Meadows, and one after the other try our prentice hand at public speaking. Another ploy was to visit those churches which after the sermon on Sunday evenings invited everyone interested to stay on for a discussion session. It was the latter we were waiting for. Trembling, but determined, I would wait my chance to get up and ask as awkward a question as I could devise.

In the subjects I had chosen for my MA degree I included Roman Law, and Constitutional History and Law. One day, reading on a university notice-board that there was going to be a competition in these two subjects, the winner to be awarded £100, I decided to have a go. Most certainly I did not expect to win. But I did. That £100 was manna from Heaven; even I, with my head in the clouds and my bookish ways, could not help seeing that my parents at home were harder up than at any previous time in my life. But the condition was that the winner had to complete the LL.B degree. I needed that £100. At a time when a penny, even a farthing, meant something, it was a considerable sum. So the only way I could get through my fourth year, when I should have been dedicating myself entirely to Moray House Training College in order to acquire the qualifications necessary before I could earn my living as a teacher, was by doing a bit of cheating. When Training College classes and law classes collided I had good friends who put in a card for my absent self at Moray House. I was not found out until many years later. By then it was treated as a joke.

I remember almost nothing of what I was taught in those law classes, but will always recall with pleasure and gratitude our Professor of English Literature. Once Professor Grierson got going, he would discard his notes, stand sideways, look upwards and soliloquize to himself. We would strain to catch his every word. I can see him as if it were yesterday, and hear the very tone of his voice, as with steel-rimmed spectacles slipping down to the point of his large nose, he intoned, *'Timor mortis conturbat me'*. Indeed that is just about all the Latin I still remember.

An odd man out among the university staff during my student days was Professor Lancelot Hogben. He talked with scathing contempt about his colleagues and liked to have a group of senior students as audience. I am not quite sure how I came to be invited to his home as I was not one of his students and we were not *sympathique*; I suppose it was because of my political activities. One evening he decided to amuse himself by prophesying what kind of career we students would have. He was highly complimentary about some of us, but when my turn came all he could say was that one day I would be the mother of a large family. His wife, who was tall and slender and wore long, dangling ear-rings, took little part in the discussions, but liked to pose by the side of the fire with her hands above her head and her sleeveless dress displaying well-groomed armpits. I thought it all a bit much; I was not amused. Hogben I remember as a small, rather effeminate-looking man, wearing a floppy black bow tie. Later I was to appreciate his academic brilliance, but we never became friends.

The two law professors who made the deepest impression on me were totally unlike in almost every way. One was Professor Harvey Littlejohn, who taught forensic medicine. He would pace to and fro in front of us, acting the part of the victim one minute and that of the murderer the next. I felt I was back in the Old Arcade theatre watching a rattling good melodrama. That year I was the only woman student in his class and plainly he would have preferred me not to be there: my presence embarrassed him. Then one day I distinguished myself. We were visiting a mortuary to observe him conducting a post-mortem. Luckily for me, I did not faint or become sick easily, so I stood up to the awfulness of the whole thing better than some of the men students. At a crucial moment when the student nearest to the Professor was too sick to hand him a sponge he had asked for, I gave it to him. After that we were reconciled to one another.

But it is Professor Macintosh who leaves the kindliest memories. I was invited, along with a number of other students, to have tea with him one Sunday afternoon. Never before had I had to cope with such a highly polished, slippery floor as he had in his drawing-room, made even more of a hazard by an occasional Persian rug. If all we had been offered had been polite conversation round the tea-table, the situation would not have been too difficult. But he and his smiling, well-rounded, quietly dressed wife had obviously decided to ignore Sabbath taboos and, still more daring, to bridge the generation gap. We were invited to play games. Games on that slippery floor? I was sure any moment I would disgrace myself by falling flat on my back. The last thing any of us wanted was this kind of 'jolly romp', but they were such a genuine couple, so utterly well intentioned, that we played up as we were expected to do, keeping our comments and our laughter until afterwards.

In my fourth year I had a marvellous piece of luck. I was able to take over from Pauline, a medical student, her attic flat at 53 George Square, only a few doors from the University Women's Union. I was now on my own for Eveline had a serious illness that year and had had to return home. As she felt lonely and isolated, cooped up in a Perthshire farmhouse, I tried to keep her in touch by writing to her about everything under the sun almost every day. If I were now depending on memory alone to recall my fourth year at Edinburgh University, most certainly I would not be able to do so with the candour and immediacy of those letters. The last thing on earth I had in mind was that one day they might be read by anyone else. Each generation in turn blunders its way through the traumas of adolescence. Nor are the generations so different from one another. In external mannerisms, yes. In the inner reality of our struggles to find ourselves, no. My lot had to conform to profoundly secretive modes of behaviour and took longer to reach maturity. At least so it would seem by the way young ones now talk. Sex in particular was a taboo subject. I am not writing of Oxford or Cambridge, for from what I have since read there were apparently gilded youths who lived apart from the more pedestrian students and, protected by their wealth, could flout the conventions as much as they pleased. But my university was in the capital of the country of the unco' guid – but also, don't forget, of Robert Burns.

In my first letter to Eveline from 53 George Square in January 1926 I wrote:

I find it very nice up here. I have some gorgeous coloured leaves on the mantlepiece and two quite nice prints on the wall. Otherwise I have not attempted to relieve the austerity of the room and indeed am finding it decidedly restful. There are two defects only – the gas-fire on for a long time is apt to give me a headache and when I reflect on the bill that must be mounting up, also a heartache. All our friends who have been up find it irresistible.

On Saturday Pauline had tea with me, for I want to know all about birth control and she is the best medical for getting me the right books, etc. So far I have done no work, but this afternoon I intend to begin. Very foolishly I allowed myself to be taken to Crawford's for tea by the least objectionable of the Law crowd. Going has put me in a bad mood. He is a very handsome, ruddy-complexioned youth, and I felt I was looking my worst, not having powdered since morning. Also I asked if he would have *milk* in his tea instead of saying *cream*, which he corrected, and altogether he was a rather dud companion. My considered intention is to waste no time on persons or things that leave me indifferent, so I hope not to repeat today's philandering.

The lists are up for 'Education'. I occupy my usual place; ie, I have a first-class and come sixth from the top.

Chérie, I fear this is a most uninteresting letter. I am just writing on without taking time to think and am not in a mood for making comments, so I give you the surface of the stream during the last week to inspect at your leisure.

On my shelf I have Russell's *Analysis of Mind*, Rivers' *Psychology and Politics*, Tawney's *Education*, Brailsford's *Socialism for Today*, Wells' *Soul of a Bishop*, all waiting to be read, so I hope to settle down soon and get started.

I think I must be missing your dressing-downs. I have been told by three different people this week that I am pretty, have eyes like a cinema (save the mark!) star, which makes me think the world must be mercifully blind. The exuberance of my first few days, I suppose. But don't get alarmed. I shall be a pale, puffy student again by the end of another week. I must now courageously face the new term's work – Education and Mercantile Law, special lectures on English and History, an investigation of the education of women at different periods and examination of the Board of Education's circular on differentiae of curricula for boys and girls. (The latter has to take the place of an education essay this term.) I have also to make a speech, or rather, lecture on February 7th to the St Giles Ward of the Edinburgh Labour Party.

Pauline tells me I may be asked to speak for the Women's Union at Manchester. I would very much like that so I don't suppose it will materialize.

I am a lazy shirker, you know. I want to keep on having dazzling things happen to me instead of doing some honest work and continuous thinking.

When will you be well enough to come to Edinburgh? I have discovered a camp-bed folded up in the corner of a cupboard, so with the help of cushions and coats I might survive the night on it. Miss Fitzgerald need not even know you are visiting if these trifles upset the poor soul, and we would be quite happy. Tonight I fried steak and onions for my supper as I had no lunch proper.

Much love,
JENNIE

The Miss Fitzgerald in question was a senior lecturer who occupied a larger flat on the floor below mine. I was taken completely by surprise when she knocked at my door one afternoon and asked if I had a male visitor with me. When I said 'yes' I was curtly told this was against the regulations and must not happen again. But what about my family? I asked. Of course it was quite all right for my father or a brother to visit me, but no other males allowed. Often on those Saturday afternoons when my father did not have to go to work, he came over to Edinburgh bringing me freshly washed and laundered clothes from home and taking back with him anything I needed to have washed or mended. Besides the clothes there would be home-baked scones, pancakes and cakes, and sometimes a generous portion of potted meat. Home-made potted meat, not the poor quality stuff sold in the shops.

His usual routine, after spending some time with me, was to break his journey at Dunfermline on the way home. He would go first to visit his parents, then finish the day at what we called the penny concerts. Dunfermline is Andrew Carnegie's birthplace and as such richly endowed. The concerts were of a very high standard, for the Carnegie trustees could afford to pay for the best available singers and orchestras. For a penny you could stand at the back of the hall. For a copper or two more you could have a seat. I remember one Saturday evening when I was home from college for the weekend watching my father as he came striding up the street where we lived. Anyone who did not know him would have thought he was tipsy. His eyes were sparkling and there was a marked jauntiness in his gait. Indeed he *was* tipsy. He was drunk on music. He was returning home from Dunfermline after hearing what he said had been a particularly fine rendering of the *Messiah*.

After the warning I had received from the lady professor, I had to make sure my father did not call at my flat. So when his next visit was due I took the precaution of meeting him as his train pulled into Waverley Station to tell him I could not take him to George Square as I already had a father. We laughed together as I explained that I had met Walton Newbold by chance in the Carnegie Library on George the Fourth Bridge. Newbold was a highly thought of socialist lecturer on economics. He had often lectured in Cowdenbeath and neighbouring towns. I had been glad to see him and had invited him back to tea with me. This was the 'male' my censorious neighbour had heard talking and laughing with me in the attic above her. By this time my one real brother had emigrated to Australia, but that did not deter me from adopting one or two others.

I had no sentimental attachment to any of the men students of my own age, and only one of them caused me any serious embarrassment. He was a dark-haired, voluptuous-looking young Dutchman from Amsterdam. He discovered my home address and one day during a between-term period turned up at my home. He wanted to meet my parents and to arrange for me to meet his. His intentions were what we in those days called 'honourable'. All I wanted was to see him safely on the train going back to Edinburgh; I had not the slightest interest in him and might have forgotten him entirely if, when sorting out old papers, I had not found two large postcard reproductions of famous Dutch paintings which he had given me.

On 22 January 1926, again writing to Eveline:

George Square

Mother was here on Saturday. We had a very satisfactory afternoon and she thought my room quite all right.

I have not the remotest desire to go to any student affairs, not even to outside dance halls with the Law youth. He is getting rather 'fresh', if you understand my slang. Some of the notes he passes to me in class are not what Miss Fitzgerald would approve of. On Friday he wanted me to go to tea again, but I had more sense this time. Of course if I had nothing better to do I could have quite good fun out of him, but work is just piling up around me. I *must* settle down.

J.

Again to Eveline – 3 February 1926:

Last night I reread Rivers' *Psychology and Politics*. Tonight I have been reading Olive Schreiner's Letters 1876–1920. What a torrent of reading I want to plunge into: H. Heine, Montaigne, Hinton, Nevinson, Edith Wharton, Karl Liebknecht...

I shudder at the vanity, superficiality and littleness of my false self after hours spent as the last few have been! Tomorrow J. P. M. Millar is speaking to the University Labour Club on 'Adult Education'. Mrs Millar has asked me to go home with her afterwards for supper. Strange as it may seem to you, I may refuse to join that little supper party unless I am feeling particularly gracious towards my fellow creatures. More and more it seems to me that happiness or, if you prefer, that feeling of internal well-being is largely a matter of selecting a fitting environment, that is, one in which whatever is essentially and uniquely you finds expression. Somehow I have no spontaneous drawing towards those delightful, artistic, advanced people, who honour our movement. I want big, simple people, free from affectation, such as Olive Schreiner must have been.

I came to appreciate Mr and Mrs Millar more after attending a weekend school organized by them for their National Council of Labour Colleges. There I met Ellen Wilkinson and Winifred and Frank Horrabin for the first time. They were impressive lecturers and good company. In later years Ellen and I became close friends. She was always generous to a younger colleague. In that same letter I went on to say:

Politics, Education and Psychology, the relation of one to the other, form the background of my reading and thoughts these days. With more thoroughness than you associate with me, I am selecting, reading and relating the best books that have been written on each. More than a mouthpiece I do not presume to be, but perhaps my personal synthesis and presentation may fulfil an equally necessary function.

But why do I belabour the commonplace? Have we not discussed and agreed on these things a thousand times? One person or another is constantly asking about you. Where fitting I say you send your regards to them.

In the *Nation* there is an excellent review of a book by Sinclair Lewis. I think you would be interested in it, especially one piece of reflection about what happens when an aristocrat turns reformer. I have been unable to get portraits of Mary Wollstonecraft and Olive Schreiner. I want George Sand as well now, because of what O.S. says about her. Whenever I can I must read the two volumes of her letters. The woman, it seems, was infinitely greater than her works.

Imagine! Olive Schreiner died as recently as 1920! How strange to realize that someone so like ourselves is dead! Were she alive still, I should have made a bid for her acquaintanceship. This slovenly letter must stop now. Writing what comes into one's head without thought or selection can come dangerously near to an abuse of friendship.

Yours always,
JENNIE

I dislike my hat bought the other day. Clothes annoy me, but I am self-conscious and embarrassed if too badly dressed!!!

Although men students of my own age had no special interest for me, there were others who had the glamour of being older and, as we thought, much more wordly-wise. These were the young men who had served in the Forces and were now returning to academic life. One of them was the President of the Labour Club. The first time I took my friend, Eveline, to one of our meetings, we were the first to arrive, except for the President. I hurried to the front to talk to him, but Eveline hung back. Looking up from the table where he was seated, preparing for the meeting, he saw her at the back of the room and asked, 'Who is that shy flower?' That gives a key to the nature of this unusual fellow student. He was essentially a poet. The attraction between us was mutual. I knew so little about him. We never once discussed his wartime experiences. I did know that he was the nephew of the Rev. James Barr, another of the ILP speakers who visited us in Fife. I had a vague idea that his father was a widower and a minister like his uncle, but we never talked about his home life.

What *did* we talk about? I suppose I chattered on about everything under the sun, especially when we went tramping over the hills together. 'Tramp' is almost a description of how carelessly he dressed. His boots were splendid for walking and climbing, but more like pit boots than the kind the other students wore. He was not so much older than I since he had been called to the Army from school at the age of eighteen, but when we were together our relationship was more that of a benevolent adult playing around with someone a generation younger than that of contemporaries. He was infinitely gentle. At the end of a long climb we would rest together on the hillside. He would look down at me, lightly caressing, a few butterfly kisses at most.

Then one day I received a letter saying that he had gone off to the Continent on a long walking tour and hoped to be able to win his way back to health. I had no further letter. We never met again. I was bewildered; it was all quite outside my understanding. Much later I learned that he had had a complete mental breakdown and was confined to an asylum for the rest of his life. What had happened to him? What kind of Hell had he been through in the war years? I believed then and I believe now, that he was as surely a war casualty as men who died in the trenches.

A pard-like Spirit, Beautiful and Swift –
A love in desolation masked.

Those lines in Shelley's *Adonais* always recall for me the finely drawn, sensitive features and the lightish-brown hair above the careless clothes and hobnailed boots of Robert Eaglesham.

After my friend vanished, I did not sit aside and mope. I had my books, all kinds of books, poetry in particular. I went occasionally to dances and to the theatre, more often to the cinema, and most magical of all to see Pavlova dance in the Usher Hall. We climbed the stone stairs to the 'gods' and there, hanging like flies from the ceiling, devoured every movement, every sound. It was pure enchantment. Afterwards, taken completely out of ourselves, we did not so much walk home as float. And I was as politically involved as ever.

5. The General Strike

When the 1926 General Strike began, a few students found their way to Hillside Crescent, the headquarters of the Edinburgh Central Strike Committee, but the great majority were on the other side. Some were vicious. I heard one young fellow with whom until then I had been on quite friendly terms say that what he would like to do was drive a tank down Cowdenbeath High Street. Among the volunteers who came to Hillside Crescent there was a pleasant young man with a splendid motor bike and side-car. Just the thing to convey our strike news-sheets out to the West Lothian mining villages. After I had helped to pile the news-sheets into his side-car, he asked me rather shyly, if I would like to come with him, riding pillion. It would, he assured me, be quite an experience for me – I would meet real miners!

Then almost as suddenly as the strike had begun, it was over. All the excitement, all the believing that a new day was dawning, crumbled into bitter resentment and disillusionment. It was 1919 and 1921 all over again. In 1919 Bonar Law, the Chancellor of the Exchequer, wrote to Bob Smillie, President of the Miners' Union, in the following terms:

Speaking in the House of Commons last night I made a statement in regard to the Government policy in connection with the Report of the Coal Industry Commission. I have pleasure in confirming, as I understand you wish me to do, my statement that the Government are prepared to carry out in the spirit and the letter the recommendations of Sir John Sankey's Report.

But, of course, the Sankey Report, including the recommendation that the pits should be nationalized, was cynically set aside. It had helped to keep the miners quiet at a time when there were no reserve coal stocks and therefore when they were in a strong position to challenge the coalowners.

In 1921 Lloyd George again outwitted the miners. It was in that year, when I was still a schoolgirl, that I had my first experience of how it feels to have policemen advancing towards you with raised batons. I was cycling home from Dunfermline with a load of books on the back of my bicycle when I ran into a crowd so dense that I had to dismount. This was in Cowdenbeath High Street. When the crowd began moving backwards instead of forwards I was at first bewildered. Then .I saw what was happening. They were retreating before the advancing police. I found myself right out in front, not as a heroine leading the strikers but simply because I had no room to turn my bicycle around. I was thankful not to be hit by one of the stones a group of young miners were throwing at the police.

Although the General Strike lasted only ten days the miners held out from April until December. Until the June examinations were over I was chained to my books, but I worked with a darkness around me. What was happening in the coalfields? How were they managing? Once I was free to go home to Lochgelly my spirits rose. When you are in the thick of a fight there is a certain exhilaration that keeps you going. While I was at college, my parents had moved to Lochgelly to be nearer the Nellie Pit, where my father worked. I was delighted to find we now had a small back garden as well as a long sloping front garden. Also our new home at 12 Paul Street was much more conveniently planned than the one we had left. This we owed to the vision of Dr Christopher Addison, who in the years immediately after the First World War was Minister of Health and Housing under the premiership of Lloyd George.

In our part of the world Lloyd George was no hero. We did not forgive or forget the Khaki Election of 1918. Nor his treatment of pacifists during the war. Nor the Marconi Scandal. Nor the way he played fast and loose with the Suffragette Movement, doing nothing to oppose forcible feeding or to undo the notorious Cat and Mouse Act. 1919 and 1921 had also clearly shown where his sympathies lay. His treatment of Dr Addison was one more mark against him. Dr Addison had been one of his closest and most loyal colleagues, but when the Tories attacked him in outrageously venomous terms for having built council houses 'without regard to cost', Lloyd George threw his Minister of Health and Housing to the wolves. In the Commons he sought to appease the Tories by stating that Addison would hold office only until the end of the session. As if that were not enough, he also promised that Addison's salary would be cut not only by the £2,000 the critics were demanding, but by an additional £500. A J P Taylor, in his biography of Beaverbrook, puts the position with commendable bluntness when he states, 'Lloyd George certainly knew how to push a friend overboard when the raft was threatening to sink.' But of course Lloyd George failed to save himself. Once the war was over the Tories had no more use for him. He was an outsider, an upstart Welsh lawyer who had got above himself.

He was a wonderful orator. I have heard my father say that when he came to address meetings in Scotland you had to hold on to your seat not to be carried away. And in his early years he was deeply concerned to make life more tolerable for the poor. He fought for his social security legislation with all his boundless energy and adroitness; the only thing he was not prepared to do for the poor was to become one of them. He needed money, lots of money, to maintain a home for his wife and family in Wales and another in England for his secretary, who became his mistress and, at the end of his life, his second wife. Added to that there were constituency and party expenses to be met. One of the mysteries of the English legal system is how he was allowed to syphon into his private pocket a great deal of the money raised by the sale of honours. No doubt with his immense self-confidence Lloyd George felt that, given untrammelled power, he could have done wonders for humanity as well as for himself. But the Tory Establishment was too much for him. When peace came, the 'Hang the

Kaiser' mob saw to it that no concessions were made to those in the Liberal and Labour Parties who advocated victory tempered by mercy. In those years forces were set in motion that led to the rise of Hitler and the Second World War.

What Lloyd George failed to understand was that no man, however gifted, is a major political power in himself. He can teach, he can preach, he can make a significant contribution, but power politics is a struggle between social forces, not a duel between individuals. Winston Churchill learned that lesson during the years when he was ostracized by the Tory Establishment. When his moment came during the Second World War, he seized the chance of becoming leader of the Tory Party, in control of the Party machine, as well as continuing as wartime leader of a Coalition Government.

But it was Stanley Baldwin we had to deal with in 1926. Like Lloyd George, he took his stand on the side of the coalowners. From June to September I was ceaselessly on the go; there were endless meetings to address in any area where there were signs of flagging morale. Just as urgent was the need to collect funds to keep our soup kitchens going, which meant travelling outside the mining areas to address gatherings of sympathizers. The most important part of these meetings was collection time. I was so pleased when I returned from Dublin and Belfast with £100. Apart from a cheque for £20 from the Post Office Workers' Union, every penny was collected at meetings, usually in the open air, from men and women as poor as ourselves.

Some of the letters I sent to my friend Eveline at the time describe more graphically than anything I could now write not just what was happening to us but the highly charged emotions generated by the merciless class war being waged against us.

My letter to her of 27 June 1926 reads:

The ninth week of the strike is now beginning. I am learning how guillotines find favour in a revolutionary period. There's enough hatred burning in my own blood to keep the hell-fires burning for the other side through all eternity.

I have succeeded in protecting my own home from actual privation. On Friday I was able to hand over another £10 to Mother – the proceeds of the MacLaren Bursary, which is my latest little to-do. The chance of travel is as remote as ever. Dad, seeing me writing to the convener of the I L P Summer School saying I would be unable to attend, calmly told me to say that I was a heavy burden to my people through education expenditure. I didn't like to hurt his feelings by pointing out that in the last nine months I had earned £124, more than £3 per week, and that far from him keeping me, I had been entirely self-supporting, and also helping to keep him.

I am not of the martyr type and don't pretend to be, so I feel a genuine grouch against the family. To make a damned good show at carrying on and by way of thanks to be told that you are a burden to the family, is a piece of gross cruelty. Of course, Mother knows better, but Father deserves to be made to feel the arithmetic of the situation. Impractical dreamers may be charming people but they can also be – oh, what am I bleating about. It is just that I could weep, my dear, being a baby whose bright toy has once more been withheld from its greedy hands. Write and comfort me. Tell me I am a noble woman, a violet blushing by a stone unseen, the kind of friend you are proud to shake by the hand. If you do, I'll break your neck.

Now I feel better. I have written out my bad temper. Also I have remembered that a man in trouble has written for me to meet him and talk to him. That makes one whole again. No, it is not *Dan*. His Lordship will be sentenced to six months or a year soon, yet in spite of that powerful solvent, I am cross, critical and cool with him.

Eveline had written to me to say she was well enough to plan a holiday in Paris. I wrote back:

When the bourgeoisie are being guillotined, I won't let anyone touch you. There now. Go in peace and be happy. O, what a flood of indignation and argument you want to let loose after that last pat of mine. But you can't, you can't. There are 25 miles between us and soon there will be 125 miles. If you are not taking the weekend songbook with you, I should very much like to have a loan of it. Tomorrow I go to Edinburgh for a law exam and have nearly all the stuff to read yet. I have got to the stage now when I am writing on and on merely to put off the evil hour when I settle down to Jurisprudence again. What a life!

Much love and Many Blessings

JENNIE

In fairness to my father I ought to say that I had not remembered that I had been helping to support my parents only
during 1926 – my fourth year at university. I know now he
must have been well aware of how rebellious I felt at not having
the money to go off to the ILP summer school, where I
would so much have enjoyed the lectures and meeting new
friends and all else. In my first three university years I took all
the sacrifices my parents must have had to make to ensure I
had everything I needed with hardly so much as noticing what
was happening. Having exhausted his modest savings, my
father's pride must have been hurt when he found himself
dependent on the earnings of an arrogant young daughter.

One of the first things I noticed when I returned home in
June was the coarseness of our tea cups. Twenty-six years before, at the time of her marriage, my mother was presented
with a tea-service of fine bone china. But instead of preserving
it on a high shelf as was the usual custom, her china had been
used on high days and holidays, so only a few fragments remained. An insight into the state those mining areas had been
reduced to is given in the following passage in a letter I wrote
to Eveline at that time:

Yesterday I bought Mother a most exquisite set of china. Sounds
plutocratic, doesn't it? I made the discovery in a second-hand shop
heaped with grime. I got six cups and saucers for 2/– and a sugar and
cream jug for 1/–. The next day my mother got the other half-dozen
cups and saucers for 1/3. They are slim, elegant, modern, white with
green edging, and altogether only such a bargain as could be picked
up in an area where even shopkeepers have had a destitute summer.
Mother had been fretting about the coarse white cups we were reduced to, so we are all agreed that our tea is now twice as good.

The Dan I refer to in my letter was a young, tawny-haired,
sturdily built, high-powered organizer and brilliant platform
performer brought into West Fife to take charge of Communist activities. We met in private as well as in public and were
well aware of the attraction we had for one another. But in
argument we gave no quarter. I refused to accept his 'holier

than thou' Communist dogma and he scathingly attacked what he called my woolly-headed evangelical socialism.

On 21 July 1926 Eveline was still in Paris. I wrote to her:

Your letter arrived this morning, and I was delighted to read it. So Paris is all that it is painted. You will be making all your friends look more gauche and provincial than ever when you come back.

But I'll tell you one thing you haven't done. You haven't mounted a lorry and addressed thousands of people with a skirt to the knee and ascending even higher every time your eloquence raised your arms aloft. Poor Auntie Maisie who was in the audience was purple with shame and indignation at her brazen niece.

Need I add that it was only after the meeting I learned that the short skirt I was wearing had embarrassed my aunt. In the same letter I wrote:

I can't afford new clothes, so I have got my navy frock shortened and smartened and wear it with what Dad calls my 'Don't give a damn hat!'

Last Saturday there was a 'Votes for Women at Twenty-one Years' demonstration in Cowdenbeath. Then, in Lochgelly the previous Thursday I was pitted against Mrs Helen Crawford, executive member of the Communist Party and the greatest platform asset they have. She dresses beautifully, quotes the Bible, yet talks forcibly, so has proved most effective amongst the women.

Again on Monday there was a gigantic demonstration in Lochgelly to welcome home seven class-war prisoners. What a day! Can you imagine some of those young miners called on for the first time in their lives to make a speech! One recited a verse from the Red Army March, a dedication verse swearing that death itself would not deter him. His quiet steady voice travelled over the hushed crowd with vibrating intensity. In the evening they were the guests of the Trades Council, Mrs Crawford and myself also being invited. Dinner, consisting of potatoes, mince and beans, followed by a milk pudding, then tea, bread, butter and jam, was served by the soup kitchen staff. I sat at the right hand of the chairman and will never enjoy a banquet more. Afterwards we were singing and dancing.

The Communists are concentrating on this area and have won the support of the 'down and outs' who are to be counted by the thousand. Their best speakers, such as Page Arnot of the Labour

Research Department, have been brought up from London to consolidate the work of permanent organisers on the spot. They denounce the ILP, left, right and centre and little me is the chief protagonist on the anti-Communist side. At the moment I am not attacking them openly for we are pledged to a united front. That the CP violates this will only be one more count against them.

I oppose Communism on the ground of its internal organization, strategic position (that is, outside the Labour Party, so weaker than the ILP) and its tactics during this present strike, that is, coming to areas like this that can stand alone instead of helping the ILP in propaganda work and fund-raising in weaker areas. But forgive me, I am forgetting you are in Paris to escape from such questions for a little. Anyhow I am too lazy to write either coherently or legibly so you will find my signature on the last page if you have any doubts about who is writing to you.

Dan is in prison for four months. Thank goodness for all concerned that I had cooled towards him before this occurred. It is hell for him. I am told by one of the released prisoners that he is inside making mats, the worst, most monotonous job of the lot. In the half-hour for exercise by walking round the square, the young men make for the outside to get as much activity as possible. Dan goes crawling round the inner ring with the older men. He is still the popular idol here so purgatory will pass and the hour of triumph return. On his release it is anticipated that there will be the biggest demonstration ever seen in West Fife.

You will be surprised to learn that your weekend song-book has been well used. When I grow tired of reading or writing at my little window upstairs, I am trying to get my voice out of my throat and find singing the best way of practising. Of course if anyone approached during the performance I would feel thoroughly affronted, but I know all about the German officer who crossed the Rhine, the gypsies who came to a lady's door, my aunt who died a month ago, and oh nearly every one of the songs.

In the meantime you are basking in sunshine and varied company on a brilliant stage and I am glad with all my heart that I can picture you thus instead of ceaselessly revolving on the treadmill of your own thoughts in lonely Spoutwells.

On 4 August 1926 I was again writing to my friend Eveline in Paris, and delighted with the way her affairs were progressing. In our Edinburgh years this finely strung young woman with her Dresden china complexion and a capacity even greater than my own for agonizing over all the injustices in the world was too shy to make men friends easily. Now she was being ardently courted by a young man and writing to the fount of all wisdom, that is to me, seeking encouragement and advice. Remember, there was no easy access to information about sex matters in those days. I cannot imagine my mother so much as mentioning the subject to me. Even my knowledgeable and enlightened father did not talk to me directly before I left to go into lodgings in Edinburgh on my own when I was barely eighteen. What he did was place a book by Marie Stopes in a position in our bookshelves where I was bound to find it. That I did, but it was all a bit remote and unattractive. Some of us at that time went in for a great deal of poetry to carry us through our adolescent phase, what was then called sublimation.

But by the summer of 1926 I was twenty-one, Eveline a year older. It was time for us to begin to wake up. So in my reply to her I wrote:

If you are sure you won't lose more in mental conflict than you gain otherwise, if you are sure you are not once more idealizing a nonentity, if you are reasonably convinced you are running no risk of disease, then the question becomes simply what about possible pregnancy? Mrs J. P. M. Millar informed me that France is the most advanced country in the world in contraceptive methods. In forensic medicine we studied in detail good, bad and indifferent methods of abortion, which even orthodox doctors frequently practise. I think you can be reasonably sure, even if an accident occurred, of safely evading the consequences. Considering all those things in your position, provided my inclinations were sufficiently aroused, I cannot see myself running away from life. So far this sex business has been the background of my life with public work as the foreground. Both of us, in our own ways, are out for more than the negations of life. Better to enjoy and suffer than sit around with folded arms. You know the only true prayer? Please God, lead me into temptation.

JENNIE

So there you have it. I knew all the words, had studied forensic medicine along with medical students, made friends easily – and was still a virgin. I suspect in the present permissive age when everything is talked about publicly, even in the mass media, there are still quite a lot of youngsters who are as fastidious as we were, but don't like to admit it for that is not now the fashion.

It was the struggles in the coalfields in 1926 that shaped the whole of my after-life more than any other experience. Eveline was back in Edinburgh completing her studies in the autumn of 1926. In reply to her plea to be kept up to date on all that was happening in Lochgelly, I wrote:

Every day orderly processions led by a pipe band pass our home on the way to the pits. There have been serious goings-on these last two days. About one hundred and fifty windows of blacklegs' houses smashed, fires drawn at the pits, police fights, etc. Dad has just laughingly told me how one of his friends (Councillor Bill Crooks) described yesterday's main event.

Word reached a demonstration at the Nellie Pit that the police were batonning into subjection the people of Glencraig. Fired with this news, the rasher elements turned the pipers in that direction. Bill Crooks tried to calm the mob and hold them back but being told, 'If you are feart, gae hame' was human enough to march on with the rest. When Dad chided him for his rashness (he had an ex-service pension of 17 shillings per week which would have been stopped if he had come before the court) his reply was:

'Oh man, it was grand. A widna have missed it for a pension. When the Glencraig folks heard the skirl o' the pipes, they took fresh heart and battered into the police. Man, when the population began cheering, it was for a' the world like being in Flanders again and marching into a Belgian village while the folks hurrahed and the Jerries went skellering before ye. I couldn't have stopped from chasin' up yon scabs and bobbies though my life was at stake.'

Crooks and Stewart will bear the brunt of this. Seventeen men were arrested for doing nothing two days ago so last night Crooks was expecting to be hauled out of bed. The swine don't serve a summons in legal fashion but surround the houses of their victims in the night and remove them. Mrs Crooks is a nervous wreck. I was there until 1 a.m.

but, perhaps because the whole place was waiting and prepared, no arrest was made last night. Our house went like a fair.

'Your turn is coming' is what Dad is being told on all sides, meaning of course that when Crooks and Stewart are removed, a new scapegoat will be needed.

In another letter to Eveline at this time I describe how 'thousands of us marched to the poorhouse and claimed admittance':

This was a protest against leaving the single men and women to starve by refusing even a penny of parish relief. What a kick-up. When we reached Dunfermline there was a huge demonstration with a platform party including Dan and myself. He was in command and had every town marching separately under its own leader in military formation. Perfect discipline all the time unless when an occasional person fainted through marching so far on an empty stomach. Dan, the idiot, caught sight of me when he was marching into Dunfermline park at the head of his mighty men and in his surprise shouted, 'Jennie' at the top of his voice. A detail, you say. Yes, but a damnably embarrassing one for me. I consistently snubbed him during the meeting, so I am now waiting in amused indifference for his next move.

That was 1926. A turbulent medley of friendships and enmities, high hopes and soul-destroying wrath and despair. I longed to see a united working-class movement but again and again found that the Communists, with their iron discipline, were bent, not on co-operation with us less highly organized socialists, but on taking over total control.

6. The Aftermath

As part of his strike-breaking activities, Stanley Baldwin promised that there would be no victimization when the miners went back to work. That was one more piece of deliberate deception. My father was not reinstated – for four months he trudged from pit to pit, turned away everywhere. At last he got a manual labourer's job and came home so utterly exhausted that the most my mother could tempt him to eat were a few spoonfuls of custard with the white of an egg whisked on top; and I was all too aware that it was only with difficulty he could climb the stairs to bed at the end of the evening.

He got his job back only after a man lost his life in the section of the Nellie Pit where he had formerly been deputy. When the general manager, Mr Dawson, known to the men as 'bloody Hindenburg', began his investigations into the cause of the accident, he was furious when told that my father was no longer the deputy in charge. There was an old kindness between them as they had been boys at school together. At various times Dawson had tried to persuade my father to join the Masons and cross to the management side, but Dad was a dedicated socialist and trade unionist; there was never any question of him changing sides.

After 1926 nearly all the families that could escape to a less depressing environment did so. For us, the worst loss was seeing my father's younger brother forced to leave. The two brothers were close friends, had the same socialist outlook and both earned their living as deputies. Uncle Michael was also victimized, and sadly he came to the decision that the only thing to do was to go off to America. Lindsay, the youngest of his three children, called to pay us a farewell visit; we lived close to one another but as a special treat he was going to stay with us overnight. When I opened the front door, there stood a diminutive figure, seven or eight years old, carrying a small suitcase. He was the 'wild one' of the family and certainly did run amok at times when his mother was with him. But that last visit, when he was on his own, he was what Ma called 'a perfect little gentleman'. Like everyone else, he adored his Auntie Phem (my mother's Christian name was Euphemia). I missed the children but my father's loss was the one that was irreparable. He became a lonely man after his brother left. No one else ever took Uncle Michael's place.

Harder for my mother to bear had been the loss of her only son. He emigrated to Australia a few months before the stoppage began. I loved him dearly but did not share my mother's tears. He was barely eighteen and was working in the office of one of the Dunfermline linen factories, but he longed for a more adventurous life in a larger and sunnier country. I thought it was good for him to get away from the general atmosphere of decay surrounding us.

In September, while the stoppage was still on, I began work as a relief teacher in my own old school in Cowdenbeath. This was very congenial: I got on well with the children and could be home by four o'clock. Sometimes there were committee or public meetings I had to attend in the evening, but more often I could stay snugly beside a warm fire, reading or gossiping with friends. At the weekends I would more often than not be off to ILP meetings in other parts of Scotland. We were determined, after the ignominious collapse of the General Strike in 1926, to build a more powerful Labour movement that could be relied on to hold its ground, not run away under fire. Our hopes now lay in winning sufficient strength in Parliament to be able peacefully and constitutionally to carry through basic socialist measures.

In 1927 I was appointed a delegate to the national conference of the ILP. Some of our leading members present at the conference, notably Snowden and MacDonald, were lukewarm in their support of our programme. I was so incensed by

MacDonald's dithering that I was not even nervous when I was called to the rostrum to address the conference. Emanuel Shinwell spoke in defence of MacDonald. I followed him. We wanted ideals not idols, was my *cri de coeur*. The applause at the end was deafening. I was stunned. I had only spoken as I had done a hundred times before at all kinds of meetings, large and small. Fenner Brockway, in his book *Inside the Left*, described the scene in the following terms:

A young dark girl took the rostrum, a puckish figure with a mop of thick black hair thrown impatiently aside, brown eyes flashing, body and arms moving in rapid gestures, words pouring from her mouth in Scottish accent and vigorous phrases, sometimes with a sarcasm which equalled Shinwell's. It was Jennie Lee making her first speech at an ILP conference. And what a speech it was! Shinwell was regarded as a Goliath in debate, but he met his match in this girl David.

Making every allowance for Fenner's cordial support of the point of view we then shared, I suppose it must have looked and sounded something like that.

One of the many new friends I made at the conference was Charles Trevelyan. Arthur Ponsonby had been the first to brave the frozen hostility of the House of Commons when he rose to advocate peace by negotiation during the First World War; Trevelyan followed. MacDonald held back, only venturing to speak some time later. Many of the 'peace by negotiation' advocates had visited Fife and stayed in my home, but although Trevelyan had left the Liberal Party and joined the ILP in 1919 he had not come our way. I met him in 1927 for the first time. In the years ahead to the end of his life we were steadfast friends, and he sustained me through all kinds of stormy weather.

After the conference invitations flowed in to me to address meetings in England as well as in Scotland. It seems that what I lacked in 'polish' I made up for in ardour and it was an uncompromising socialist stance our people wanted in those years, not the timid approach of the right wing of the Party. Not long afterwards, in a by-election in North Lanark in

February 1929, I was elected to Parliament. But before that I had to fight for my political life in circumstances that almost destroyed me. It was then I had my first personal experience of how the 'dirty tricks' sections of political parties operate.

Until 1928 I had no difficulty in earning my living during weekdays as a teacher and spending strenuous weekends touring the country on behalf of the ILP. But I was getting tired of relief work because travelling time often left me with too short an evening, and therefore I was delighted to be appointed to a permanent teaching post only two miles from home. An added attraction was that I was taking on a 'problem' class. A young teacher had been taken to court by the father of one of her pupils and convicted of ill-treatment. The father had pleaded for his 'poor motherless boy' and public sympathy was entirely on his side. An older, more experienced teacher took over the class, since under the leadership of the 'poor motherless boy' it had got out of hand. After a time she felt she had had enough and applied for a transfer to a more tranquil part of the county. I was quite sure I could succeed where others had failed. Of course other teachers did not understand those children or the problems their parents were having to face in the way I understood them. Had we not marched together behind the same banners throughout the lockout months of 1926?

One factor I had left out of account was the strength of the Communist Party in this area. In Lochgelly the ILP was the dominant political force, but in Glencraig, where the school was situated, the Communist Party had the larger following. I kept my political and teaching worlds entirely apart. It did not occur to me that I might be delivering myself into the hands of my enemies. During 1926 the ILP had an uneasy alliance with the Communist Party, but that was all over: there was now a life-and-death struggle between us. They knew that they had a better chance of returning a Communist Member to Parliament for West Fife than for any other constituency in Scotland, so money and personnel were poured into the area from as far afield as London. They did in fact win the

seat in the 1935 General Election, their one and only gain in
Scotland. In the hectic period leading up to 1929 one of their
main tasks was to discredit the Labour Party, the left wing in
particular. We were their only rivals. By fair means or foul,
the public had to be turned against us.

My father was their first victim. Over in Clackmannanshire,
where I was now well known but he was not personally
known, mining audiences were told that Jennie Lee's father
had blacklegged in 1926. One evening two stalwart working-
class matrons came to our door and asked if they could talk to
us. They had come over from Clackmannanshire to find out
the truth. After a pleasant hour round the fire, with Mother's
hospitable tea-table well to the fore, they left, fully satisfied
and vowing vengeance on the scandalmongers. It never occurred to me that one day it would be my turn to be rescued by
women of that same formidable, indomitable breed.

Before going to teach in Glencraig I had had no great difficulty in keeping order in any class in my care, but I had now
to face a much tougher set of circumstances. The boy, whose
father had made him a hero by taking his teacher to court and
winning his case, was up to every mischief. The headmistress,
a plump little lady who was due to retire at the end of the
year, ordered me to purchase a 'strap'. I was outraged at the
very idea and curtly refused. Then one day she entered my
classroom, brought several of my pupils to the front of the
class and punished them. I was livid with rage. Of course a
few of the children were rowdy, but I wanted to deal with
them in my own way. I wanted more time. I am not proud of
what followed. At the first opportunity I waylaid her in her
private room and harangued her about the iniquity of her behaviour to such an extent that she broke down and cried. But
the children had got my measure. I was a softie. They could
do what they liked and would not be punished.

Most afternoons when I returned home I was so exhausted
that, like my father returning from hard manual labour in
1927, I had to lie down and rest before I could eat. There was
a bald spot on top of my head as big as a large egg. Fortunate-

ly I had lots of hair so it could be covered over. 'Alopecia' is
what our doctor called it. Nothing before had taken this kind
of toll of my strength. Then breaking point came. The
'motherless boy' who was the storm centre of all the restlessness in the classroom was in the front row, where the most
backward pupils sat. He was having a long-distance quarrel in
sign language with a boy in the back row. Then, to my horror,
he lifted a slate and was just about to throw it. I caught him
by the scruff of the neck, railroaded him into the staff retir-
ing-room, put him over my knee and spanked him with all the
force I could muster. I had lost my temper completely. That
was the last time I had any trouble from him. But the local
Communist Party, hearing what had happened, decided that
their moment had come.

'Kind, kind and gentle is she' was chalked in large letters
on the pavements. They knew perfectly well that every other
teacher in that school used the 'tawse' as a matter of course.
They knew too that I was wholly opposed to corporal punishment. They were not concerned about that. A 'poor motherless boy' who had been ill-treated before by a teacher was
again the victim of a woman not fit to teach. That was their
story. They were moving in for the kill! I was to be hounded
out of public life. I insisted that the Director of Education
should make an investigation, and after doing so he demanded
an apology on my behalf, but no apology was given. I was
offered a transfer. That I could not accept. It would have been
too like running away.

The climax came at an ILP meeting in Lochgelly Town
Hall, where I was one of those billed to speak. The news
reached us that Glencraig Communists were joining forces
with Lochgelly Communists to wreck the meeting. I had no
stomach for this kind of in-fighting. I wanted to get on with
the main battle of fighting the coalowners and all the Establishment forces on their side. I must have shown my nervousness
as I stood in the ante-room waiting for the meeting to begin,
for a wise old collier, one of the ILP committee organizing
the meeting, took my arm and said, 'Lassie, if ye will think

mair o' your subject and less o' your self you will no be sae nervous.' How right he was. It was myself I had been worrying about. His gentle rebuke helped me to pull myself together. Then the miracle happened. When we walked on to the platform I saw that the front row of the crowded hall was filled with the mothers of some of my pupils. They too knew what was afoot. I was told afterwards that they had warned the would-be wreckers that if they did not behave themselves they would 'get what for'. The meeting was orderly and enthusiastic.

Later in the year the old headmistress retired and was replaced by a younger man. I knew from the gleam in his eye the first time we met that he was a 'good Labour man'. Sometimes I had gently to propel him to the classroom door when he was inclined to linger and to chat about all manner of things when I wanted to get on with my work. The whole atmosphere of the school was transformed, although of course there were still difficult moments.

It was the raucous bitterness in the homes of many of those children in the aftermath of industrial defeat that was the biggest unsettling element. Also I am afraid most of their parents had little knowledge or understanding of my high-falutin educational theories. One day, meeting the mother of a likeable but incorrigibly rowdy youngster, I asked her if she would have a word with him. Her reply was, 'Robert pays nae heed to his faither or me, but he thinks the world of you. Just give him a good leathering.' What could you do about that kind of response, especially as the same Robert presented me with a magnificent Christmas present that had taken him many weeks to produce with the help of an older brother? They had made a heart-shaped wooden frame, at least a foot long, decorated it with fancy papers of every colour, and across the centre there was the seasonal greeting 'Merry Xmas'.

I had a vivid illustration of just how much the home conditions of these children varied when I sent my two cleverest girls home to ask permission from their parents to be allowed to accompany me to Edinburgh after school hours one evening. As soon as the school closed I hurried to Lochgelly station, and there was one of them, little Rita, waiting for me, wearing her best Sunday clothes, complete with a muff and a purse. But where was Greta? Just when I thought we would have to leave without her, I saw an eager little face peering in through the outside railings, but not venturing to come right on to the platform. She was the same unkempt little mortal she had been when I sent her home to ask for permission to accompany me. I had a comb, a small towel, soap and nail-brush with me, as I knew I would have no time to wash before hurrying to the station. These helped me to avoid hurting Greta's feelings for I told her we would *both* have a good wash on the train. First I got her clean and tidy, then sent her to our compartment to join Rita while I too had a wash.

Now we planned our campaign. As soon as the train reached Edinburgh we had to hurry up the Waverley steps and cross Princes Street to Jenners. I was giving myself the rare treat – indeed this only happened once – of having a costume made for me in this, at that time, very posh shop. Each child was given a shilling and told to go down to the toy fair in the basement, complete with Santa Claus, while I hurried upstairs to the fitting-room. They knew we had to count every second if I was to get there in time to keep my appointment before the shop closed. They also knew to come upstairs and wait for me when they had bought themselves a Christmas present. When I presented myself and my appointment card, the superior young lady assistants took my measure – my ordinary-looking clothes, my non-U Fife accent. I was frigidly conducted to the fitting-room. But when I re-emerged the atmosphere was transformed. I saw two small girls with shining eyes embedded in an enormous sofa so large that their legs were straight out in front to them. They were showing their presents to three or four young lady assistants, who were bending over them in friendly interested fashion, all the haughtiness gone. Even I now got a smile.

There was time for a leisurely tea with buns and cakes before our train was due to take us back to Lochgelly. When we

got there Rita's father was waiting for her on the station platform, and after thanking me courteously, went off with his
youngster. There was no one, needless to say, waiting for Greta. I went with her in the tram to the Glencraig terminus, then
she darted off through a labyrinth of sub-standard houses
to her home. She clearly did not want me to go beyond the
terminus. Rita was an only child; I cannot even remember
what present she bought for herself. It was Greta who was the
miracle-worker. With her shilling she had bought Christmas
presents for all her small brothers and sisters, as well as for
herself. For twopence a time in those days you could buy a
selection of gifts that delighted children. Please don't think of
Greta as having a chip on her shoulder. Not a bit of it. She
was happy and proud as she rushed home, hardly able to wait
to get there in order to distribute her gifts.

Two mornings later Rita brought me a Christmas present of
a box of chocolates. You don't encourage that kind of thing,
but when it happens all you can do is accept gracefully. I mention this because of the sequel. Next day I had another chocolate box dumped on my desk. Greta was not going to be out-
done. It looked a bit grubby, and when I took it home and
opened it, I discovered what I had guessed had happened.
The child had found an empty chocolate box, bought twopence worth of mixtures, and thumbed each sweet carefully
into place. Children? What can you do about them? One moment they break your temper, the next moment the plight of
some of those children just about broke my heart.

Even the poorest parents did everything they possibly could
to send their children to school well wrapped up in cold
weather and adequately shod, but there were times when at
least half a dozen arrived blue with cold and with leaking footwear. Most members of the staff considered themselves a cut
above the colliers' children they were teaching and were Conservative in their views, but one thing I did appreciate was the
trouble they took to keep a cupboard well stocked with the
cast-off clothes and footwear collected from the homes of
better-off children. This meant that in wet cold weather there

was a fairly good chance of finding something to fit a shivering child who came to school inadequately clad or with wet feet. There were hot-water pipes at floor level around the classroom. Squelching footwear, some of it only rubber sandshoes, and the damp socks inside, were dried along the pipes. While this drying process was going on, in a quite literal sense the stench of sad, sour poverty pervaded the very air we breathed.

1928 ended for me very differently from its stormy beginning. I was no longer living beyond my strength. School problems still existed but were greatly eased. And home, as always, was an oasis of peace and security. Writing to Eveline just before Christmas I record:

> This is one of those blissfully peaceful Sundays here. I have been at home so seldom at the weekends this winter that I appreciate it enormously. Dad and Ma are bantering in the kitchen in their usual style, and through here only the ticking of the clock breaks the perfect stillness, and everything from a blazing fire to the snowdrops on the polished table is just as I would have my home to be.

It was also my good luck that now and then I could escape to pleasant places where I had made new friends. The Socialist International Conference in Brussels in August was the high spot of the year. My speech at the ILP national conference in Leicester at Easter was paying rich dividends. I was appointed one of the fraternal delegates from the ILP. Never had I seen such bands and banners and colourful processions as were mustered in Brussels from more than a score of different countries.

We discussed disarmament, the fight against the rising tides of fascism, the need to establish an eight-hour working day and much else of a similar kind. But it is not the conference hall, not even the concerts and receptions and processions that have left with me all through the years the most vivid memory. What I best recall is Charles Trevelyan packing as many of his friends into a taxi as it would hold, then taking us to the field where the battle of Waterloo had been fought. To my amazement Charles knew the position of every regiment during the battle and guided us around with all the zeal of a small boy playing at soldiers. Where was the near-pacifist, the stern upholder of 'peace by negotiation', the serious senior statesman? At that time I had not yet visited Wallington, the family home of the Trevelyan family. Later I discovered the secret. The whole of an immense attic floor was laid out with literally thousands of toy soldiers. Every one of the regiments that had fought at Waterloo was represented. Charles, his historian brother George, and his poet brother Robert may have disagreed on many things. But they were united in the joy they took in this relic of their childhood.

The conference was over in six days. I had still some free time before the end of the school holidays, so instead of returning with the rest of the delegation, I went off over the Harz mountains and down the Rhine as far as Cologne. I had been persuaded to join a youth group from Berlin University who, after the conference, had planned to go on a walking tour. They treated me more like a pet mascot than as just one more of the company, and they got as much fun from my strange ways as I did from theirs. The first evening, at the end of a long tramp, I was so exhausted that when we reached the inn where we were to spend the night I tumbled into bed and fell sound asleep. One after another they came up to my bedroom to have a look. The inn-keeper's lady had told them she did not quite like to wake me. What should she do? I was sleeping under a great red eiderdown, not realizing that I should have waited for the bed to be properly made up with white sheets. It was the first time I had seen this kind of bedding, and, on the principle when in Rome do as the Romans do, I had simply slipped under it.

When we reached Cologne every room in every hotel was occupied. There was an International Trade Fair being held there at the time. At last, on the outskirts of the city, down by the waterfront, we found what seemed to me all we were looking for. It was an inn with a plain restaurant and bar on the ground floor, and bedrooms on the upper floors. And it was spotlessly clean. I had at that time some knowledge of French, if with an execrable accent, but all the German I knew was '*Ich habe mein hertz in Heidelberg verloren*'. This they had taught me and whenever we came to a new town I had to change the name. I could not understand the fierce argument going on as to whether we should settle in here or not. When consulted I said, yes, yes, of course. Their difficulty was that this was the kind of joint where sailors could bring women they picked up, no questions asked and that evening there was spare accommodation as the Fleet was out at sea. But how could they ask the young 'English lady' to stay in such a place? The young 'English lady' had no idea what the argument was about, but after a long day's march was only too thankful to have found a place to stay. I slept like the dead.

Remembering all the kindnesses and the songs and the laughter as we walked across the Harz mountains, then down the Rhine Valley, I often worried and wondered about the fate of my socialist friends after Hitler came to power. I learned very little – just a hint or a rumour now and again.

In those years another new world was opened up for me by a young Chinese intellectual. He was the London correspondent for some Far Eastern newspaper, and had already had his first book published, *China in Revolt*. Like Jomo Kenyatta, Julius Nyerere, and so many other young men and women who came to this country to study from parts of the world fighting for their independence, he found his best friends in the ILP, especially among those who had first-hand knowledge and experience of Far Eastern affairs. Before meeting Tang Liang-Li at an ILP conference I followed as best I could everything that was happening in revolutionary Russia, and I was keenly committed to the Indian Congress Party's struggle for independence. But China, Japan, the Middle East and the Far East were far-off exotic countries I knew nothing about.

Tang had a flat on the edge of Bloomsbury and most of his friends lived in the same area. I enjoyed an occasional jaunt to London to be with them all, travelling overnight on Friday, then returning overnight on Sunday in order to be back in time for school on Monday morning. It was Bunny, as we affectionately called her, that is Hilda McNulty, later to become the wife of Sir Selwyn Clarke when he was Governor of the Seychelles, who was the organizer and chief provider of hospitality during those hectic weekends. She worked in the ILP research department and besides being infinitely kind, had a wide knowledge of the problems of the countries which later came to be called 'the third world'.

On one visit, I persuaded Tang to take me to Chinatown in the East End. After assuring me that a particular pub which was then famous was just a tourist racket, he good-naturedly agreed. But Bloomsbury and Chinatown were worlds apart. Colonel and Mrs L'Estrange Malone, Bunny McNulty, Margaret Louis, Fenner Brockway, and many more of his friends gave me my first tentative insight into some of the problems of parts of the world where the lot of the poor made conditions in even our worst-hit mining areas seem affluent by comparison. I had been given wings. The Fife world I returned to began to look more and more drab. What should I do? Escape as so many others had done? Tang had a plan for me. He had an independent income of £500 a year in addition to whatever he earned. If I would give up my teaching job, come to London to live, I would soon be able to earn my living as a freelance journalist. I would not be taking any risks for he would find a room for me in the Bloomsbury area and provide me with £200 a year as a base to build on.

Tang took the problems of the world seriously, but not solemnly. He had a puckish sense of fun, and was very popular with his English friends. But I did not want him running my life for me. He expected to return to China by the late autumn of 1929 and wanted me to go with him. He would find a college lectureship for me to go out to, then if I did not like living there I could return to Britain with all the added experience and prestige of my travels. He had everything carefully planned and hoped that instead of returning home I would by then be willing to marry him. That was never even a remote possibility, but I valued his affection and concern for me, and was happy when he wrote from China early in 1931 saying he was working on another book and had married a Chinese girl who had had, like himself, a Western education. In a letter dated 19 March 1931, to Eveline who also knew him well, I say, 'He is a dear! I remember him with the greatest affection and would love to visit him in China some time – especially if there were Chinese babies with his eyes and funny ways.' Alas, the good news did not continue. Tang was a socialist, not a Communist. In the internal struggles that convulsed his country he was one of the many who went under. The last I heard of him was a message from Fenner Brockway saying he was in gaol. We were powerless to help.

Personal friendships and foraging expeditions into unfamiliar parts of the world gave spice to life. But nothing, and no one, could move me from my centre of gravity. I had no intention of running away. In July the previous year I had been adopted as parliamentary candidate for North Lanark. The Tory majority was only 2,028 and there was seething discontent in the heavily populated mining parts of the constituency. I had been entrusted at the age of twenty-three with what was regarded as a winnable seat. If I could win my way to Parliament I would be fighting the enemy eye-ball to eye-ball.

Looking back, I now know that if, like so many of the girls who were my school-friends, I had been sent to work in a factory or at the pit-head when I was fourteen years of age, I would not have been selected to contest North Lanark in face of competition from powerful trade union nominees who offered to pay all election expenses. But Scottish folk had a reverential attitude to education. They were as much impressed by my university degrees as by my oratory. And just as important, I came out of the right stable. I was Michael Lee's grand-daughter. As a schoolgirl I had often listened enthralled to stories of the fearful odds pitted against Bob Smillie, Keir Hardie, my grandfather and others like them when they were struggling to build a Labour, trade union, and co-operative movement. But those were old, far off, forgotten things and battles long ago. By the time I was old enough to be noticing what was going on around me, Grandfather Lee was dispute secretary for the Fife and Clackmannan Miners' Union. The head office of the Union was in Rose Street, Dunfermline, and his home was in easy walking distance of his office. Far from regarding my grandfather as a down-trodden proletarian, he was the great grandee of my youth.

There was, for instance, the world-shaking occasion when he went off to Budapest for an international miners' conference. On his return he had presents for all of us. The two I remember are the long hookah pipe for my father and the Hungarian doll in native costume for me. And the stories he brought back with him! In case you think I am presenting my grandfather as a kind of plaster saint, let me make him a bit more human. Let me describe how he came to sign the pledge. There was the authorized version and the unauthorized one. According to the authorized version, which I heard my grandfather himself tell more than once, one Saturday evening when his cronies called, expecting him to accompany them as usual to the pub, he said, 'I am not going with you. I have three sons growing up in this house, and never let it be said that it was their father's example that led them astray.'

Authorized version. Now what really happened. One evening Mrs Reid, who owned the village pub, put her shawl round her shoulders, and went up through Lochgelly High Street to my grandparents' home. 'Margot,' she said to my grandmother, 'you had better come down with me and bring your man home.' The two women were friends and neighbours. My grandmother found my grandfather in the back parlour of the pub, slumped over a table, dead drunk, and piles of money on the table around him. He was treasurer of the local miners' union; earlier in the evening he had helped to collect from his workmates their union contributions and also the penny or two a week they subscribed in order to maintain their own independent doctor, because they could not trust the company's doctors, especially when compensation cases were involved.

The miners' committee must then have retired to the back-room of Mrs Reid's pub, where they counted and checked the money they had collected. Afterwards they no doubt had a convivial dram or two, then they went off leaving my grandfather to gather up the money and take it home with him, to keep it safe until it could be put into the bank the following day. After a long hard day's work underground, collecting the money in the early evening, counting and checking it in the pub parlour, my grandfather could quite well, although I cannot know this for sure, have thought he would have 'a wee doch and doris' before wending his way home. Anyhow, there he was, slumped over a table in the back-room of the pub, lost to the world.

When he sobered up, what had happened so alarmed him that the most important thing in his life was that it must never happen again. He was terrified by the thought that his work-mates' money might have been stolen. He signed the pledge. 'A sober man is a thinking man' he was fond of saying.

Have I bashed his image by telling about his moment of weakness? For myself, when I was old enough to be told about his early life, I loved him all the more dearly.

Between 1926 and 1929 much that I myself had experienced gave the hardships of those early years a new reality. This was not just past history. Men were again walking from pit to pit, blacklisted everywhere for their trade union activities. Some children came to school hungry and ill-clad. Mothers died prematurely because they had not had proper nourishment and medical care, leaving behind young families. And there was so little I could do, cooped up with restless children in a classroom with pea-green walls, looking out on a slag-heap that towered above us immediately outside the playground railings. All my hopes were centred on Parliament, and I was going to get there sooner than I had thought possible, for in February 1929 the Conservative Member for North Lanark died. Preparations for a by-election were at once begun.

7. Member of Parliament for North Lanark, 1929–1931

In the North Lanark by-election a Tory majority of 2,028 was transformed into a Labour majority of 6,578. Any Labour candidate could have won the seat in the political atmosphere in the west of Scotland at that time, but the party managers were leaving nothing to chance. All the leading members of the party flocked to my support, as a General Election was due any moment, and North Lanark became a preliminary trial of strength. The Tories could not attack me on account of my youth for all the political parties were angling for the flapper vote.

When the General Election came women between twenty-one and thirty years of age would be voting for the first time. I now had my first encounter with party managers; they had written an election address for me, but when I read it in the spartan Glasgow hotel where accommodation had been found for me I tore it up. I can see now that they had a case. The miners' vote could be taken for granted; it was the middle- and lower-middle-class voters we had to impress, so my university background was written large and my mining background played down. But I was not having it. This was a reversal of my values. So, laboriously, with the cold marble slab of the washstand as a table, I rewrote my election address.

Our next collision was when I was told I would be introduced into the House of Commons by Miss Margaret Bondfield and the Chief Whip, Tom Kennedy. Again, I was not having it. I had no grudge against either of them, but I did not know them personally and had already arranged for my grandfather's lifelong friend, Bob Smillie, to be one of my sponsors. The other was James Maxton, an ILP friend I had known from my childhood. When I arrived in London in the early hours of the morning on the day I was due to be introduced into Parliament, nearly the whole of the Trevelyan family was waiting for me on the station platform. Even earlier they had gone to Covent Garden, and off we went to Great College Street in triumphal procession, the Trevelyans carrying boxes of fruit, flowers and vegetables on their heads. A short time before I was due to leave for the House, Lady Trevelyan had an inspiration. Standing at the far end of her long L-shaped drawing-room, she told me to go to the other end and come slowly towards her, three steps at a time, bowing as I advanced. I needed that rehearsal for otherwise I might have made a most ungainly parliamentary debut, bowing from the waist as I walked towards the Speaker's chair, but forgetting to lower my head.

Now I had to find somewhere to live. Clifford Allen (later Lord Allen of Hurtwood) had a small furnished flat at 28 Dean Street, Soho, which he wished to rent. That became my first London home. The former occupants had been Elsa Lanchester and Charles Laughton. I made friends with a spinster lady living in the flat below who wore mannish clothes, had a closely cropped hairstyle and had been a militant suffragette. It was as well for me that we became friends for I was country bred, not used to locking doors, especially doors with double locks, London-fashion. Sometimes I mislaid my key and had to ring her bell late at night. She had a comfortable divan in her sitting-room and never hesitated to offer me hospitality when I locked myself out.

The one good deed I could do for her in return was to free her from the nuisance of water seeping from the floor of the flat above, through her sitting-room ceiling. There was no fixed bath in my flat, only a large hip bath that was kept in a cupboard and pulled out when needed. I was most careful not to fill it overfull, for the bane of her life had been the times when the Laughtons miscalculated and had the floor swimming with water. At one time Karl Marx and his family had lived at 28 Dean Street. I hope they had a bit more space than the two rooms divided by a curtain which was the extent of the accommodation when I lived there.

As soon as I had an independent roof over my head, I was ready for battle. Alas, that 1929–31 Parliament was downhill all the way. In 1930 we lost the one Scottish Member who could have given effective leadership to the left of the party. We were mourning the death of John Wheatly. As Minister of Health and Housing he had been the outstanding success of the 1924 Labour Government. MacDonald, in 1929, fearing his robust, competent, socialist approach, excluded him from his Cabinet. It may very well be that, even with Wheatley, the tides of timidity and reaction would have been too much for us. It never occurred to me, when I rose to speak in Parliament for the first time, to keep to the convention of being non-controversial. I was in too big a hurry to say what I had come there to say. Winston Churchill was at that time Chancellor of the Exchequer and I directed my attack mainly against his budget proposals. Later in the day, in the Smoking Room, he came over to me and congratulated me on my speech. He assured me that we both wanted the same thing, only we had different notions of how to get it. The richer the rich became, the more able they would be to help the poor. That was his theme and he said he would send me a book that would explain everything to me. The book duly arrived. It was *The American Omen* by Garet Garrett, a right-wing economist who was despised by most of us for his extreme views.

I was being initiated into the urbanities of parliamentary life. In this rather claustrophobic atmosphere, friendships and enmities cut across party lines. Attlee's dislike of Herbert Morrison, Philip Snowden's comtemptuous attitude towards Ramsay MacDonald, the hostility of the trade union group towards the left of the Party, and quite a few other criss-cross relationships, were all too evident. There were similar personal and political tensions in the other parties. The Asquithian Liberals detested Lloyd George. Beaverbrook, even with the Conservative Bonar Law in tow, was regarded as a vulgar brigand by the landed aristocracy of the Tory Party. For many long years the Tory Establishment had just as low an opinion of Winston Churchill.

When Parliament rose for the summer recess I was stale and spent. From the by-election in February to the General Election in May I had been given no respite. It was meetings, meetings all the time, culminating in a spectacular Albert Hall Rally on the eve of the General Election. Besides coping as best I could with the problems of a score of villages in a large county constituency, I was under constant pressure to speak in other constituencies, in particular in 'marginals' we hoped to win in the General Election. I had to get away. But where should I go? And with whom? I decided that I was not fit company for man or beast so I would go off somewhere alone. And to have any real privacy it would have to be somewhere abroad.

During the Socialist International Conference in Brussels the previous year, I had listened fascinated to the tales the Austrian delegates told of the wonderful workers' flats they were building in Vienna and I knew that if I went there I would be given a warm welcome. My plan was to go to Vienna, book myself into a hotel, rest for a few days, then contact my socialist friends. But before I got round to doing so, Frank Wise, my favourite parliamentary colleague, arrived. I thought this was a pleasant coincidence. If I had known Frank better I would not have been so easily deceived. He was at this time, besides representing a Leicester constituency in Parliament, chief economic adviser to Centrosoyus, the Soviet Trading Mission in London. He was one of the brilliant young civil servants promoted over the heads of less able senior colleagues by Lloyd George in the critical days of the First World War. One of his duties was to act as economic adviser to the Prime Minister on Russian affairs.

His decision to leave the civil service and undertake the precarious task of advising and guiding largely inexperienced Russians on how to develop an export market in a hostile world was not an easy one. But Frank was an incorrigible optimist. With his generous, idealistic temperament he

believed devoutly, as so many others of us did, in all that Russia
sought to do. All it needed was time. But for a few days, he
too was seeking to escape from the pressures of the work he
had just left in London and the equally strenuous work waiting for him in Moscow. Knowing I was in Vienna, he thought
it a good idea to join me there before going on to Russia.

Vienna in the summer of 1929 had luxuriant flowers in the
window boxes, orchestras, large and small, playing in the
open-air restaurants, a wealth of cafés providing sweet cakes
and *café au lait* and lots of newspapers and magazines for
leisurely customers. It had recovered from the devastation it
had suffered during and after the First World War. Its handsome socialist mayor was proud of its Opera House and still
prouder of the splendid new flats, children's nurseries, and
other amenities that were giving new standards of comfort and
dignity to working people. I had made a good choice. Frank
and I could play truant for a few days, climbing the surrounding hills to sip the new wines, and in the evening dancing to
traditional Viennese music. Tragic times were to come again
all too soon to this lovely city, but for the moment Vienna was
bathed in sunshine and hope.

When a reluctant Frank moved on to Moscow I got out my
address book. A few days later I had left the hotel and was
staying with the hospitable Scheu family. They had worked
with Philip Noel-Baker under Quaker auspices in the hungry
years following 1918. Philip had written to them so I was expected and, as soon as they had my address, they came to call
on me and insist that I move out to their charming home in a
quiet tree-lined suburb. I was only too happy to do so. Along
with their son, Friedl, his friend Walter Wodak, and other
young Austrians, I went swimming in the open-air swimming
pools during the week, and at the weekends we would be off
down the Danube or climbing the surrounding hills.

On one occasion when the mayor took me on a sight-seeing
tour of the famous new flats, Walter and Friedl got me to
make some mild criticisms that they thought would come better from me than from them. The mayor was Walter's em-

ployer and he was a little in awe of him. The young fellows
thought some of the ornate decorations detracted from the
style of the buildings. It was the usual generation gap. We
young ones had a more streamlined notion of what constituted
good design. But it was all so very friendly. There was a whole
new world to build, and we were determined to build it. We
were dreaming and scheming about that new world, and we
were not going to allow anyone or anything to stand in our
way.

I returned from Vienna sunburnt and refreshed, ready to
resume the serious business that was the central purpose of
my life. But the friends I came back to in the villages of North
Lanark had not been away anywhere. No refreshment for
them. Just the daily grind, remorselessly, day in, day out,
year in, year out. Our only hope was to work to the limits of
our strength to persuade Parliament to come to their aid. But
the parliamentary atmosphere after the summer recess was
just as discouraging as in the earlier months. We on the left
urged pressing ahead with basic socialist measures, accepting
defeat from the combined Tory and Liberal vote, then going
to the country in circumstances in which we could evoke the
enthusiasm and hard-slogging support of the grass-roots 'faithful' who carried the brunt of electioneering. MacDonald,
Snowden, Thomas, the majority of the Parliamentary Labour
Party, took a very different line. They were determined to
soldier on, jettisoning most of their election promises and
trusting that the electorate would understand they were forced
to do so because they were only a minority Government.

One of my infuriating memories of this time, arising from
the greatly varying educational and income standards of
Labour Members of Parliament, was Beatrice Webb taking it
upon herself to teach the wives of the poorer Labour MPs how
to dress, how to curtsey, how to behave generally when invited to Buckingham Palace or any other grand social occasion. The homely, plump wives of two elderly miner MPs told
me how nervous they were about all this. I said there was no
need at all to be nervous, just wear your Sunday best and you

will look and feel fine. 'Yes,' they said, 'but you will be there wearing a proper long evening dress.' Of course they were right. From college days I was in the habit of wearing a long evening dress on special occasions. But to reassure them, I said, 'No, I shall wear an afternoon dress with long sleeves.'

It cost me more than I could afford to buy dark-brown silk material and have it made into a long-sleeved afternoon dress as I had promised. But when the great day came, and I joined the guests mounting the gilded staircase, I was the odd one out. My poor friends had accepted the Webb guidance. They were anxious not to do the wrong thing. Of course some of our working-class women had helped their husbands in the struggle to win local government and, later, parliamentary seats; they were used to the accompanying social occasions. But most of them had been tied to their homes, all their energies absorbed in caring for their husbands and young families. Now they were suddenly exposed to the full glare of the cruel eyes of high society. I could have wept when later on in the evening I looked over the banister and saw one of those innocent, inexperienced women sitting on a divan in the hall below. She was waiting for her husband, no doubt. But the flesh was bulging over the top of her too-tight corsage, her bare arms were large and red, and altogether she looked a picture of exhaustion and discomfort.

A joke that at that time was going the rounds was about the wife of Jimmy Thomas, who, waiting for her Cabinet Minister husband towards the close of an official reception, was asked if she would not like to stay a bit longer. 'No,' she said, 'I want to go home. My shoes are tight, my stays are tight and Jim is tight.' Of course this story was an invention, but it was thought very funny indeed by people who had been brought up to certain standards of dress and grooming, and were insolently insisting that others should imitate them. I was saddened that our poor women should have been so bamboozled by the Webbs. They had their own natural dignity, their own best clothes for special occasions. But these things Mrs Webb did not understand. There was a great deal she did not understand. We met again in Russia in 1932. No one could have been more ingenuous. It was treated as a great joke among sophisticated Communist officials when the Webbs got out their notebooks wherever they went, and wrote down, uncritically, everything they were told. But of all this later. In the meantime we were muddling on to the pitiful denouement of our electoral defeat in November 1931.

One of the people I met for the first time in that 1929–31 Parliament was Aneurin Bevan. It was conceded on all sides that the rapier thrust of his deadly attack on Lloyd George was the most brilliant of the speeches made by any of the newly elected Members. One summer evening, when the House was sitting late, we walked to the far corner of the Terrace, talking as we leaned together over the parapet. We were comparing notes. In spite of his brilliant parliamentary debut and his left-wing stance, I was in two minds about him. For one thing I did not like some of the company he kept. He delighted in the Beaverbrook menage and talked exuberantly about slumming in the West End. Was he too clever by half? Would he stand the pace or had he the makings of another Victor Grayson?

That summer evening I came to know him better. We had all the time in the world. It looked as if it was going to be an all-night sitting. Comparing notes, I could tell him of the stand my father took during the First World War, of the active part he had played in the miners' Reform Committee Movement and of his sceptical syndicalist outlook. I had often heard him say, 'It all comes off the point of the pick,' and he would refer to Parliament as 'the gas-chamber'. Aneurin Bevan, although belonging to a younger generation, had become involved in trade union and political affairs at such an early age that he had gone through every one of those experiences. But we had been defeated on the industrial front in 1919, 1921 and 1926. We were both now pinning our hopes on political action. We were eager to test to the full the possibility of bringing about basic socialist changes by peaceful, constitutional means. If we could avoid direct industrial confrontation, leading to a civil war in which our side almost certainly would be the weaker, that would be a consummation devoutly to be wished. Some other countries had no choice, Russia for instance. But maybe our people could be spared the agonies of civil war. Even Lenin had said that in England this might just be possible.

Nye always had a word for everything. I think that was the first occasion I heard him say, 'It is better to count heads than to break them.' At the same time we were both damning and blasting the drift of affairs under MacDonald's flaccid leadership. I knew it was no use asking Nye to become less of a lone wolf, to work more closely with the I L P group to which I belonged; he simply could not take James Maxton, the leader of our group, seriously. Nor could I. I had become mordantly critical of my old childhood playmate. Maxton had charisma and compassion. He loved everyone. He was a man of deep feeling, but there was no hard metal in him. Once when I tried to persuade him to leave the Smoking Room and speak in a particular debate, he said to me, 'Remember the leader who may be the right man for one stage in the journey is not necessarily the right leader for the next stage.' How true! And how well he knew himself!

That summer evening, when the division bell rang and we hurried inside to register our votes I said, 'You know, Nye, we could be brother and sister.' Looking at me with a mischievous gleam in his eyes, he quipped, 'Yes, and with a tendency to incest.'

When I was returned to Parliament for the second time in one year, that is in the May General Election of 1929, I was already quite at home. Indeed my first reaction to the House of Commons had been that its debating standards were inferior to our University Union debates – we students took great care to prepare our speeches. Also I had come to know many Members of that Parliament in earlier years in my home, at ILP conferences and elsewhere. When Nye arrived at Westminster he was a stranger in a strange land. He relished this new experience and was keen to pit his wits against the ablest of his political opponents as well as arguing with friends. Edward Marjoribanks, a young Tory Member, stepson of the first Lord Hailsham, approached Nye after his much publicized savaging of Lloyd George in his maiden speech. Beaverbrook, who was always a great collector of talented young socialists, had apparently asked Marjoribanks to bring Nye along with him to dinner one evening. Nye thoroughly enjoyed those rumbustious occasions. He was at all times contemptuous of the type of colleagues whose socialist roots were so shallow that they were afraid to venture into the company of high-powered Tory opponents.

Nye became friends with this brilliant young Conservative, who seemed all set for a successful parliamentary career. But, alas, the strain of completing a biography of Marshall Hall, and making his first contributions in Parliament, had reduced him to a state of nervous collapse. He was engaged to be married and confided to Nye that he was dreading the approach of his wedding because he felt he was impotent. I do not know whether he went into the gun-room of his stepfather's country house with the deliberate intention of committing suicide or whether he killed himself by accident. Either way, it was a tragic waste of life. Nye was bitter and angry and felt that if he had been treated more sympathetically by his stepfather, he might not have ended his life. I know nothing of all this directly, I only record how little Nye ever allowed himself to be cut off from people because of political differences. On the contrary, having his values challenged refreshed and exhilarated him.

I did not know Marjoribanks, nor did another brilliant newcomer, John Strachey, play any part in my life. But John was intrigued by the young collier from South Wales, who could more than hold his own in conversation on almost any subject. Another bond between them was a love of the Welsh hills. Nye became a frequent visitor in the home of John's older sister, Amabel, and her architect husband, Clough Williams

Ellis. The countryside around their home in Portmeirion became almost as familiar to him as his own Tredegar countryside.

I had my own quite different set of friends, who belonged mainly to Frank Wise's world. I might be off with Frank to a lecture at Chatham House while Nye was quite likely lecturing to the company around Beaverbrook's dining-table. Or I might find myself hauled down to Toynbee Hall along with Frank and his great friends, Margaret and Ted Lloyd. In these years, Jimmy Mallon was the presiding genius in this East End Community Centre, which, among its many other functions, catered for privileged young Cambridge University men concerned to find out how the other half lived. I had no need of this kind of schooling, but once Jimmy got hold of you there was no escape. I would find myself lecturing to a group of American Congressmen or to other well-heeled visitors, who, besides being curious about this unfamiliar world, had a social conscience. The object of the exercise was twofold: first, to expose the appalling living conditions in the East End; secondly, to attract as much cash as possible from visitors who could well afford to make substantial contributions.

I did not much care for some of Nye's new friends, but right from the start we were both fond of Frank Owen, a young Liberal Member who was also making a name for himself. There was no tortuous neurosis about that charming companion. He was full of the joys of spring in an honest-to-God straightforward way. For a time Nye and he shared the same flat. It was a hilarious affair. Our friendship with Frank Owen went on through the years, but in the nature of things Nye's intimacy with Strachey was bound to be short-lived. John was a brilliant expositor and in his work for the Left Book Club made an imposing contribution to the political education of a great many people on both sides of the Atlantic. The trouble was that he had no compass on his ship. He was all over the place; he lived entirely in a world of abstract concepts. When his pro-Mosley association ended, he was as contemptuous as ever of the broadly based Labour movement, and found a new role for himself as a leading exponent of Communist theory and practice. Later on he wended his way back into the safe embrace of the official Labour Party he had so much despised, moving, according to changing fashions, from left to right.

Another bright light in this 1929 Parliament was Sir Oswald Mosley. Early on he gave a dinner party in the Harcourt room. Frank Wise and I were among his guests. When the first course was served I found myself looking with distaste at half a dozen slobbery grey oysters. We had a wonderful selection of high quality fish in Scotland in those days, but I had never eaten oysters. Our host had placed me next to himself at the large round table and with great good nature saw I was in some difficulty. 'Let me show you,' he said, and proceeded to pour tomato sauce and some other condiment over the oysters, explaining that this was a good way to begin to have a liking for them.

Our next encounter was not so successful. I contrived to corner him in the division lobby while a vote was being taken, and as we were hemmed in on all sides by other Members he could not evade my importunities. I was indignant at the Government's delay in providing a road-work scheme which had been promised to ease the desperate unemployment situation in my constituency. Oswald Mosley was the Junior Minister in the Department dealing with those matters. I wanted no more dilly-dallying, nor was I in any way appeased when in dulcet, soothing tones he looked down on me from his superior height and tried to calm me. His tone would have been quite all right for reciting poetry in the moonlight, but it simply added to my wrath on this occasion. As a back-bencher I was already openly attacking Government dilatoriness. As a Minister he was not at that time free to do so although, to be fair, as I later came to know, he was fighting his boss, Jimmy Thomas, inside the Department as hard as we left-wing ILPers, were attacking openly on the floor of the House. But the fatal flaw in his character, an overwhelming arrogance and an unshakable conviction that he was born to rule, drove him on to the criminal folly of donning a black shirt and surrounding himself with a band of bully-boys, and so becoming a pathetic imitation Hitler, doomed to political impotence for the rest of his life.

A pleasant interlude in that strenuous, confusing, disappointing time was spent journeying through Russia in the summer of 1930. Fascination with all things Russian had still a strong hold on socialists, whether left, right or centre. I was eager to see for myself and delighted that I would be able to do so in privileged circumstances; not for me the carefully conducted tour, the official run-around. I travelled to Russia with John Strachey, George Strauss, Nye Bevan, Magda Gellan and Celia Simpson, but they all knew that once there I planned to leave them in order to accompany Frank Wise on a journey that would take us from Moscow to the foothills of the Caucasus. As it was his job to negotiate business deals with tough capitalist concerns, it was no use feeding him with fake statisics. He could not sell goods that did not exist; he had to have accurate first-hand information as to just how much wheat, timber, tobacco and other commodities were available for export.

I brought with me to Moscow a good supply of silk stockings and fine quality soap. These were presents that Frank intended to give to Madame Litvinov and to his Russian secretary. I had been promised a party, but that party did not materialize. His Russian friends were afraid to meet me: the ban on fraternizing with foreigners had been tightened. Before returning to London I was taken to visit Frank's secretary. This charming, highly cultivated Russian lady was living in one small room of the mansion where her parents had been sole occupants before the Revolution. The main furniture was two single divans, an elaborately carved chest and a table set for tea complete with a large silver-plated samovar. Was she a convinced Communist, or just making the best of things? How could I know? But one thing was clear: she was not wasting any time on self-pity. She radiated that warm Russian charm that many of us have known on both sides of the barricades – among penniless refugees living from hand to mouth in foreign capitals, and among those others facing up to all the rigours of a post-revolutionary situation.

Comfortable accommodation had been arranged for me in one of Moscow's hotels for visiting VIPs. But I was very much aware of the poverty and tensions that washed right up to the hotel door, and how strange it was to see the main streets of a capital city so very quiet, hardly any private cars, a tram car trundling past now and then, packed to suffocation inside, and with passengers clinging to the outside as well. I was not so foolish as to have expected anything different. A vast peasant country was struggling to build an industrial base and had none of the advantages Britain enjoyed in the early years of our Industrial Revolution. We had been in a position to command cheap raw materials from a vast colonial empire, but even so, children of five, six and seven years of age were forced by hunger to work until they dropped in our factories and coalmines.

Walter Duranty, the doyen of the American press group in Moscow, told me always to remember that Russia was a country in a state of siege. The same judgements could not be applied to her as to countries to easier circumstances. Louis Fischer and Maurice Hindus were two more American Moscow correspondents who talked with knowledge and considerable sympathy about all that was happening around them. One evening, when we were due to dine with our Ambassador and his wife, Frank was happy and excited for he had learnt that two high-ranking Russian officials and their wives had accepted invitations to the dinner. There was no lonelier job in all the world than running the British Embassy in Moscow at that time. This was a welcome breakthrough and Frank had been mainly responsible for it. One exception to the rule that Russians would not fraternize with foreigners was Karl Radek. We spent several evenings in the company of this loyal Bolshevik and accomplished journalist. He got around in a way few other Russians dared to emulate. Alas, like many others, he was later purged.

Before we left for Tiflis I was taken by Russian interpreters to see some of the hopeful, forward-looking projects that had been begun, best of all some fine nursery schools. It was no use pretending that such schools were being provided for all children – my Russian guides knew better than to make that kind of claim – but these were flags in the wind, the way Russia wanted to go. I knew only half a dozen words of Russian, but I did not need language to delight in the Russian ballet, nor in the Moscow Arts Theatre for the acting was so superb it transcended language.

By the time we left Moscow for Tiflis, I had talked with journalists and diplomats, Russian and Western; I had visited schools, theatres and much else. I was now keenly looking forward to the next stage of our journey. But, before I left, I was glad to have met the remarkable English woman who had become the wife of Litvinov, former London Ambassador and now a senior official in the Foreign Office. Madame Litvinov appreciated Frank's gifts every bit as much as his secretary. We dined pleasantly in her flat and although no doubt commodious in terms of the Moscow housing situation at that time, to London eyes it looked spartan and small. Its brightest ornament was a handsome, dark-haired young son who insisted on accompanying us downstairs when we left and on opening the door of the waiting car for us with truly princely grace.

I now live in a world where you have to be careful to close windows and doors at night and to lock your suitcase when you are travelling. But I was not brought up that way and my careless habits persisted. Somewhere between Moscow and Tiflis my suitcase was lost. I was dismayed when I remembered that I had not bothered to lock it. Frank reported the loss to the train attendants and to the station master at the next stopping place. His command of the Russian language was adequate to cope with this kind of problem and it was a matter of pride with him to travel unescorted as much as possible; and of course wherever we arrived, courteous officials were waiting to receive him.

We were travelling rough, Russian fashion, for most of the journey as there were few trains with wagon-lit compartments in the areas we had to visit. This was just what I wanted. I would be able to see revolutionary Russia with the lid off. And so I did! The caviar, bread and biscuits our Russian friends brought to the station for us as we were leaving Moscow soon vanished. How could you do other than share with emaciated mothers holding out starving babies, as we passed through stations in the famine area? At one point I lay on an upper wooden berth, so weak from hunger I did not want to move. Frank, with the help of a group of young comsomols who were travelling to a youth conference in Tiflis, brought me down from my bunk and out of the train. The comsomols guided us to a restaurant hidden away in a back street of a desolate grey village. Bortsch, red cabbage soup, shashlik and other foods were being served. The engine driver was also one of this select company, very select indeed: this hide-out was for 'official' personnel only.

At first the comsomols had looked at us suspiciously. How was it that two foreigners were travelling through a forbidden area, and travelling without their movements being supervised by a Russian guide? Once Frank explained who he was and the nature of his work, their young faces lit up with a mixture of awe and warm fellowship. They adopted us. Like Walter and Friedl and all the other young Austrians, like the Berlin youth group I had tramped with through so many miles of beautiful Belgian and German countryside, they were wildly excited about the future. The hardships around them were inevitable: they would pass. Then all Russians, not just a few, would come into their true inheritance. There would be food, and homes, and schools, and theatres, and foreign travel for everyone. One day they would visit London; they were looking forward to that very much. But first, they said, they had a lot to do at home.

The last stage of the journey south was a physical endurance test. We travelled all through the night sitting on planks in an open goods wagon. But we had good company. The comsomols, too, were being sent on in this fashion. We were the privileged ones. The rest of the passengers were left marooned in the middle of nowhere in a train that had broken down. On arrival at Tiflis we were at once taken to the station master's room. To my embarrassment, there were the contents of my suitcase, spread out on the floor. How I wished I had not stuffed unwashed hankies and one or two other odds and ends into a corner of my case. Had not my mother always insisted that you must never go out with a hole in your stocking for you might be run over and taken to hospital? Anyhow, not a single item was missing. I had to sign a document stating this was so, then my case was repacked and handed over to us.

In those years, and it may still be the custom, Russia's leading Ministers and others carrying exceptionally heavy work loads did eleven months hard labour then went off to the Crimea or to the foothills of the Caucasus for a month, living in sanatoriums. These had been the preserve of the wealthy in Tsarist days and combined every kind of medical supervision and treatment with luxury hotel accommodation. After the rigours of the journey south, I now found myself in the type of 'sanatorium' reserved for Russia's top brass. On waking, the morning after my arrival, I was astounded when my bedroom door opened and a man in a white uniform approached my bed. He knew no English, I had only six words of Russian, but it was clear that he was a doctor and had come to check my blood pressure and heart condition. I thought a mistake had been made. But it was no mistake; it was the routine examination given to all new arrivals. How very sensible. After the first shock, I fully approved.

One evening in a village in the foothills of the Caucasus, I had another glimpse into the immensity and complexity of the problems facing those who were seeking to change, root and branch, the living conditions and thought processes of this vast country. We were the guests of the mayor. He had an exceedingly assertive wife, who did most of the talking and left me in no doubt about the contempt she felt for the unemancipated women of the capitalist world. In Russia, by contrast, women were absolutely free and equal. It was a warm evening. We strolled along the village street and were resting on a grass verge at the foot of the hills. Looking up I saw a splendidly garbed Cossack swaggering down towards the village, his wife some paces behind him – and carrying all the luggage. I enjoyed my hostess's discomfiture. Century-old customs are not changed overnight.

8. Collapse of the Labour Government

Back again to a parliamentary situation drifting from bad to worse. There was no way of reconciling MacDonald's complete dependence on the advice of bankers and senior Treasury officials with the views of those of us who did not share his abject terror as to what would happen if we went off the Gold Standard. Nor did we believe that making the poor poorer, and cutting back on public expenditure could have any other effect than to turn a bad situation into a worse one.

It was in this atmosphere that the Mosley Manifesto was published. It was drafted by Allan Young, John Strachey, W.J. Brown and Aneurin Bevan. Most of its proposals were in line with what the ILP had been preaching for years; Allan Young, who had become chief economic adviser to Mosley, was formerly an active ILP member. If Oswald Mosley had had a little humility, and any real knowledge of the Labour movement, its strengths as well as its weaknesses, many of us on the left could have come together and, in time, offered effective alternative leadership. But after resigning as Junior Minister under Jimmy Thomas, who, God help us, had been appointed by MacDonald as Minister for Employment, he left the Party and went off to form a fascist party. Aneurin Bevan did his best to prevent John Strachey from following Mosley. He failed but before long John found he had made a mistake and retraced his steps.

We had not long to wait for the final collapse of this pathetic Parliament. MacDonald, frightened out of his wits, agreed to form a National Government. When the election came, we were reduced to a number of warring splinter groups. MacDonald, Snowden and Thomas were the prisoners of the

Tories. Some Labour Members went with Mosley. Others, either openly or clandestinely, transferred their allegiance to the Communist Party. The silliest decision of all was made by the ILP. Instead of remaining in the Labour Party and seeking to strengthen its hold there, under Maxton's poor leadership we went into self-imposed exile.

I had not a single really close friend among the pro-disaffiliation ILP members. My most intimate friends remained in the Labour Party and made frantic efforts to keep me with them. I loathed the thought of disaffiliation but I was a prisoner of geography. The most dedicated, unselfish elements in the Scottish Labour movement were so revolted by the record of the 1929–31 Parliament that they insisted on going their separate way. How could I desert my friends? How could I make common cause with the right-wing leaders of the Scottish party with whom I had quarrelled so often and so bitterly? There was also an element of cowardice in my decision. I could not bear to be branded a careerist, as someone ready to betray old comrades for the sake of personal advantage.

The atmosphere of that November 1931 Election was very different from the two I had fought in 1929. There were still crowded meetings. There were still eager canvassers ready to work until they dropped. But the hostility of some of the right-wing local miners' leaders, a hostility which had not surfaced two years before, began to make its influence felt. North Lanark was a miners' seat. I had stolen it from them. At the selection conference I had beaten their nominee. All that and disappointment with the Government's record had its effect. But by far the strongest opposition I had to face came from the Catholic church. Every Member of Parliament who had voted against the Scurr amendment was blackballed.

John Scurr was a right-wing Labour MP whose loyalty to the Catholic hierarchy took precedence over his loyalty to the Labour Party. Sir Charles Trevelyan's Education Bill made provision for Catholic schools. But Scurr was not satisfied. The Scurr amendment asked for more than the Government thought right to give. Trevelyan was the only friend we left-wing ILPers had among Government Ministers, but that did not deter Maxton, McGovern and Campbell Stephen from failing to support the Bill he cared so much about and had worked so hard to achieve. They did all they could to pressure me into joining them. When the vote on the Scurr amendment was about due, they got hold of me, literally got hold of me, to explain to me the 'facts of life'. In the west of Scotland I could challenge the authority of the Labour Party and still survive, but if I also antagonized to the Catholic vote, there was not the slightest hope I could hold my seat.

I was livid with contempt. They were prepared to desert not only their friend, but their principles. If they had genuinely believed in the Scurr amendment that would have been a different matter. But no. All they cared about was saving their seats. They succeeded. I went under. In Ebbw Vale Aneurin Bevan had been returned unopposed. He spent the whole of the campaign helping me in North Lanark. But no amount of effort could overcome the powerful forces against us. A Tory was elected with a majority of 4,693.

When it was all over I could at last go home to Lochgelly, where all I wanted was complete rest for a couple of days. One of the first letters I wrote was to Charles Trevelyan. I was dismayed that he had been defeated, but the vote against him was so decisive that I knew his taking time off to do some meetings in North Lanark had not decided the issue. Then and always I wrote to him in completely uninhibited fashion, never for a moment dreaming that those letters would be preserved and one day returned to me. On 29 October 1931 I wrote:

All along I have been mentally and emotionally adjusted to defeat in North Lanark. It was just as well I was steady, for yesterday, in the villages, was terrible. Both men and women were weeping and cursing, being taken completely by surprise. I went round after the poll and nursed the wounded as best I could, finishing with a funeral service in Shotts which brought a mixture of cheering and tears from crowds who blackened the streets by their numbers. I am terribly,

terribly sorry about those stalwarts who worked like slaves through all the rain, and for the moment are simply broken. Personally, I was so certain of the result that I bundled Mother off to Fife on Wednesday morning before the results were out and would not let Bevan or others wait at the County Buildings. I hate people around on an occasion like that who may seem to be sheltering me from the crowds.

When I came out there was wild cheering, so I got on top of the car and spoke for a few minutes. I think it bucked them up a bit for they felt that anyhow we were not running away. The victorious candidate was got quietly away by a side door, while two rows of mounted police were necessary before I could get through to the car waiting for me. To the crowds of course I said the expected things about fighting again and winning, but when Bevan departed for Wales before I set out to tour the villages he cheerfully said 'Goodbye for five years this time', and I think he is right. With such a majority the Tories will not dream of appealing to the country earlier.

When the fight was on it was splendid having so many good pals around and difficulties were mere trifles. But one's very attachment to them made their grief the more trying.

On Sunday I must return to Glasgow for municipal election rallies. I simply must do so, for the candidates I am speaking for worked like slaves throughout my campaign and are banking on some of us seeing them through their job.

I know you will be troubling about me, but please don't. Apart from the inevitable amount of disappointment that all of us must face, I am surprised how well I have stood the wear and tear. My voice is almost back to normal and with two days sleep, I shall be quite fit again.

A week or two later Frank and I were at Wallington together. This was one of the few places where we were completely safe from malicious gossip. And there was always a warm welcome. Not a single one of Frank's letters to me have survived. But Charles Trevelyan kept all our letters. In writing to Charles soon after we returned to London, Frank gives a pretty clear picture of the problems, personal and political, we were trying to solve. On 23 November 1931 he wrote:

A request from Jennie to give a signature for your visitors' book reminded me to my disgrace that I had not written to thank you for a pleasant interlude which your hospitality made possible at Wallington ten days ago. It was pleasant indeed to see you and Jennie though you were under the weather – and good to find she wasn't despite the election.

I am very sensible of all she has meant to me in happiness, in inspiration and in sound political sense in the past two years. And it won't be my fault if we don't find a way round the external difficulties that confront us, though they are very far from simple at present. J, as I daresay you well know, is very clear-headed and achieves an amazing combination of cool detached judgement with the warmest possible feelings which at once bewilder and delight a mere Englishman, even one accustomed to many foreign races. I presumed to think, erroneously, that the Scotch were unexciting. But she never loses sight of her main objectives. Nor generally do I. So we'll probably attain what we both want.

Meantime she seems to be piling up introductions and encouragements for her American tour which I expect will be a terrific success. I am wistfully hoping that business may call me across the Atlantic at the same time. But so far I've not been able to find sufficient excuse.

I gather that the Labour front bench is still weighed down by the disrepute of its period in office and that Aneurin Bevan is about the only really useful parliamentarian yet emerging from the back benches.

When I looked back on the previous two years I was grateful. It had not been hard slogging one hundred per cent of the time. Now and again, for a brief spell, one could escape to pleasant places, secure friendships, days in the country, an occasional evening at the theatre.

The most magical theatre occasion had been when I was taken to see Paul Robeson's *Othello*. I was enchanted by the deep strong cadences of that wonderful voice and felt that this was not only a great artist but also a most unusual and distinguished human being. When Lady Trevelyan heard me raving on in this fashion, like any latter-day pop-star fan, she said, 'I see I shall have to arrange a party.' So one warm sunny afternoon in the first summer of the Labour Government, all eyes on the Terrace of the House of Commons turned to the table where the traditional tea, with strawberries and cream, was

being served to Sir Charles and Lady Trevelyan, Sybil Thorn-
dike and Lewis Casson, Paul Robeson, his wife and myself.
The centre of attraction, of course, was Paul Robeson. Ramsay MacDonald, still in the first flush of success, sauntering
by, stopped to pay his respects. So did others. And many
more looked shyly in our direction but did not venture to in-
vade our privacy.

The only other time I met Paul for more than a passing
minute was when Nye persuaded him to attend the Welsh Eis-
teddfod the year when it was held in Ebbw Vale, Nye's constituency. We spent a pleasant evening together with lots of
laughter and good talk in the home of the friend who was
providing hospitality. Then the following night there was the
opening concert with Nye in the chair, Paul the chief solo
singer, and the whole of that great audience singing with a
fervour and joy that is one of the most endearing of Welsh
characteristics. It breaks the heart to think of all the suffering
inflicted on Paul Robeson in his later years.

Most evenings in that 1929–31 Parliament, we were
chained to the House, for every vote was needed when the
division bell rang. It was a great treat, therefore, to be invited
to dinner at the Trevelyan home in Great College Street,
which was near enough to Parliament to have its own division
bell. When that sounded those of us who were MPs had to
scurry across to the House, getting there just in time to vote.

There was only one dinner party that turned out disastrous-
ly. Charles had invited H.G. Wells to dine with him and
asked if I would like to join them. Of course, of course! H.G.
was one of the bright guiding stars of my youth. I read avidly
everything he wrote. That day in Parliament there had been a
violent debate about all the issues that meant most to me – the
cruelty and indignities of the Means Test, failure to get on
with the building of urgently needed houses, schools and hospitals, and all this against a background of hundreds of
thousands of unemployed building workers. I arrived at Great
College Street brimming over with indignation. The only
other guest that evening was H.G. Lady Trevelyan was at Wal-

lington. If she had been present, we might have got ourselves
sorted out. As it was, H.G. brushed aside anything I tried to
say, returning obsessively to the teaching of history in schools.
We began glaring at one another with growing hostility. So
this was H.G. Wells, this dumpy little man with the squeaky
voice, totally indifferent to the problems that concerned the
great mass of ordinary people.

It was many years later before I met Wells again. Nye and
he had become friends. We were invited to a Sunday buffet
supper at his home in Regent's Park. What had happened at
our first meeting was that Trevelyan, as Minister of Education, had invited Wells to dinner, as Wells believed, to talk
seriously about the teaching of history in schools. H.G. wanted
to get on with this without constant interruptions from a brash
young woman hopping from subject to subject. If Charles had
told me to come and listen while he talked with Wells I would
have understood and gladly concurred. But I was not told this
– hence the misunderstandings. Now all was sweetness and
light; before the end of the second meeting, H.G. was telling
me how much I resembled his favourite grand-daughter!

After the 1931 Election I now had to solve the problem of
earning a living. In January I was due in America on a lecture
tour, but would Americans want to listen to a defeated candidate? I wrote at once to Mr Feakins, my lecture agent, in-
structing him to cancel all contracts with colleges, women's
organizations, town forums, and the rest where the slightest
reluctance was shown to have me as a lecturer. I need have
had no fear. There were only one or two cancellations. So I
sang for my supper from coast to coast and had my first experience of how overwhelming American hospitality can be.
When I was about due to return to London, a telegram from
Graham Spry in Ottawa invited me to go to Canada to lecture
under the auspices of the National Canadian Clubs. This was a
complete surprise, but as I had nothing better to do, I happily
accepted. Graham was club secretary; it is possible that his
friend Stafford Cripps had suggested sending me that invitation, but I do not know for sure.

Another surprise was when I found myself sitting between W.B. Bennett, then Prime Minister, and Mackenzie King, Leader of the Opposition, at a club luncheon in Ottawa. I was hastily told that they were not on friendly terms, and it was up to me to do my diplomatic best to keep everything going smoothly. Both remained after the lunch while I addressed the gathering on 'The Younger Generation in Russia'. All on the strength of my one short visit there! The mystery of this double honour bestowed on my unimportant self was not solved for me until AJP Taylor published his biography of Beaverbrook in 1972. Bennett had not been expected at the lunch, but he turned up after receiving a letter from his friend, Max Beaverbrook, telling him he must look after me. Just how topsy-turvy can human relations be? I was not one of Beaverbrook's entourage: politically we were poles apart. Yet he took the trouble to write to influential friends on my behalf, in his usual cryptic style, 'Jenny is a great young woman. She follows Maxton, quarrels with the Labour Party, hates MacDonald; loathes Snowden; loves Russia – and may go to gaol.' To another friend he wrote:

She is pretty. She has brains. She very nearly became a first-rate figure in the House of Commons... She is Maxton's darling. I mean his political darling, for Jim Maxton has no darlings in the sexual sense, poor fellow.

By that time I had become sadly critical of Maxton and, far from loathing Snowden, I was deeply sorry for him. But it was all well meant. So too were Bennett's attentions. I was taken home to a family dinner to meet his sister, I was shown with pride the signed photograph of Mussolini in his study, and when leaving he insisted on kneeling down to help me fasten my fur-trimmed Canadian snowboots, of which I was very proud.

Crossing the United States from New York to Hollywood, then back again, followed by a Canadian lecture tour that took me from the East Coast to the West Coast and back again during the first three months of 1932 gave me a many-sided view of the Great Depression of that year. Part of the time I was splendidly looked after by prosperous Americans with apparently a passion for being lectured to on every kind of subject. 'Depression' did not mean that everyone was on the bread line. Indeed if I had not made friends with the Reuther brothers in Detroit and with a high-spirited compassionate group of socialists and liberals in New York and in several other cities I would have seen little or nothing of the victims of the Depression. They made sure I saw a great deal. In New York I was taken on a conducted tour of shanty-town, or Hooverville as it was sometimes called. Homeless families were living in shelters made from old rags, orange boxes, any scrap materials they could get hold of. Then there were the centres where endless lines of destitute men queued for a bowl of soup. I turned my head away as I could not bear the embarrassment of invading their privacy.

In Canada as well as in the United States the same sights recurred. Somewhere in the Canadian Middle-West, at one of their rescue centres, to which compassionate friends who were trying to do what they could to help, insisted on taking me, I heard a broad Scotch voice shouting, 'Jennie, Jennie', and turned to greet the son of one of my best friends and political supporters in North Lanark. He was glad to see me, and, being young and strong, was quite sure he would get over this bad patch. No whining. But before we parted he made me promise that I would not tell his 'mither' where I had met him. As if I would! In America at that time, just as in Britain during the Second World War, there was a certain camaraderie, a certain breaking down of social barriers, although that kind of claim can be carried too far. My most embarrassing moment was when I returned to New York after a cross-country journey and had not a single dime in my pocket. I was standing helplessly on the station platform as I had a portable typewriter, books and other luggage with me that was quite beyond my strength to carry. A tall, strong, Negro porter came towards me. I told him I was sorry, but I had no money to pay him. 'That's all right, miss,' he said, and with an angelic smile carried my luggage to the taxi rank.

Afterwards I tormented myself worrying whether he understood the nature of my dilemma. Did I or did I not explain my situation to him? I was not short of cash, but with bank closures and all other kinds of difficulties, for the moment I had imprudently left myself without ready money. Once I reached the hotel in Gramercy Park Square where I was in the habit of staying and was known, there was no difficulty in paying the taxi-driver. Although I was on a commercial lecture tour, it never so much as occurred to me to avoid meeting liberal and socialist circles, totally unconnected with the money-earning part of my visit. Apparently all too often they were cold-shouldered by visiting socialist lecturers who made the excuse that their lecture contract prevented them from doing unpaid work. Friends I met then for the first time remained my friends all through my life, a rich reward for stepping out of line, leading, if you like, a kind of double life.

On returning to London, Charles Trevelyan and Frank Wise insisted that I must not simply throw myself around on ILP propaganda platforms. I must settle down to serious study. They urged me to qualify for the English Bar. I already had my Scottish LL.B. One comical by-product of this was that I would be required to eat only half the number of dinners that beginners have to eat as part of the ritual of preparing for the Bar. I made a start: I ate some dinners in Middle Temple and passed one examination. But my heart was not in it; I was too deeply involved in the day-to-day struggles of the Labour movement.

9. Russian Interlude

Apart from political involvements, the one thing I wanted to do in 1932 was to return to Russia. This time I did not want just to meander around the foothills of the Caucasus. I longed to climb to the summit, then to journey slowly down into the valleys on the other side. I had never the least interest in organized games but loved walking and climbing, and I thought I was pretty good at both.

In the summer of 1930, when Frank and I had looked up from the lower slopes of the Caucasus to the mountains towering above us, he said that he had promised himself that one day he would take time off to climb to the top. The question was, could I go with him? He had spent holidays climbing in the Swiss mountains and was strongly built. I loved the hills of Scotland but was too ignorant to realize that I knew nothing about the hazards of serious climbing. Another snag was that I had never ridden so much as a donkey on a holiday beach, but would have to be able to sit on a horse without falling off, even if it were only a tame mountain mule.

We had agreed that while crossing Canada earlier in the year, I should take every opportunity to learn to ride. Frank was most anxious about this. I wrote to him from Canada saying:

I don't know how or where I shall be able to have riding lessons. My outfit is too cumbersome to trail around and the chance of finding horses and riding opportunities, especially at this time of year, are few. I shall not miss any opportunities that come my way, and anyhow you need not worry. I shall stick on all right if I have to. You wait!

Originally I had planned to return from the United States in the middle of February, but invitations to lecture both in Canada and the States kept flowing in so I was not able to sail home until 26 April. I was only too grateful to my transatlantic friends for enabling me to earn enough to keep me going for at least a year, all the more so because my father had been seriously ill and needed the month's holiday I arranged for him. I also took good care to send home a monthly cheque of £25 to ensure that my parents had any modest comforts they needed. When invited to Canada, I had not realized that the National Canadian Clubs were very much a top-brass affair. Until then only leading Establishment figures among Conservatives and Liberals had been their guest speakers; I was their first socialist guest, but soon I became used to having the red carpet spread under my feet wherever I went. Writing to Frank just before returning home, I said,

> I am so used now to travelling like Royalty and having every detail worked out for me that I shall be as awkward to handle at first as some of these horses you are playing around with. But no doubt, with a little tact and skill you will be able to reproletarianize me.

After May Day meetings in Lanarkshire I had just time to go home for a day or two, have my luggage put in order, then off to Moscow. Frank left London a few days ahead of me, so by the time I arrived he had completed his business affairs. As before, we were travelling Russian-fashion and it was all very primitive and friendly. Whenever the train stopped everyone rushed out to the platform to fill billy-cans with boiling water so that we could make tea. There was no food on the train: each little group carried its own rations; 1932 like 1930 was one of the famine years. There were starving people begging for food at every station.

Then, total contrast. On arrival at Kislovodsk we were met and escorted to one of the luxury VIP sanatoriums. A Cossack regiment was stationed just outside the town; Frank made friends with the officer in charge, who invited us to accompany him any morning we would like to have riding practice. I would be in no danger, for the horses were so well disciplined that the leader set the pace and the others obediently followed. For the first few mornings all went well. We meandered along almost at walking pace, the two men obviously enjoying talking to one another. I knew too little Russian to know what they were talking about and, in any case, I was concentrating on the business of holding the reins properly, gripping with my knees as hard as I could and keeping my feet in the stirrups. Then something went wrong. I was too dazed at the time to know quite how it happened. All I knew was that the horse I was riding set off at a mad gallop. I had not enough strength in my arms and thighs to control it properly; all I could do was lean back as far as possible, and by a miracle I kept my balance until the two men rescued me.

This incident gave me a wildly inflated notion of my skill as a horsewoman. I was in no danger while riding tame mules but just escaped breaking my neck when I returned home, boasting that I had been taught to ride by a whole Cossack regiment. One painful tumble was enough. I vowed I would never mount a horse again and I never have.

But we had not come to the Caucasus to linger in Kislovodsk. We were both keen to be on our way and all arrangements had been made for us. Our luggage, except what we needed for the climb, had been forwarded to Baku, and we were to join a group of Russian climbers who were making the first crossing of the year. They were professionals whose job it was to check what damage had been done to passes over the mountains by avalanches in the winter months. For five days, while we were negotiating the top of the mountains and beginning the descent on the other side, we would have to be prepared to travel on foot.

The night before the climb began there was little sleep. Frank was warmly welcomed as a member of the team, but a passionate argument began concerning the female with him. Two tough proletarians from a Leningrad film factory were not taken in by my splendid outfit, not even by my fine leather riding boots. When evening came, two mattresses and rugs were allocated to Frank and myself on one side of a wooden partition; the Russians were similarly provided for on the other side. Through the thin dividing wall Frank could hear and understand the interminable argument going on among them. I curled up and went to sleep. By morning the two Leningrad realists were still holding out against me, but they had been overruled.

As I set off with a large rucksack on my back, I laid down the law in my usual high-handed fashion. Under no circumstances must Frank try to carry any of my climbing gear and he must leave me to climb in my own way and at my own pace. For the first day or two we trundled up the easy part of the climb in horse-drawn carts. Then the carts and their drivers departed. We were now ready to tackle the mountains in earnest. The beauty of this fairyland of ice and snow was so exhilarating that I do not remember feeling either cold or fatigue during the first day's climb. Our leader knew every step of the way and in the evening he guided us to a primitive hut where a great fire was kindled, food prepared, and then to sleep.

My first discomfiture was when I tried to put my boots on in the early morning. They had been soaked the previous day as we tramped through snowdrifts, dried during the night by the fire and were now as hard as boards. No amount of tugging was any good. They had to be abandoned. Fortunately, I had a pair of gym-shoes in my rucksack. The Russians wrapped around them the kind of cloths that peasants had walked and climbed in back through the centuries. My new footwear was quite comfortable. So on we went. It was my pride and resolve that I would never hold the others back, never be last in line. My special friend was a Red Army soldier with a pleasant, worn face who had some kind of heart trouble. I understood that he was climbing against doctor's orders, but loved the mountains so much that he was determined just once more to take part in this kind of adventure.

All my life I have found that when there is something you have to do, you find strength somehow to do it. So up we climbed until I had one more mishap, this time much more serious. We were feeling our way along a narrow ledge, in circumstances that I learned later no responsible Swiss climbers would have tackled unroped, when I slipped and was slithering down a steep incline with a frozen lake at the far distant bottom. The leader climbed down after me. Everyone was roped together now, and the rest of the party pulled us back to safety. No one reproached me. We were all good friends. But by now I was living on my nerves: I could not eat. In order not to worry Frank I accepted my share of the evening meal, then went out of sight and threw it away.

At last the blissful moment came when we saw the first sign of human habitation on the other side. A flag was flying in the wind over a mountain hut; the local people knew we were approaching and were waiting to welcome us. The flag was for us. At one stage I had blisters on my heels, then other parts of my feet became painful, but the extraordinary thing was that later on the discomfort vanished. My feet were encased in a soggy mass of rags and were not unbound night or day. As we approached the welcoming hut, one of the young Russians came smiling towards me and made to remove the rucksack from my back. It was a friendly gesture but I was not parting with it. We were now a deliriously happy band in a tipsy kind of way, although we had drunk only cold spring water during the climbing and tea in the evening.

Then the strangest thing of all happened. As soon as I unloaded my rucksack and lay down on a mattress on the wooden floor of the hut, I began to weep convulsively and uncontrollably although I was very happy. Never before or afterwards have I known that total separation of mind and body. Also, although I was lying on a level wooden floor, I had the sensation of rolling over and down a forty-five degree incline. Frank was as bewildered as I was. I told him to go away, leave me alone, I would soon be all right. To my surprise the plain soldier with the heart condition came over to me, knelt beside me, began taking my pulse, then looked up smilingly to Frank, assuring him there was nothing to worry about.

What I did not know until then was that he was not only

an experienced climber but a high-ranking Red Army officer and a qualified doctor. Before beginning the climb Frank and he had introduced themselves to one another and the leader of the party knew all about both. But before he knelt by my side feeling my pulse. I had not a clue; he had not wanted his identity known during the climb, but of course Frank knew I was being carefully guarded by the most competent of mountaineers. Any time a halt was called I thought it was so that he could rest because of his heart condition. Maybe sometimes it was because he decided I needed to be rested. A dainty ballerina who had been trained by Isadora Duncan was his travelling companion. She was tiny but immensely fit and had not so much climbed as floated over the mountains. The four of us were natural companions. It was arranged that after we had rested, horses would be brought for us and we would travel together during the next part of the journey.

In the meantime, our party went off to wash soiled clothes in the sparkling water of a fast-running stream. That is, all except me. Once my feet were unbound they were a mass of raw red flesh. I could not walk as far as the stream but found a basin in the hut and hobbled out to the veranda with it. But I was not allowed to do my own washing; the earlier well-justified hostility of the squat, powerfully built factory hand from Leningrad had vanished – she was now all friendliness and smiles. In spite of my remonstrances, she insisted on running off to the stream with my washing.

The following day, clothes washed and dried, an ironing-board was produced and I was quietly ironing a few garments when my new friend approached. A quite ridiculous wisp of a white lace embroidered hankie had turned up among my clothes: the sort of thing you don't buy for yourself but are given as a Christmas or birthday present. She looked at it so admiringly that I held it out to her. We had only sign language between us. She refused, but just as she had overruled me and run off with my washing, now I insisted she accept it. First she held it in front of her, then tried it on her head. This was not something for everyday use: it was a precious decoration, a piece of sheer luxury in a land where such as she were unused to any kind of luxury. Watching her response to this minute crumb of beauty I had to be careful not to show what I was thinking and feeling, but under my breath I prayed to the God I did not believe existed to be gentle with her, to give her a fair share of the beauty and love she needed just as much as any superficially more attractive woman.

The professionals prepared to return to where we had started – they had completed their survey. Fond farewells were said all round. By now I had had my fill of the beauty and terror of the mountain tops, I was more than ready to be on the move again, especially as the melting snows thundering down the mountainside crashed in our ears all day, all night, without a moment's respite. To travel from the snow line right down to a land that looked a picture-book illustration of the Old Testament, all in a few short days, was wonderful beyond belief. We walked or rode through a countryside where the oxen were grinding the corn, where figs were ripening on the trees and people were living lives that had remained unchanged century after century. And the sheer luxury of not having to carry anything; the mules were our porters. When the time came for our soldier friend and his girl to go their separate ways, a ragged scarecrow of a man became our guide. We were assured we could trust him, that he knew everything there was to know about both the terrain and the local people.

Once we were alone with him, our guide began talking to Frank on the assumption that the English gentleman was a conservative and hated the new regime as much as he did. Until the Revolution he had been a priest. That was very handy for us as he knew where to find food. A small stone house which looked as inhospitable as any house could look changed character when the family saw that it was the priest who was arriving. These were secretive mountain people. No strangers travelling on their own could have won their trust, but for their priest and his friends, eggs, chicken and bread miraculously appeared and quite a feast was soon prepared.

There was only one shadow marring our journey. As soon as we left the mountains behind us and reached the populated areas, there seemed an endless number of beggars, some lame, some with missing limbs, many of them emaciated children with hideous eye-sores.

I was now looking forward to reaching Tehran. I thought that once we had sailed across the Caspian Sea from Baku to Persia there would no longer be those pitiful sights. But in Persia the beggars were just as much in evidence, and just as abysmally naked and hungry and diseased. The only difference, I told myself, was that Russia was trying to overcome the poverty and oppression inherited from the past. It was also seeking to free women from centuries-old subjection. Persia, as we then called Iran, was making no such effort.

In the streets of Tehran, for the first time I saw women swathed from head to foot in hideous black garments, only the eyes showing. One day I went out in the mid-day sun, all alone, bare-legged, wearing a short sleeveless white dress. That was a very ignorant thing to do but I had not stopped to think; I wanted to buy a small rug in the bazaar that I could have made into a saddle bag I needed for extra luggage. The stall-keepers in the Bazaar were asleep. The silence was broken only by a growl from somewhere, not loud, but not pleasant. An American with a damp cigar in the side of his mouth appeared as I was preparing to retreat to the safety of the hotel and said, 'Say miss, you can buy cheaper in London. Here is an address. No need to cart a carpet all the way there and you will have to pay duty on it at the Customs!' Being obstinate, I returned later, properly chaperoned this time, and bought a very small but very lovely Persian rug that I cherished through the years.

10. End of an Era

A delightful by-product of my American tour in the early months of the year was that I could now afford to rent a one-bedroomed top-floor flat at 19 Guilford Street. Sitting-room, bedroom, bathroom, kitchen, were all well proportioned and the rent was £2 10s per week. I find it impossible to equate money values then and now. Also Great-Grannie Pollock's great-grand-daughter had no use for old-fashioned furniture. One day I would revert to a love of old things, but in this phase it had all to be in the contemporary mode – light weathered oak. Settling into a real flat of my own and the labour of going around finding the essentials I needed balanced my disquiet with the way political events were moving.

In July the ILP finally disaffiliated from the Labour Party at a specially convened conference in Bradford. The vote was decisive – 241 for, 142 against. I had to go one way or the other. For reasons or if you like emotions I have already described, I remained with the ILP. To cut ourselves off from the main stream of the working-class movement was madness. I made no secret of my hope that the left inside the Labour Party would gain sufficient ground to make it possible before too long for all of us to be in the one party again. Fenner Brockway was the great peacemaker among us; after disaffiliation he still had a difficult job trying to reconcile our varying points of view. Ten years later, describing those who in 1932 tried to prevent us cutting our own throats, he wrote in *Inside the Left*:

It was Frank Wise who troubled me most. Despite my admiration for his knowledge and long-view constructive mind, we disliked being lectured to at length from Olympic heights showing his contempt for the contributions of less educated and more emotionally elementary colleagues and forgetting that the working-class experience of comrades around him might be as valuable as his civil service experience and his mastery of economic facts.

Frank had immense self-confidence but he was not arrogant in any harsh sense. He was the kindest of men. I was completely on his side both in his analysis of the economic issues facing us and in the constructive proposals he put forward for dealing with them. Part of our difficulty in the ILP was that most of the fine men and women who were attracted to it were preachers, dreamers, idealists who, whether they called themselves Christians or humanists or agnostics, were by temperament deeply religious. They belonged to the tribe of Abou Ben Adhem. They loved their fellow men. They longed for the day when there would be no more war, no child would be undernourished or denied educational opportunities and no man denied the right to work. I was as impatient as anyone else to reach the Promised Land; but I was also fascinated with the practical problems that would have to be faced and overcome if we were ever to get there.

Frank was one of the few who had practical as well as theoretical knowledge of the business world. On one of the first occasions when I had dinner in his flat, the only other guest was Max Beaverbrook. Frank's ILP comrades became restive when he tried to explain to them the economic facts of life and the realities of power politics. Beaverbrook was more worldly-wise. He found it worth while to clamber upstairs to Frank's top-floor flat in John Street in order to inform himself on the current state of the Russian economy. Beaverbrook advocated many crazy policies in his time but his attitude towards Russia, in season and out of season, was that instead of trying to crush the Revolution, it would have been better for us as well as for Russia if we had ceased to interfere with its internal affairs and had concentrated instead on developing sound trading relations. Unfortunately he was not able to convert either Churchill or Lloyd George to his point of view.

Year after year, first Italy, then Germany, then Spain went

under the heel of the fascist dictators. While all this was happening the main energies of the Labour movement were turned inwards, not outwards. There were the various wings of the Labour Party. There was the ILP. There was the Communist Party. There were the all-powerful, right-wing, trade union bosses who controlled the vote at Labour Party Annual Conferences and provided most of the funds at election times. We were all so busy fighting one another that there was little time or strength left over for any other kind of fight. A pamphlet published then by the Socialist League and written by Frank Wise, *The Control of Finance and the Financiers*, argues the case for a planned socialist economy in terms that are still relevant. J. A. Hobson, Harold Laski, Brailsford, G. D. H. Cole, R. H. Tawney – we did not lack brilliant theoreticians pointing the way we ought to go, but the essential conservatism of the trade-union-dominated Labour Party ensured that we could only hobble along on leaden feet. And all the time the growing fascist forces throughout the world were carrying everything victoriously before them.

At Easter I was once more in Germany. Eveline was now living and working in Berlin, her flat a haven for her socialist friends who were under ever-increasing threat. Apart from being anxious to find out as much as possible about the real state of affairs there, I had the practical incentive that my main income came from lecturing in the United States in the early months of each year. I needed first-hand, up-to-the-minute information both for lectures and articles. I saw no likelihood of being returned to Parliament in a by-election so was trying my prentice hand at writing. I contributed unpaid articles to the *New Leader*, our weekly ILP journal, and was in perpetual motion travelling all over England, Scotland and Wales addressing meetings for the ILP. This was a labour of love: train fare paid but not a penny more, so I had to keep some kind of balance between paid and unpaid activities.

The odd times when I could return to London, and the luxury of having my own independent flat with Frank's flat close at hand, kept life from becoming too grim. We each worked under immense pressure, Frank in particular, but we also contrived to be together as much as possible. I enjoyed this arrangement but Frank was becoming increasingly restive. Before we met, he already had his London flat, and his wife Dorothy and his children lived in a comfortable roomy house in Wendover. They had agreed to live apart. Dorothy and I felt that the *modus vivendi* we had reached was the best compromise we could make in the circumstances. We both opposed Frank's pressure on us to agree to a divorce. That would have allowed Frank and me to live openly together without all the secrecy that public opinion at that time enforced unless we wanted to commit political suicide. There was never any question of Frank withdrawing his protective love and care from his wife and children; divorce would not have altered anything in that respect. But I felt he underestimated the damage divorce would do to both of us, to myself in particular. Dorothy, too, shrank from the embarrassments and inevitable unpleasant gossip we would all have had to face if divorce proceedings had gone forward.

Returning from America on the *Leviathan* on 8 March 1933, I thought I would have it out with Frank before I arrived and was once more under strong emotional pressure. I wrote:

Frank Dear,

All is quiet on board now so I have time at last to write to you about our personal affairs. But I don't know what to say. I seem as far as ever from any certainties. Looked at from the outsider's point of view first, I feel that divorce and marriage would do both of us immense harm. Certainly public non-Catholic opinion is becoming more tolerant about divorce, but in triangles where all three parties are fairly equal as to age and other matters. The situation where a man has lived with one woman for twenty years, and becomes attached to another woman about twenty years younger, is too painfully common, and associated with too many unpleasant types, to be lightly accepted. Nearly all men between forty and fifty turn from women of their own age to the younger generation of women. That in itself is often humorously overlooked, but where he goes so far as to break up his family life and seek remarriage – well the hounds are apt to be at both their heels.

Imagine either of us ever trying to make a speech with any reference to the welfare of children or of family happiness. Immediately the malicious or the merely critical would want to know what regard we had shown for the family life closest to us. We could easily be painted as depraved home wreckers. Now I know, dear, that as you read you are protesting, but remember I am putting the situation from the outsider's point of view. To them there is nothing unique about you and me, so they fit our relationship into its generalized group – and the group is not a pleasant one.

Next how do I personally feel? The thought of being separated from you fills me with panic. It takes away what has been the very centre and base of my life for the past three years. And I want a definite home of my own in addition to whatever public work and activities I shall be doing. If you had been free and we had been in the same political group, I would have married you before now. Even the difference in our ages would not have stopped me, and that is quite an important item. But I cannot, at twenty-eight, feel and behave as if I were forty-eight or even thirty-eight. All in good time but for a few years more at least, I am liable to be a rather over vital animal with the temptation to love others as well as you. If I felt it was wrong to do so, I would act accordingly, but because I love you better and more completely than any other man, does not still my curiosity and even temporary infatuation for others.

The border-line between friendship and passion in the relationship of any man and woman who are fairly attractive animal specimens is always precarious. I want to be honest about those things, and that is the hardest thing in the world. Even although in fact what is called faithful to you, I would resent and protest against any suggestion or act of yours that might imply I was compelled to be so, and if ever you had a fit of jealousy and surrounded me with an atmosphere either spoken or unspoken that suggested I had not kept faith, I would be torn with too many mixed feelings to be sure of acting wisely – and that I know applies equally to you.

I have already seen you sullen, ready to leave me with a sense of your injured innocence on quite trivial matters, and it has been me, not you, who has made the peace, made it because I loved you too much to see you go off to a restless unhappy night, because of your own self-tormentings. But remember, married, I would be too proud to do any such thing, so if you wanted to go on tormenting yourself, there would just have to be two of us separately miserable.

All that means, that leaving everything else aside for the moment and thinking only of the physical and emotional basis of our marriage, we must face the fact that there is, say, a fifty-fifty chance of our making a great success of it, but an equal chance of failure. We are both rather self-centred, stubborn in our principles and points of view, both sensitive and proud which is all delicate material to build on. Apart from public consequences, a free relationship is by far the better for such as us. I think we have made a success of it so far, apart from the surrounding worries, and know we could go on doing so, except that public opinion would prevent us running a *ménage à deux*.

When Frank was around I had eyes for no one else, but when he was abroad on business or immersed in Socialist League activities I had other companions. Nye was a favourite. He knew everything I was up to and I knew just as much about his various light-hearted affairs. When he paced the floor of my flat saying, 'No hostages to fortune', I knew exactly what he meant. Both our lives were shaped by the same revolutionary disciplines. Celibacy was no part of our creed, but marriage was something to be avoided at all costs. Passing affairs were quite all right but permanent ties were dangerous for these could make cowards of the best of us if torn between concern for dependants and situations in which we must be free to pursue our socialist objectives, whatever the personal consequences.

Our dedication was real and profound. All revolutionary movements, whether inspired by religious or political fervour, attract young men and women prepared to sacrifice everything for the cause they believe in. That is the meaning of Christ's command – he that loveth father or mother more than me is not worthy of me. And he that taketh not his cross and followeth after me is not worthy of me. He that findeth his life shall lose it, and he that loseth his life for my sake shall find it.

Our main preoccupation was how best to advance our socialist objectives, but we did not make heavy weather of it. There was lots of laughter and pleasant times as well. I enjoyed the skill with which Nye got himself out of entanglements with one or two lovelorn young women who could not believe he was serious in his resistance to marriage. He was always devastatingly explicit in stating his point of view. He never cheated. But of course, unless an infatuated young woman had the same driving compulsion as we had to remain free to face whatever hazards the future might bring she just could not understand. At the same time, Nye knew better than anyone else how much I was torn between my love for Frank and my determination not to become involved in divorce proceedings which could quite well have made it impossible for me to continue my chosen life's work.

What neither of us could foresee was that both our lives were going to be drastically altered by Frank's sudden, utterly unexpected death. On Sunday evening, 5 November 1933, Frank Owen telephoned from the *Daily Express* office to tell me that the news had just come in that Frank, who was spending the weekend at Wallington with Charles Trevelyan, while walking in the woods, had collapsed and died.

It was all too unreal. I could not believe that anyone so vital, that Frank, at the height of his physical and intellectual strength, had ceased to be. I was half-unconscious all night long. No drugs, no drinks of any kind to dull the pain. No one to talk to.

In the morning when my door bell rang, Kate, my elderly Cockney daily help, answered the door. Charles Trevelyan had travelled on the night train from Newcastle, had gone first to Frank's flat to collect letters of mine and any other odds and ends I might have left lying about. He had hoped to reach Guilford Street before the news of Frank's death reached me. I was still in a state of shock, more dead than alive, an inert mass, incapable of moving. Together Kate and Charles got me on my feet, washed, dressed, breakfast set out.

The next thing I remember is being gently propelled by Charles into a jeweller's shop. Part of that nightmare night was that my one clock was not working and I had lost my wrist-watch. Fastening a new watch round my wrist was almost a symbolical act. Life had somehow to go on. It was not easy; this was the first death I had known. It helped that I had public engagements I must not break. I had to go on as if nothing much had happened.

A few weeks later, I wrote to Eveline:

Frank's loss does not grow less. Aneurin and Hubert Griffith are both good pals. They take me anywhere I want to go, but they are not Frank. Did I tell you that Ni* wants to share a cottage with me in the summer? Frank was solid gold. Ni is quick-silver. He is as unreliable as Frank was reliable. He is moody, self-indulgent, but in a curious way he is a brother to me. Our mining background, our outlooks, hopes and despairs are most similar. If I do decide to share with him it will be an emotionally and financially rocky business, and perhaps I am merely seeking another kind of pain to kill the one that is with me. But by April when I return from America I count on being sane enough to make sensible decisions.

How little I knew Nye. How blind I was to his true character.

*Ni rather than Nye was the spelling I and his family and closest friends always used.

11. A New Life Begins

It was a relief to leave for the United States on one more lecture tour on 18 January 1934. I had let my London flat and had no wish to hang around London when I returned; I had told Nye that after spending a few weeks putting everything in order at Guilford Street, I planned to rent a country cottage not too far from London so that I could still keep in touch with ILP and anti-fascist activities, but have country things around me and peace and quiet for reading and writing.

As so often in my life, the problem was solved for me in a most unexpected way. Hubert Griffith's mother had a beautiful farm in Kent, lived herself in a converted barn, let the main farmhouse and surrounding fields, and now had converted a stable into a tiny rural *pied-à-terre* which she wished to let. She must have been a great beauty in her youth. She had exquisite taste, a witty, astringent tongue, and did wonders on the housekeeping front on a modest income. At the weekend Hubert and other friends joined us, which meant that instead of brooding on my own in a lonely cottage, I was surrounded by lively company and as soon as Mrs Griffith had assured herself that I had an entirely platonic relationship with her son, we became great friends. She was as charming to me as she was bitchy to any girl friend he brought home with him if she sensed that her son was in danger of being 'nobbled'. H.G., who was dramatic critic for the *Evening Standard* at the time, had a passion for classical music and was a devoted ballet fan. He was very warm-hearted, and little Browning's duchess had a roving eye – he liked whate'er he looked upon, and his looks went everywhere.

I did not join the Griffith household until the end of July. I stayed on in my London flat as I had a good many things to attend to in town. Nye, who hated London and was off to his Welsh mountains as soon as Parliament rose, this year rented a flat near mine during the Whitsun recess. By now, he had had enough. He had come to the end of his patience. One day when I called on him I had a rough reception. He was determined to force me to stop floundering around like a blind bat and make up my mind: he wanted us to live together. I liked him well enough and the chemistry was all right between us, but I could not believe that there would be the security that Frank had given me for a few short years, and that I had always known in my parents' home. So I floundered on for a bit longer.

One of Nye's favourite haunts was the Café Royal. Always he was avid for good talk, for the companionship of those who, like himself, enjoyed what he called 'star tapping'. That meant leaving the obvious behind and moving into the realm of the unknown. Good conversation was a form of exploration; you did not begin by arriving at your destination, you tried out ideas, some preposterous, some vaulting so far ahead of what was acceptable to mere earth-bound mortals as to be incomprehensible to them.

In those days you did not have to have a lot of money in order to spend an evening in the Café Royal. There were expensive dining-rooms, but there was also a large open room which was yours for the whole evening for no more than the price of a coffee and a sandwich. Jacob Epstein was one of the many writers and artists we met there; when he saw Nye he would beckon him over to his table. One evening Nye arrived in a mood of high excitement; we had been to a Matthew Smith exhibition, which was a new experience for both of us. Nye, seeing Jacob Epstein at one of the tables with a number of friends around him, rushed over and, in voluble Welsh fashion, gave them a lecture on the wonders he had just seen. One of his phrases was 'the birth place of colour'. When he stopped for breath, Jacob said, 'Let me introduce you.' An insignificant-looking man, with a bad cold that evening which did not enhance his appearance, was sitting beside him. This was Matthew Smith!

On another occasion Nye said we were going to have dinner proper at the Café, so I put on my best dark-green velvet dress. When we went into the posh dining-room, waiters were hovering around the table for two that Nye had reserved for us; he had left nothing to chance, carefully ordering both food and wine before we arrived. I did not say anything, but maybe a raised eyebrow conveyed what I was thinking: this was quite outside the range of what we could normally afford. Quick as lightning, Nye answered my unspoken question with the retort: 'You can always live like a millionaire for five minutes.' This was what made Nye irresistible. He could make you laugh even when you wanted to cry.

Later he came to the main business of the evening. He said we must get married. It would do him no good in his Welsh non-conformist constituency if it became known, to use the language of those days, that he was 'living in sin'. And while he could no doubt survive, it would be fatal for me if gossip got around in North Lanark, where I was I L P candidate and expected to fight the next Election. I could feel no certainty about the future, but there was no point in handicapping ourselves by defying the conventions. We had more serious work to do, and, of course, I would never be a stumbling-block in his way.

When Parliament rose at the end of July, Nye did not come with me to my charmimg stable in Kent. Instead he was packed off to New York to take part in a mock trial on the theme of the Reichstag fire, which had taken place in February 1933. This was a propaganda and fund-raising project on behalf of the victims of fascism. John Strachey, who had made a great reputation for himself in America as well as in Britain after the publication of *The Coming Struggle for Power* and other Marxist publications of that kind, was the first choice of the London committee. But John was not the stuff that martyrs are made of. When we failed to persuade him to undertake this uncomfortable and unprofitable task, Nye was our next choice. I was a member of the committee and was asked to use my influence with him. He was looking forward to escaping to the country, but we both felt he could not refuse. There was no quick hopping across the Atlantic by air at that time. He would have to travel by sea; but allowing for that and about a week in New York, we reckoned he would be back before the end of the month. Instead it was more than two months before he returned; the New York committee persuaded him to do a coast-to-coast money-raising speaking tour on the plea that if he returned immediately after the New York meetings the money raised would be very little once his travelling expenses were deducted.

Soon after he got back we were spending the evening with Pat and George Strauss. Nye was at his wittiest best, entertaining us with a racy account of his many adventures when crossing from the Atlantic to the Pacific. At one point, when he said it was bloody hot and uncomfortable, but he felt he had to bring back a decent sum, George quietly interrupted him by saying, 'But Nye, *I* paid your travelling expenses.' We had not known this, but now the story was told. Countess Karolji, who was fluttering around London at the time and was very much *persona grata* with the Communist Party, had gone to George saying that his friend, Aneurin Bevan, was not in a position to pay his own travelling expenses, but as he was contributing his unpaid services would George like to make a donation that would take care of Nye's boat and train fares. That was the kind of underhand trick the Communists played on us, again and again, in big matters and small. The London committee, under Dorothy Woodman's chairmanship, was socialist-controlled. What I did not know was that in New York, it was the Communists who were pulling the strings.

As the forces of fascism drove on from strength to strength and the British Government welcomed rather than sought to restrain its advance, some of us were only too anxious to form a broad alliance from Liberal to Communist in the desperate hope that we could win sufficient public support to compel the Government to change its policies or make way for a Government that would. The General Election did not come until 1935 and once again we were defeated. We socialists prided ourselves on being the great internationalists. At crowded meetings we sang the *Internationale* and the *Red Flag* –

Come dungeons dark or gallows grim,
This song shall be our parting hymn.
Let cowards flinch or traitors sneer.
We'll keep the red flag flying here.

But while we preached internationalism, it was the fascist powers, ably abetted by their capitalist allies everywhere, who practised it. They did not talk, they acted. We collected food and bandages to send to Spain. Hitler and Mussolini sent arms, and the Popular Front Government in France closed the frontiers between France and Spain, thus making it impossible for the Republican forces to receive arms from abroad. No experience in those years cut so deep as the martyrdom of the Republican forces in Spain; gallant individuals tried to make amends for the behaviour of their Governments by volunteering to fight on the side of the Republicans.

I was in Barcelona when George Orwell arrived. The day before I had visited the Aragon front, and was horrified when I saw the old-fashioned makeshift weapons with which the socialists were facing the fascists. The heavy fighting had not yet begun, only sporadic exchanges of gunfire. That was alarming enough on the occasion when the farmhouse in which I was sheltering was under direct attack, but it was child's play compared with what was to follow. I had been sent to Spain by the ILP. My job was to collect as much first-hand information as I could in order to help us decide what was most needed; then I had to return to take part in meetings all over the country, whose purpose was both to inform and to raise funds.

George Orwell came over to the large round table in the Barcelona hotel where a number of us were staying, as he had recognized me and thought I knew him. At that time I had no recollection of meeting him, but gradually it became clear who

he was. He told me he had made a new contract with his
publisher so that his wife would be provided for. All he
wanted to know was where he could report for service. This
lanky figure with the sallow complexion had large feet and was
taking no chances with his footwear: he had a pair of tough
boots slung over his shoulder. It was also clear that he had not
come either through the ILP or Communist network. Both
parties arranged tickets, passports and other essential first-aid
for volunteers anxious to fight in an unknown land where they
did not know even a single word of the language. George
apparently had made his own unaided way to Spain. *Homage
to Catalonia* tells the story of the heroism, muddle, squalor,
amateurishness he encountered, and tells it in his own inimit-
able style.

At least, at the end of the day, he survived to record it all.
Bob Smillie's grandson was not so fortunate. I had a special
fondness for this brave, able, unpretentious youngster. He
was in the fighting line, but we had decided to recall him because an authentic first-hand account of his experience would
bring home to our British audiences just what was going on
and how we could best help. Later on, if he had insisted on
returning to Spain, he would have been free to do so. But
young Bob died in Spain. He was arrested on his way home
and died in prison. He became ill and had an appendix operation in circumstances that never became clear. Was there foul
play, or was there neglect? Certainly he would not have died if
he had been operated on in a Scottish hospital. These were
only two of many. But their courage, and the food and bandages we sent was all chaff in the wind compared with the
Moorish troops who marched through Torremolinos and the
ample arms supplied to Franco by the fascist powers.

I hear that Torremolinos has become a crowded, over-
commercialized tourist centre. When Nye and I spent the early weeks of January 1935 there, it was a small, unspoiled village. We had prudently gone along to a registry office before
Parliament reassembled in the autumn of 1934, but put off
taking a holiday until the Christmas recess. All his life Nye

enjoyed complaining that I cost him two guineas: that was the
fee for a special licence. Our intention was to get the marriage
ceremony quietly over when no one was looking, but we had
reckoned without our friends. John and Marion Balderston,
who had belonged to Frank's world, not only continued to
look after me but adopted Nye as well. John was doing very
well at the time, as he had added to his laurels as a distinguished international journalist by becoming a successful play-
wright. They had a house in Trevor Square and without our
knowledge had invited thirty guests to their home on the
evening of our marriage. They were determined to have a
celebration, and they got one in full measure. The word had
got around among friends and acquaintances, so instead of
thirty twice as many turned up. Ample food and drinks were
produced for all. Don't ask me how it was done. I don't
know. Maybe by a shuttle service to a nearby restaurant
where John and Marion were well known.

Only Marion Balderston and Nye's closest friend, Archie
Lush, had been invited to accompany us to the registry office.
When we arrived there, the uninvited guest was Nye's older
brother; he was dressed to kill, looking as a proper wedding
guest ought to look, but he was in an awkward mood. Five of
us instead of four went off to a private room in the Ivy restaurant, where the proprietor, our friend Abel, had prepared
lunch for us. Billy Bevan refused Abel's best champagne and
best wines and insisted on a special brew of beer the Ivy did
not stock, causing so much fuss and bother that we wanted to
strangle him. After lunch Marion went home to Trevor
Square. Archie, Nye and I returned to Guilford Street, and we
left brother Billy to go to the devil.

We had accepted an invitation to have an evening meal with
John and Marion, and I had an idea that one or two of our
friends had also been invited. But the mob that greeted us
when we arrived took us completely by surprise – I mean took
Nye and me completely by surprise. Archie had been in
Marion's confidence. The biggest surprise of the evening was
to see brother Bill handing around cocktails on a silver salver

and oozing Welsh charm; Marion had taken him home with her and had completely tamed him.

When Parliament rose for the Christmas recess, Nye and I went off to Spain. Sir George and Lady Young had invited us to their home in Torremolinos. Lady Young was a charming hostess, but in a sedate English county manner. Some evenings when supper was over and we were supposed to have gone upstairs to bed, we slipped out quietly and made our way along the coast to the port of Malaga. It was this first contact with Spain and Spanish people which gave a special anguish to our emotions, as our friends were not so much defeated in battle as massacred. Madame Vandervelte, widow of the former Socialist Belgian Prime Minister, was living in retirement in Torremolinos when we were there. After the fighting, when she visited London, she told us how the Moorish troops marched through the village streets, looting and killing wherever they went. As they approached, some village people came to warn her, crying in despair as they clung to her, 'Los Moros! Los Moros!' I can hear the tone of her voice as clearly as if it were yesterday, as she repeated those words to us.

Another unforgettable memory of that time was the behaviour of the Labour Party when it met in Edinburgh for its Annual Conference. Nye was a delegate. I was at the press table reporting for the *New Leader*. I would have been very willing to rejoin the Labour Party, as Nye urged me to do, if I could have brought myself to do so, but the block trade union vote, in spite of the opposition of the overwhelming majority of the delegates from the local Labour Parties, ensured a victory for 'non-intervention'. I was totally antagonized, so just had to go my own way. It did not satisfy me, but at least those of us in the ILP, however lacking we might be in political muscle, however forlorn the hope that we could ever take over the leadership of the Labour movement, were no party to the betrayal of our friends in Spain.

After the conference we spent a few days in Lochgelly with my parents. It was love at first sight between Mother and Nye. Later on, when she came south to look after us, I can see

him, before beginning to carve a Sunday joint that she had
cooked to perfection for us and as many of our friends as we
could squeeze round our refectory table, looking at me pen-
sively and saying to the joy of the assembled company, 'I had
to marry the girl to get my mother-in-law.'

In his courtship of my father Nye had to go more warily,
but the two men enjoyed themselves hugely on their first encounter – at my expense. As we sat around the fire after one of
mother's fine meals Nye enjoyed so much, Nye began attacking me. Did Dad know what I had done to him? I had
brought him back a box of cigars from New York that no man
in his senses would dream of smoking. Then he went on, in
high spirits, to explain that he had impressed on me to stick to
Romeo and Juliet. Now remember, he repeated, Romeo and
Juliet. Don't go wandering off to any other brand. I knew
nothing about cigars, but when I saw some costing only five
cents each I felt I could afford to bring back a whole box for
my father and another for Nye. After Nye's tirade, my father,
his eyes twinkling, said, 'Follow me.' Nye followed him upstairs where from the back of a drawer in his bedroom he
produced a box of what were called Robert Burns cigars. Like
Nye he had found my bargain-basement cigars unsmokable,
but never a word had he said.

On this first time together in Scotland I enjoyed showing
Nye the countryside around Edinburgh and around Lochgelly
which held so many pleasant memories for me. He was warmly appreciative but it was the Duffryn valley, the road over the
Black Mountains, the lovely Welsh hills quite close to
Tredegar that meant most to him, then and always. From earliest boyhood they had added grace and spaciousness to his
life. Always when we drove to Wales, as soon as the Welsh
hills appeared in the distance, he began singing 'Home To
Our Mountains'. And unless the weather was quite impossible, we spent most of the daylight hours walking and climbing.

In the General Election of 1935 the Conservatives won
North Lanark with 22,301 votes; I followed with 17,267

votes; the Labour Party candidate came third with 6,763 votes. As I was no longer a member of the Labour Party, it was perfectly entitled to run its own candidate, but it did so against the wishes of the great majority of Labour supporters in the constituency: given a straight fight, I could have won. The Labour Party bosses in London, however, decided a Tory victory was the lesser evil. In North Wales they behaved differently; the Labour candidate was withdrawn from Megan Lloyd George's constituency in order to enable Megan to win. Such were the priorities in the bitter feuding of those years. A Liberal was better than a Tory, but a Tory was to be preferred to a left-wing socialist!

Nye did many brave things in his life but none braver than when he decided we were going to be married. In some ways we had the same background, the same early memories – that was true of external circumstances, but at the heart of our lives we had been brought up very differently. I had not been woken in the early dawn when I was barely fourteen years old to trudge off to the pits. I had not had to educate myself by reading late at night and into the early morning hours after a hard day's labour. I had never known the terror a young boy knew as the underground trams came hurtling towards him – escaping death by reaching a manhole just in time.

I did not stammer. I was rather too articulate. I was not left-handed nor had I had a sadistic schoolmaster's ruler torturing my young hands as punishment for writing with the 'wrong' hand. I had not risen in wrath from my place in class to throw an inkwell at this same schoolmaster because he was humiliating an inoffensive schoolmate in front of the whole class. When asked why he had not come to school the previous day, the piteous reply was that he had no boots. Instead of a little ordinary human sympathy the boy was taunted and jeered at.

At the age of seventeen, when Nye attempted to speak at a miners' union meeting, he had to face ridicule because of his speech impediment. But he would not give in. He forced his critics to listen to him, stammer and all.

After working underground for six years Nye won a scholarship to a Labour College in London, paid for by the Welsh Miners' Union. On returning to Tredegar after two years away from the pits, no colliery would employ him: he was blacklisted everywhere. The coalowners never relented but they were forced to accept him as check weighman; this was the one job the rank-and-file pit workers controlled. For three years, between returning to Tredegar and taking his place on the pit-head to check that the men were not being cheated, he had to face the humiliation of being 'on the scrap heap'. Nye had been grateful enough for two years during which, with immunity from hard manual labour, he could give himself entirely to study, but he did not enjoy London. He was very much a loner, preferring to study on his own rather than attend classes he found dull.

Afterwards of course, he could be very amusing about some of his adventures as an innocent abroad. A young woman picked him up in Earl's Court Road and told him about the little boy she had to support and how she had been deserted by the father of the child. Nye was full of love and sympathy. The next morning he woke up to find that she had vanished, taking with her every penny he possessed; it was the whole of his monthly allowance, not much, but all he had to live on. Years later when he came to London as a Member of Parliament, a waitress in a restaurant he entered fainted at the sight of him. This was the lady who had walked off with his pocket book.

The London I first knew was entirely different. I had my Bloomsbury friends waiting for me with a warm welcome. Then when I arrived at King's Cross station on the morning of the day I was due to be introduced to Parliament, the Trevelyan family was on the station platform to greet me and take me home with them.

I don't know what would have happened if Nye and I had remained too long cooped up in a one-bedroomed London flat, but we were determined to make do with Guilford Street until we found a home outside London. It took us two years to find it. I was almost as happy and excited as Nye was when this happened. Now he had his heart's delight: a home in the country. The only one who was dismayed was Nye's mother. When she visited us and found we were living under a thatched roof with bare polished wooden or tiled floors and plain white walls, it seemed to her that her impossible son was bent on going backwards just when he ought to have been moving forwards. After a life time of selfless hard labour, bringing up a large family and supplementing her husband's wage by running a millinery business in her parlour, she was now living in a solid stone house in the centre of Tredegar. No more ancient cottages for her. Mother and son were both strong-willed. She wanted her family to 'get on' and kept telling him that he ought to look after himself instead of always getting into trouble looking after other people. For her, our old thatched cottage was literally as well as metaphorically the last straw. And fair enough, on that first visit we had barely begun the renovations we were planning.

12. A Home in the Country

For the next two years I was a prisoner in the country but a willing prisoner. It had to be one of us and Nye had his parliamentary duties to attend to. These did not deter him from driving home late at night or in the early hours of the morning for we had no place of our own in London and could not have afforded one. On the occasional nights when Nye had to stay in town he was as welcome in Paulton's Square with Kay and Hubert Griffith or with other friends as they were our welcome guests in the country.

Nye was planning the renovation of our old thatched cottage with the same total abandon he gave to his crusades to save the whole world. The first essential was to knock down the dividing wall between the entrance hall and the main sitting-room. That would give us a long low room, lots of light from three front windows and another on the wall beside the fireplace. Then we must have a large open log fire. When we removed the hideous oil stove in front of the fireplace we found to our delight that it was all we could wish for in depth. The only snag was that it smoked like the devil. Nothing dismayed, Nye assured me that once the dividing wall was removed, the length of the room would be greater than the height of the chimney and that would cure the smoke nuisance.

We lost no time in contacting the local builder, a very religious man, known as 'Glimpse of Glory Johnston'. This gentle old craftsman quivered with horror when asked to remove the unwanted wall. He begged us to remember that this was a genuine Elizabethan cottage and the whole thing might fall down if that supporting wall was removed. Nye overcame his scruples. The wall came down, a great oak beam across the ceiling took its place, and to my relief nothing catastrophic happened. The next triumph was that the log fire behaved admirably.

But there were more hurdles to cross. The first night we slept in the cottage I was woken by the noise of an army trampling across the attic floor above us. Just a few mice, Nye said soothingly. I am not particularly cowardly but I dreaded and detested mice; now we understood why the lady who sold us the cottage went around with two large cats at her heels. We quickly acquired Samson, a lively young tomcat, then Delilah, a delightfully playful kitten, to keep him company. That helped, but we had to face the expense of getting rid of the tatty old thatch. It was replaced by what was called Norfolk reeding, the work being beautifully done by the type of skilled craftsmen who at that time were still available. With a sound roof, no more mice, a log fire at one end of our main room, a hospitable refectory table (our favourite wedding present) at the other end, and a small study completing the ground floor, we were getting into shape.

Having acquired Samson and Delilah the next addition to the family was little red-headed Joice. She was fourteen, had just left school, was looking for a job and had heard that I wanted someone to help in the cottage. Nye was present when she timidly knocked at the door. Her first question was would she have to wear a uniform? 'Wear what you like, whiskers, come in the nude if you want to,' said Nye, beaming down on her benevolently. At that Joice fled. There had been no talk of how many hours she would work, how much she would be paid. What was to be done about Nye? There seemed to be no way of governing that impish unruly tongue. To my surprise, Joice turned up next morning ready to begin work. Why? Maybe she had decided we were a couple of lunatics but at least not stuffy Home Counties gentry against whom her proud young spirit rebelled.

Renovating the cottage was a challenge but one that never damped our spirits. The garden was a different matter. It was large, almost three acres, most of which was a wilderness. If we had only had to deal with weeds and shrubs which had got out of hand, that would have been easy – just a matter of time and hard labour. But years ago there had been a grass tennis court in the centre with the usual high surrounding wire enclosure. All this had been allowed to collapse into the ground, so it was not just a matter of using a strong scythe to cut through a tough undergrowth of vegetation; we had to cut through wire entanglements as well. Joice's older brother, Joe, a strongly built young farm-worker, helped us in the garden in his spare time. Then our many friends who liked to descend on us at the weekend had all to do their stint. The only parasite among them was Archie. He would stride up and down, issuing orders and doing never a thing – except keeping us convulsed with laughter. He was far from well at the time and shortly due for a dangerous thyroid operation. Nye kept a weather eye on his friend to make sure that he kept strictly to his role of licensed court jester.

When we moved from Guilford Street to Brimpton Common we invited Kate Sneezum, our daily help, to come with us. Kate was terrified at the very thought of being in the country, she was Cockney born and bred. Once we were in reasonable order, we coaxed her into paying us a visit. Apparently she had arrived at Paddington station hours before the train was due to leave and, during the evening, while we did all we could to make her feel at home, she was clearly uneasy. In the middle of the night she was sick. Next day Kate was safely back where she knew she belonged.

When working for us in London she arrived at 8 a.m. in the morning and left no later than 2 p.m., earlier if we were both out at lunchtime. One day I was surprised to return from a meeting in the country to find Kate still busily washing up in the kitchen although it was about three o'clock. I knew how much it mattered to her to be off promptly no later than two for she met some of her cronies and they went off to the 'pictures' together. This they did every change of programme and, as she explained to me, they enjoyed themselves sitting through two rounds for the price of one. They were warm and comfortable and had time for a really good talk.

At the time of the Jarrow hunger march we were still living in our London flat. Nye was one of the London contingent who marched to the outskirts of London to welcome our friend, Ellen Wilkinson, Member for Jarrow, and all her brave band, and lead them into the centre of the town. When the men arrived and catering and other arrangements for them had been settled, Nye took Wal Hannington and one of the other leaders home with him for a brush-up, a quiet talk and something to eat. Kate had not expected either of us to be in for lunch that day, but she rose nobly to the occasion. Bacon and eggs and tinned tomatoes and whatever else she could find in the larder were quickly cooked and served. When Wal Hannington and the other leader, who might have been Arthur Horner, but I am not sure of that, were ready to leave, she insisted on giving each of them an apple and an orange to put in their pockets. Dear Kate! Hers was the spirit of ordinary decent folk towards one another. She told me with an air of militant virtue when my surprised self found her still in the flat about three o'clock, that she had never enjoyed so much serving a meal. Generals don't starve. It is their job to keep alive and lead their troops to victory. But that thought was quite outside the range of Kate's experience. All she knew was that Nye had brought home two of the starving hunger marchers and she was going to make sure they left Guilford Street with full stomachs.

Life would have been easy for Nye if he had joined the hunger marchers with the support of the official trade union movement. Instead he had to face the bitter hostility then shown towards any activity such as this that meant joining forces with Communists. The National Unemployed Workers' Movement was Communist-led. It need not have been. This small party, with so little hold on mass support that it was never able to elect more than two Members of Parliament and those only for a short time, filled the vacuum orthodox Labour left vacant. Nor were Nye's relations with the

Communist Party easy. They wanted no divided leadership. They wanted to maintain a Communist Party monopoly. But, of course, wherever the marchers arrived, rank-and-file Labour people broke through official prohibitions and did all they could to help them on their way. Not least was the help given all along the route by the motherly solicitude of the Women's Co-operative Guilds.

The story of the hunger marchers was repeated on the political front. Not only the I L P and the Communist Party were outside the pale. The Socialist League, which had struggled so manfully to maintain its point of view yet remain within the Labour Party, was forced to disband. By these draconian methods, the year before war broke out all the leading rebels had been brought to heel except Stafford Cripps, Charles Trevelyan, George Strauss, Edgar Young and Aneurin Bevan. When these five were expelled, Noel Brailsford wrote requesting that he be given the honour of also being expelled as he agreed entirely with his friends.

In the same way official Labour left Victor Gollancz to look to Communist intellectuals for his main support in promoting the Left Book Club. Its steady stream of books and pamphlets galvanized left-wing opinion in the years leading up to the Second World War and on through the war years. It is true that Harold Laski, as well as John Strachey (who by then was in his Communist phase), were on the editorial board. But at weekends it was Harry Pollitt, not Clem Attlee, who was the honoured guest in Victor's country home.

Nothing apparently could rouse the right wing of the Labour Party to the urgent need to assemble under its leadership every anti-fascist element from Liberal to Communist. If it had had the will, that could have been done. By the end of July 1938 a baffled and exhausted Stafford Cripps felt he could do no more for the present. He set out with his wife and two young daughters on a world tour that lasted a year. Nye did not grudge Stafford his sabbatical year. He felt he richly deserved a break but then, and all through the years, he rather wistfully wondered if he would ever be given a time of peace, a time for quiet reflection, a time for the renewal of his vital energies. The nearest he ever got to that was the country life he now so enthusiastically enjoyed.

My mother was anxious to come south to look after us. For a long time she had been eager to be with us and it was a great day when at last she arrived. Her one son was in Australia. Her one daughter was living in the south. Her idea of the good life was to have her family around her. Shopping and cooking and cleaning and gardening all day long never seemed to tire her or bore her. She was the most contented human being I ever knew and radiated well-being all around her. When she had been with us for some months I asked Joice if she could understand Mrs Lee now. There had been some difficulty at first as Ma had a broad Scottish accent. Quick as a flash the little red-head said with a wicked grin, 'Yes, but they don't understand me at home.'

Bringing my parents south required skilful diplomacy. How could we persuade James Lee to leave his own job and his own independent fireside and sit as a pensioner in another man's home? That was out of the question. It could not be done. But building materials and building labour were cheap in those days; I enjoyed designing a simple, two-bedroomed cottage in the far corner of the garden, and had it well begun before we invited my parents south to spend a holiday with us. They enjoyed their visit. For my father maybe best of all was the beauty of the surrounding countryside. Before they returned to Scotland, he said he would 'give it a thought'. That was progress. But the final decision came when he was once more in hospital. I had been worrying about his health for several years: he was far from strong. At this point Nye said to me, now realize, if your father goes to work underground again, it will kill him.

That settled it. I put on the pressure and my proud father was prevailed on to agree to come south. We had the red carpet spread out waiting to welcome them. Their own cottage was not yet complete but soon would be; all seemed to me to be better than well. A few days later, to my utter bewilderment, Nye took me aside and said, 'Don't you ever again dare talk to your father like that.' Never before or afterwards had Nye spoken to me in a voice of cold hard hostility. If he had I would simply have walked out of his life. I was stunned. I had said something to my father that had frightened Nye out of his wits.

No wonder nations don't understand one another and go to war. The Welsh could not understand the Scots. There was nothing Dad and I enjoyed more than a good upstanding argument, no holds barred. We had enjoyed our pillow fights when I was a child, and all through the years pummelling one another was a special kind of bond between us, but of course it became verbal instead of physical. When I came home from college, for instance, and pitted my smarty new-found knowledge against his old, hard-earned wisdom, he would cut me down to size and I would hit back.

What had I done? What had I said? Had Nye heard me call my father a moron, a silly old man, an ignoramus? That would have been quite mild language between us. But Nye was scared. He had had a gentle father with whom he talked about everything, but not in our barbarous northern fashion. He knew my father's proud stomach, and my parents were now in our care. More gently Nye went on to explain to me that we could go off anywhere in the world, but they had come to us in trust. They no longer had a home in Scotland to return to: they must never be hurt. I was overruled. I no longer talked back to my father; he was at all times treated with perfect courtesy. What Nye did not realize was that he had spoiled something between us. But maybe he was right. It was all very puzzling, but I accepted that I had now to be careful what I said and how I said it.

Day by day my father grew stronger and was obviously enjoying the soft south. Mother made friends even with the surly neighbouring farmer, who had held aloof from us two foreigners from London. Years later, leaning over the hedge as Nye and I lamented that the orange pippins we had planted were not doing well, Farmer Benham said, 'In these parts they be shy bearers'; but he had taken a sardonic pleasure in our mistakes when we first arrived. This same farmer and his son cut their way from their farmhouse to the back door of our cottage through a long intervening field one winter when the snow was piled mountains high everywhere. They knew Nye and I were in London. At that time they had no telephone, and they were worried about my parents and wanted to be sure they were not in trouble of any kind. Such odd, contradictory creatures we all are!

The added bonus for me once my parents were firmly in control was that I was again as free as Nye to come and go. There was no danger now of him ever having to return to a cold, cheerless fireside. Home was our life line; it kept us sane as we failed again and again to make any headway in public, while fascist troops trampled underfoot one European country after another. The Chamberlain Government had no will to resist; there was too much they secretly admired in the fascist philosophy. Would we be their final victims? Would Hitler cross the Channel? That catastrophe was something that in the atmosphere of those times Nye said could not be ruled out.

It was against this background that he set about organizing a Welsh resistance movement, which had both an educational and a paramilitary side to it. Among its objectives was the encouragement of physical training among workers in order to be ready to meet any demands that might be made on them, and to form first-aid units in every group whose duty it would be to succour all workers victimized, persecuted or in distress and to make sure that no worker was defrauded of his or her legal rights. These were not toy soldiers. They were in the main hard-bitten colliers who knew how to face the hardships that came their way in the course of their daily work and who never failed to go to the rescue of workmates in danger. Among the group leaders there were older men who had seen active service in the First World War.

One warm summer day, as Nye was leading his troops on a route march across the mountains, Archie Lush, full of mischief as usual, could not resist playing a trick on him.

Archie was small in stature and wanted to rest, and so while Nye led the way, head in the air, Archie, following close behind, simply sat down. All the others sat down as well. When a discomfited Nye discovered what was happening, Archie explained, amidst general laughter, 'You see, Nye, an important element in military strategy is that the general must never go too far ahead of his troops.'

The comradeship and the laughter and the practical jokes were all there, but so too was the deeply serious determination that if England went under, Wales would fight on.

I had twice visited Russia in glorious summer weather, but I did not hesitate to return there in the winter of 1936, when commissioned by the *Daily Express* to write a series of articles on different topics that had considerable current interest. There had been a news item in some newspapers stating that Schiaparelli had designed an exclusive outfit for Russian women. Was this true and was it going to be mass-produced? That was good *Daily Express* stuff. So too was curiosity about how Stalin's children were being educated. What kind of school? Were they bright, backward, just ordinary?

I knew I could pick up all this information quite easily in Moscow, but what I most looked forward to was venturing into the unknown world of the Donbass mining area. This was not popular 'copy' in the same sense, but because of the extraordinary claims that were being made on behalf of the Stakhanovite movement it was agreed I could write about it. These Stakhanovites were the pacemakers in the coalmines, and their activities were widely publicized and handsomely rewarded as an inducement to less zealous workers to follow their example. The output claimed on behalf of these pacemakers was greeted with total derision by Nye and others like him who knew what they were talking about.

Before leaving London my main problem was how to prepare for the intense cold of a Russian winter. I was given a wonderful piece of advice by Hubert Griffith, who was travelling to Moscow and Leningrad at the same time; as theatre critic for the *Evening Standard* he was covering ballet and opera and had many friends in the Russian theatre and musical world. He advised me to go to the men's second-hand department in Moss Bros's store in Covent Garden. With any luck I might be able to find a genuine sheepskin coat – not one of the dude kind – as they had had army surplus coats in stock when he had bought himself a warm Moscow-going winter coat there a short time before. I was certainly in luck. I treasured my sheepskin coat for the next twenty-five years, and only then reluctantly allowed a young relative to grab it. In North Lanark and elsewhere it saw me through many a cold winter's day. The fact that it was a bit too big for me made it all the more impressive.

I was also careful to pack thick woollen pants that I could pull over silk under-pants, since I had the kind of skin that reacted badly to wool and flannel. These were a source of embarrassment and annoyance to Hubert. Like other bohemians I have known, he had his prim side and disliked being used by me as a screen as I quickly and discreetly removed them along with all my other outdoor garments on entering an over-heated restaurant or theatre and tucked them into the sleeve of my coat. This to me was plain common sense; I could not withstand the cold out of doors without them, nor could I bear their warmth indoors. It never occurred to me to wear trousers; it was only during the rigours of the Second World War that we women got round to that.

The luxury part of that trip was seeing the dazzling beauty of Leningrad under snow, and evenings at the ballet or theatre. Hubert and I were both in Russia as working journalists. My political contacts were helpful to him, and his theatre contacts guaranteed tickets and VIP treatment any evening I was free to accompany him to the theatre. In 1936 I was astonished to find Peter the Great the hero of a popular play, something which could not have happened in the Moscow I knew in 1930 and 1932. Patriotism as well as Marxism was now very much the order of the day.

The non-luxury part, indeed the severely testing, physical part of this journey, was leaving Moscow and travelling the hard way into the mining areas. Once there, I did not find it at all easy to gain permission to go underground to see for myself what was happening. The local officials had apparently been expecting a solid middle-aged man, not a pert young woman. But when the interpreter travelling with me explained that I was not only collier-born and bred, but third generation at that, the grand-daughter of one of the founders of the Scottish Miners' Union, their attitude towards me changed. I gave myself a further boost by assuring them that going underground was no new experience for me, and that by underground I meant going right to the coal-face. All this on the one and only time when I plagued my father until he agreed to take me down the pit with him.

It was while I was an Edinburgh undergraduate spending the holiday periods at home. On Sundays, when repairs had to be carried out, coal getting was reduced to a minimum, so it was possible for my father as a safety inspector to arrange for me to go underground. I insisted on going right to the coal-face, having no real notion what I was letting myself in for. It was a joy-ride to begin with, hurtling along in an open truck with whitewashed walls on either side and a roof so high that I could quite easily stand erect. Then the endurance test began. We had to crouch in a half-bent posture that was back-breaking, and we were climbing at an angle of forty-five degrees. I don't know how long this part of the journey lasted but it seemed endless. Now and then my father would look behind to see that I was still following – but never a word. That was my Dad! I had asked for it, so now I was getting it. What a relief when we at last came to the place where the men were at work. Some were working in seams so low that they had to kneel or lie on one side as they used their picks; I was able to sit down comfortably and talk to them. The Russian miners were fascinated by my description of working conditions in a Scottish coalmine. We were now getting on famously.

In 1936 one of the first questions visitors to Russia were liable to be asked was how they earned their living. This was the era when the bourgeoisie had to be trampled under foot and the downtrodden victims of Tsarist oppression raised on high. In biblical terms, the last should be first and the first last! Once underground in one of the most famous of the Donbass coalmines, it soon became evident how the Stakhanovite output figures were reached. A whole team was geared to the needs of the leading man: everything was done to help him achieve his spectacular output. The snag was that this was all right for a short time, but no way in which to keep a reasonably steady flow of coal reaching the surface. I was not tactless enough to discuss this with my hosts. That would simply have renewed all their earlier aloofness towards me.

At the time it was the claims of the Stakhanovites that were the centre of my interest, but when Hitler's storm-troopers crashed through the Donbass, I wept as I remembered the youngsters I had met and talked to in the neighbouring technical college. These young men, all in their teens, were going to be the highly trained cadres of the mining industry. They were also receiving their military training, and there was no doubting their profound patriotism. Few, if any, could have survived the onslaught that was part of the price Russia had to pay for holding Hitler at bay.

By the time I left I was on very good terms with the local miners' officials. My generous hosts exchanged my third-class return ticket for one in a de-luxe compartment in the international first-class section of the train. I was quite used to travelling 'rough' and, apart from the money saved, enjoyed the experience. It is one thing to put up with discomfort if it is only for a short time, quite another if you feel it is your lot to be an underdog for the rest of your life.

The letters I wrote to various friends at that time were a kind of thinking aloud, arguing with myself as I tried to grasp the meaning of all that was happening around me. Another of these letters has miraculously survived. In writing to Ethel Mannin, who was at that time closely associated with Maxton and the ILP, I describe my return journey in the following terms:

It is quite true that most of my travelling companions were Red Army officers of the higher ranks. But why not? It seems to me just plain commonsense that the men and women who are carrying the heaviest responsibilities should have the machinery of life made as smooth as possible. The private soldiers travelled in another part of the train. But a Russian General has the thinking and planning and worrying to do as well as the ordinary routine.

Another travelling companion was a doctor from Tiflis. He spoke fluent French, so along with my rotten French we managed to get on pretty well. He was travelling to Moscow in search of some instruments he required for his work. He supervises three hospitals, earns a lot of money, but works like a slave. He could work less hard, but that would mean medical service withheld from many who depend on his care. He is waiting and longing for the time when his hospital equipment will be better and a younger generation will have come to his aid. At the moment there is a scarcity of first-class medical men. That seems to be the position all round in the skilled jobs. Time will remedy such shortages, but in this awkward hiatus between the old and the new, I can think of no one better entitled to travel restfully and comfortably than my doctor friend. I got the general impression that taken by and large, the people who are most privileged are those who are holding key positions and serving the State most effectively. What more can we ask or expect from a country which is surrounded by enemies and makes no claim to have reached as yet more than a half-way house to Socialism?

Once in Moscow I hastened to contact my friend, Philip Rabinovitch, whom I had met several times with Frank in London as well as in Moscow. I thought of him as a cross between a Cabinet Minister and a Big Business Executive. He had a strong physical resemblance to Lenin. When I was having supper with him and his wife in their modest flat, I said to him 'Philip, get out the army, get out the GPU, take whatever emergency steps may be necessary, but find me that Schiaparelli model.' He rose from the dining table, lifted the telephone and made one or two calls, his eyes twinkling merrily all the time. The Schiaparelli outfit did indeed exist. It was housed in what had formerly been the Moscow Stock Exchange, now a warehouse where samples of goods imported

from France were stored. The following day, armed with a
pass Philip had given me, I tracked it down. Very nice too. A
black dress of fine wool, a matching reversible coat, black on
one side, bright scarlet on the other side, and a jaunty little
fish-net beret to complete the ensemble. As with so many
other things large and small in Russia in those days, there was
a reversal of policy. Schiaparelli was left mouldering in the
corner of the warehouse. The plan to have it mass-produced
did not materialize.

Remembering so many kindnesses from my Russian friends, I
am saddened by the sequel. What happened to them? I do not
know, and I tried again and again to find out. Philip and his
distinguished professor wife spoke perfect English and were a
joy to talk to. They were true Bolsheviks and great patriots.
He represented his country when abroad with dignity and
utter integrity, but these qualities, it would seem, did not save
him during one of the subsequent purges. I cannot be sure
even of that. All I know is that no trace of him was to be
found either at his office or at his former home address.

13. Outbreak of the Second World War

In the gathering political gloom of the years preceding the Second World War, I thought, for a passing moment of time, that France was going to be our saviour, was going to light the way for all of us. In the early summer of 1936 I had been in Paris reporting the Front Populaire election for the *London Star* and *Reynolds News*. There was a glorious feeling of optimism in the air, from Communist to Liberal, all the anti-fascist forces had united. In central Paris, in the suburbs, out into the county constituency of Gaston Bergery, I attended meetings large and small.

A night or two before I left London a number of us were spending the evening together – Hubert Griffith, now married to Kay, John and Frances Gunther, Constance Cummings and Benn Levy, Nye and myself. Hubert and John set themselves up as great experts on where to stay in Paris. I was not going on a spending spree, I was going on a money-earning job, so where could I stay that would be clean but not expensive?

Constance, who was between theatre jobs at the time, said she would like to come with me. That was marvellous. Instead of going by train, we motored all the way, arriving in Paris in the early evening. Now we studied the addresses given us. It had been many years since Hubert, as a student at the Sorbonne, had lived in the hotel he recommended, and John Gunther's advice was just as out of date. Those hotels, enshrining their fond early memories, were now dilapidated doss-houses. After trying several other places, we just about settled on one. This was in the early days of a life-long friendship between Constance and myself; neither of us wanted to appear too fussy to the other. But I did feel there was something peculiar about the woman with the ravaged face and hair dyed a garish red, in charge of this hotel, who eyed us in a rather strange way when we said we wanted two double bedrooms, as our husbands were joining us at the weekend. We followed her upstairs. One look around and my common sense asserted itself. We got out quickly! It was a brothel, and not a very savoury one at that.

All ended well. We telephoned a Parisian friend, who shrieked with horror when we told her where we had been, then directed us to a 'respectable' establishment, where we were very comfortable for the rest of our stay. When Benn and Nye arrived at the weekend, politics were forgotten for a couple of nights. I can see the four of us sitting in front seat stalls in the Folies Bergère, Benn and Nye putting coins in boxes in front of their seats in order to obtain opera glasses. They were not going to miss a thing! And I was not going to spoil their fun by explaining that we had arrived far too early. The only other occasion when I had been there was with Frank. It was time enough to get there after supper, stroll around the gallery floor, and stay only long enough to admire and applaud the fabulous, one and only Josephine Baker. Nye had to take so much punishment in public, always fighting against tremendous odds, that it was a joy to see him so happy. He could do nothing by halves. At work or at play he gave himself entirely to the mood of the moment.

Our Paris weekend was soon over. The one thing we could not possibly have foreseen was that Leon Blum's Popular Front Government, far from halting the advance of fascism, was going to assist Franco to victory. In July of that same year, when the Spanish Civil War began, the frontier between France and Spain was open so that arms could be got through to the democratically elected Government of Spain, faced with an attempted coup by rebel generals. Leon Blum's sympathies were with the Spanish Government, but though Prime Minister, he was not in control. The pro-Franco elements in France, the encouragement given by the Pope to Catholics everywhere to support Franco (though many of them did not do so), the relentless pressure of a Tory Government in Britain, the rallying all over the world of capitalist interests, bludgeoned the French Government into closing the frontiers.

By now the British Labour movement had come to its senses. Attlee went out to Spain to give the Republicans his moral support, for whatever that might have been worth! But while making this gesture towards Spain, official Labour was as blind as ever to the growing menace of Hitler. The only hope of rallying sufficient strength to reverse Tory policy was to build a powerful united front of all our various anti-fascist parties. If there had been enlightened leadership, big enough to face up to whatever risks were involved, the powerful Labour and trade union bosses could have harnessed all those smaller elements to this central purpose. Instead, they considered every attempt at building this kind of unity as an act of war against their authority. The venomous hostility of Ernest Bevin, Arthur Deakin and the other Labour and trade union leaders who called the tune inside the Labour Party had to be experienced to be believed.

After the death of Frank Wise, Sir Stafford Cripps became Chairman of the Socialist League, and he fought to the limits of his strength to unite the anti-fascist forces both inside and outside the official party machine, thus becomimg the chief whipping boy of official Labour. Sir Charles Trevelyan, who had expected to retire to his Wallington estates, gave most of his time and strength to supporting the unity campaign. The ILP and Communist Party, uneasy bed-fellows as ever, were got to agree to come together along with the Socialist League. All were hoping to arouse public opinion in time to avert the dangers ahead.

These were endlessly strenuous days for Nye. He had nothing like the prestige of Stafford Cripps, but was fast gaining a reputation both in Parliament and on the public platform for lucid, passionate exposition of all the great issues about which he felt so keenly. He did not speak glibly. His stammer meant that often he had to pause to find the word that said what he wanted to say and at the same time that he was able to pronounce. Over the years he never quite conquered this speech impediment. When he was over-tired it would come back. But it became less and less marked.

Much harder for Nye was the strain imposed on him in helping to promote *Tribune*, the weekly journal first conceived following the Edinburgh Labour Party conference. At that conference some of us were sick with shame after the pro-non-intervention vote. Sir Stafford Cripps and George Strauss provided the capital that, along with the unpaid contributions of Nye and others of us, made *Tribune*'s birth possible. Writing did not come easily to Nye. It was not part of his early training. Also, having been forced to write with his right hand, which he did, his writing was almost unreadable. Some notion of the intensity of his activities in those years can be found in his questions and speeches in Parliament, his weekly contribution to *Tribune* and the reports of the conferences and great public meetings he addressed all over the country. And always his concern for the plight of the unemployed was as tirelessly and vividly stated as his obsession with the international dangers he foresaw.

When, after all Chamberlain's bumblings and blunderings, war was finally declared, Nye and I were at home in the country. Our mood that day is best described in a postscript to a book that I had written, *Tomorrow is a New Day*, just before the outbreak of war. The American edition was renamed. *This Great Journey* and the American publishers pressured me, rather against my will, into carrying the story forward into the war years. I wrote then:

Aneurin and I were at the cottage that Sunday in September when war was declared. We tuned into the one o'clock news for official confirmation that the fight had really begun. We had discussed all this so often and so much. Now at last it had come. Our enemy Hitler had become the national enemy. All those who hated fascism would have their chance now. They would have their chance to fight back. No more one-sided massing of all the wealth, influence and arms of international reaction against the workers of first one country then another.

I thought of Spain. I had a guilty feeling about Spain. I said something to Aneurin that must have indicated the drift of my thoughts. He had been pacing up and down our long, low, whitewashed cottage room, for once too excited for words. He stopped walking up and down to rummage in a corner among a disorderly pile of gramophone records. He found what he was looking for. He found records we had not dared to play for more than a year: the marching songs of the Spanish Republican armies. Now we may listen to them again. We need not be ashamed... Later in the day Aneurin became too restless to remain in the country. He set off for London... Ni home again, full of news and views and gossip. Funny driving today, says he. Everyone went a little faster, more erratically, more recklessly. *C'est la guerre!* We may not be a danger to the Germans yet but we are sure trying our 'prentice hand on one another'.

It was a time of tense emotion for some of us, but day after day passed, week after week, month after month, and there was nothing apparently many of us could do. We were expected to carry on quietly as if nothing special was happening. It was 10 May 1940 before Chamberlain was at last thrown aside and an all-party Government established with Churchill as Prime Minister. Now perhaps we could begin to fight the war in earnest. The seriousness of the military situation was kept from the general public until the fall of France. Now there could be no hiding the truth: the barbarians were at our very gates.

Both in personal and political relationships life brings many curious twists and turnabouts. I was more grateful than I can say when Lord Beaverbrook's gruff voice on the telephone told me there was a job he wanted me to do, to call at his office as soon as possible. The arch-appeaser, the man whose newspapers lulled the public into a false sense of security throughout the whole of the Chamberlain era, had been appointed by Churchill to one of the most sensitive posts in the Government. As Minister of Aircraft Production he had a solemn duty to ensure that our air crews were adequately and properly supplied with whatever type and quantity of equipment they required.

I had seen very little of Beaverbrook in the years before the
war. Nye, Michael Foot, Frank Owen and W. J. Brown enjoyed the rough and tumble of his dinner parties but I steered
clear. I was not attracted by his brash, staccato conversational
style and I had other interests and quite other kinds of
friends. But the opportunity to do a useful job was what I had
been longing for. When I arrived at his office his first greeting
was, 'You and I were against this bloody war. Now we have to
win it for them.' He was still thinking of me as Maxton's 'girl',
a supporter of Chamberlain and Munich, although nothing
could have been further from the truth. Beaverbrook had a
habit of getting his facts wrong and his conclusions right. I am
referring of course only to his decisions during this particular
phase in the war and, following that, his insistence on full
military support for Stalin once Hitler brought him on to our
side by invading Russia.

My job was to go to any factory where the workers stopped
work once the sirens warned of approaching enemy planes.
Beaverbrook expected them to work on until the last possible
moment, which was a reversal of the heavily publicized government instructions asking everyone to seek cover as soon as
the sirens sounded. I had also to find out the cause of delay if
essential deliveries did not arrive on time. Was it men, management or lack of materials? A number of us were employed
as glorified messengers moving directly from and to the Minister. The great point was that we were not paid, not slotted
into any civil service grading scheme and so could move fast
and cut through a great deal of red tape. Beaverbrook's
methods were weird and wonderful. But they worked. They
wrenched priority from the Army, Navy and every other
claimant on scarce materials, at a time when the approaching
Battle of Britain could not have been won by a law-abiding
Minister who no doubt would have got round in time to doing
whatever had to be done; but the essence of the situation was
that there just was not that kind of time.

After my first foray into one of the aircraft factories I returned to the office and asked the secretary allotted to me to

take down my report for the Minister. She was a nice young lady but she had no shorthand or typing experience, as these menial tasks were done by a lower grade of civil servant. As I had no intention of having my report delayed while she informed the typing pool and I waited their pleasure, I brought my own portable typewriter to the office and typed my reports while the nice young lady looked on helplessly.

Beaverbrook had given instructions that he wanted no long-winded documents sent into him. Short words, short sentences, short paragraphs. That was the order of the day and it suited me perfectly. Nor did I trust any of my reports to official messengers; I carried them by hand to Beaverbrook's room, usually finding a queue outside his door waiting patiently for him to keep his appointment with them. I would gently peep into his room and as soon as he saw me he would roar, 'Come in, come in, sit down.' Then he would go on talking to one or two senior Air Force officers or other officials, he sitting at his desk, they standing in front of him on the other side of the desk. No wonder so many of them hated his guts. He was not a gentleman. He had not been to the right schools. He had never been taught to play the game. May I add on my own behalf that, whatever else he may or may not have been, he was a shocking show-off. Of course he enjoyed exhibiting his powers as I looked on, but I got what I had come to ask for and I got it promptly.

His way of doing business suited me very well. The high, serious purpose uniting all kinds of opposites such as Beaverbrook and a modest messenger like myself was that we believed in what we were doing, in its urgency, and had not the slightest respect for the tripwires laid down by civil service rules and regulations. There was trouble in a Reading aircraft factory, for instance. The cause of the trouble was that, although there were good air-raid shelters in the basement of the factory, as soon as the sirens sounded, work was disrupted because some of the men rushed out of the factory and across the fields to their homes. Their wives and children were living in flimsy houses with no air-raid shelters. When I talked to the men they were perfectly reasonable. If I could give them peace of mind, the knowledge that their families had reliable air-raid shelters, there would be no question of them rushing off home.

'Hell!' said Beaverbrook when I told him I had promised shelters for their homes. 'Where are we going to get the cement?' There was an acute shortage at the time; but he got it for me. This was just one of the many times when he nipped in quickly and had supplies intended for the Army or Navy diverted in his direction before the rightful recipients were fully awake. The great point was that he never let you down. You chanced your arm, made a promise, and he was prepared to move Heaven and Hell to help you keep it.

One great asset I had when talking to shop stewards or to the entire assembled workforce was that they did not see me as someone from the Ministry. My Labour and trade union background stood me in good stead. On one occasion several workers said they wanted a private word with me. 'That bugger,' they told me, 'is a bloody Nazi.' They were referring to the factory owner. What in fact was happening was that work had come to a standstill because material that should have arrived from the United States was at the bottom of the sea. There were serious production delays from losses during Atlantic crossings. Ironically we were staring at Herbert Morrison slogans on the factory walls enjoining everyone to 'go to it'.

Some managers knew how to communicate with their employees. But a woeful number did not know how to overcome maybe shyness, maybe snobbery, maybe ingrained habits of mutual hostility and distrust. I remember saying to a group of workers in this factory, 'Make the most of your leisure, for you are going to have to pay for it dearly later on. You will be working seven days a week and working till you drop – and in the meantime, don't ask silly questions.' They understood what I was saying. The materials they had been waiting for had been delayed. There must be no careless talk. They were adult and sensible: they did not press me to be more explicit.

The important thing was they were now assured that their boss was as anxious as they were to get on with the job and that he had not been the cause of the hold-ups. It was all a matter of trust. They had no reason to be suspicious of my motives, for they knew that like themselves I was wholly and urgently concerned only with ensuring that the men in the air should have all the help the men and women in the factories could possibly give them.

That was how the Battle of Britain was fought and won. Of course there was a time limit to this hectic, chaotic way of waging war. During these critical summer months, Beaverbrook was ready to starve the Army and drown the Navy, which were no concern of his, provided he got all the planes and spare parts through to the fighter pilots on time.

When the worst was over, I had had enough. Would I become his balloonatic-in-chief, I was asked? This was promotion. He was pinning a great deal of faith on barrage balloons. I was not convinced. Anyhow I was no strategist, knew nothing of military matters and was increasingly concerned not just with winning the war but with the duel that was beginning to be fought between Churchill and Nye about the purposes for which we were fighting. I had an easy war. I went from one interesting job to another. It was Nye who had to stand out in the cold, abused, lied about, spied upon, as if he were an enemy agent. Believe it or not M15, in its infinite wisdom and understanding of the social forces at work, employed members of their staff to worm their way into Nye's confidence, even into our home.

What were they looking for? If they had opened the bottom right-hand drawer in Nye's desk they would have found an Iron Cross and a Uhlan officer's revolver. That should have helped them on their way! These belonged to our beloved Mumpitz, that is to Dr Lothar Mowrenwitz. Mumpitz at that time was lodging in London with Hubert Griffith. During the Battle of Britain Hubert was in the Air Force, his wife, Kay, and Nicola, their baby daughter, were safe and sound in Dad's cottage. It had been completed, but there was no question of the old and the new cottages becoming two separate principalities. We were a combined home and refugee camp. When forced to flee from Germany Mumpitz arrived in London middle-aged, penniless and far from well. But even when his health and fortunes were at their lowest ebb, he was a joy to all of us. Our spirits used to rise, not fall, when he came into a room. He was a brilliant raconteur. With a background of inherited wealth, having enjoyed all the leisure and pleasure of a cultivated European upbringing, this owner of a distinguished publishing house, because he was Jewish, had to leave Germany and face exile and poverty.

When war was declared we took care of his few possessions, including the Iron Cross and revolver. We loved the story of how he won that Iron Cross: in the First World War he was serving in an Austrian regiment which was ordered to advance. Mumpitz declared he was never able to read maps, had no sense of geography, so that when he reported back to headquarters he found himself a hero. He had advanced so far that he was behind the positions occupied by the British.

He was granted British citizenship even before the end of the war in recognition of the valuable work he was doing. In the days before the war when he sometimes despaired of having his application for a passport granted, I would say to him, 'Why do you want to be English? I don't have a drop of English blood. Nye is not English.' He would retort, 'If they ever give me my passport I shall say to you, "Bloody foreigners".' The day when I answered the telephone and heard a jubilant, excited Mumpitz say over and over again, 'Bloody foreigners, bloody foreigners, bloody foreigners,' I knew his great day had come. He was a British citizen. He could now travel freely and with dignity wherever he might want to go.

Before the war began, Mumpitz was slowly and painfully beginning to make a living as a literary agent. This was the world he knew. Before the war ended, he had his own flat, and one sultry summer evening a number of us were visiting him. The blackouts over the windows were suffocating and I

said, 'Let's draw back the curtains and open the windows.'
'Yes,' said Mumpitz. 'No,' said someone in alarm. 'Yes,' said
Mumpitz, adding with mock seriousness in his slow, stilted
English, 'and if the police knock at the door, I shall say to
them, it is quite all right. There will be no raid tonight. And if
they ask how do I know there will be no raid tonight, I shall
say to them, "I know there will be no raid tonight" – pause
for dramatic effect – "because I am a Gherman!"'

One weekend when Mumpitz was expected at the cottage,
he telephoned to ask if he might bring a young Austrian girl
with him. That is how Trude came into our lives. As soon as
Ma saw this pale, slender eighteen-year-old, she tucked her
under her wing and there Trude remained for the rest of time;
wherever Ma was, Trude was always welcome. When
Mumpitz met her she was being hopelessly exploited as a
seamstress in the East End of London. Her father, who was
Jewish, had gone to Israel; her mother, who was not Jewish,
remained in Vienna in order to hold on to their home and
family business. Trude and another seventeen-year-old gave
up their university studies and escaped to London. In time
she became a successful West End dress designer but Ma
never noticed the difference; she would arrive for the weekend
without make-up and looking anything but smart. She had
had more than enough of fashionable clothes during her
working week.

IIsa was another who was promptly put under Ma's wing.
She was one of the last to leave Barcelona when the
Republicans were finally defeated. As she could not go back to
her home in Hitler's Berlin my friend Eveline told her to
make her way to Lane End Cottage, Brimpton Common. In
the last few days she had been literally without food, existing
on a handful of olives, so that when she arrived at the cottage
she was hardly more than a pair of large, beautiful brown
eyes. With Ma's care, IIsa was soon fit again. Now came the
problem. How to make it possible for her to remain in Britain
and to earn her living? Archie Lush, who was working in
adult education at the time, came to the rescue. His Man

Friday, or office boy, or whatever you like to call him, was a romantic young Welshman called Horace Haigh. Archie decided it would be good for Horace to have some impediment put in his way to prevent him rushing into a hasty, unsatisfactory marriage, so the wily Archie told the gallant Horace of the plight of this young German girl. Until we could find a husband for her she could not become a British citizen, which meant she could not earn her living.

The first I heard of all these goings on was when I answered the telephone and a high-pitched Welsh voice at the other end said, 'This is Horace. I am coming up to get married.' Ilsa and Horace met for the first time on the day they were married, when Nye and I accompanied them to the registry office in Reading. There was no fooling around at this stage in the proceedings. Nye was extremely formal, but the registrar very likely sensed the general air of unease. When we left the office. Nye driving, myself in the front seat of the car beside him, Ilsa and Horace in the seat behind, I heard Nye's voice curtly rap out, 'For God's sake, Horace, put your arm around Ilsa and give her a kiss.' Through the car mirror Nye had seen the registrar at his office window thoughtfully watching our departure.

My mother had a splendid lunch on a beautifully set table waiting for us when we returned after the wedding ordeal. After lunch Horace went for a walk in the woods with my father and confided to him that he had thought he might have had to wheel his bride to the registry office in a bath chair. He had no idea what she would be like. He was simply the perfect knight rescuing a lady in distress! Later in the day Horace went off to an evening concert in London. Under his arm he was carrying our César Franck records. He had enjoyed so much listening to them that Nye insisted he take them home with him. Ilsa and Horace never lived together as man and wife, but they were always tenderly concerned for one another's welfare. In due time their marriage was dissolved. Horace married his true love and their first child was called Ilsa.

I hope this gives some idea of the sinister company Nye was keeping in the summer of 1940.

Lane End Cottage was where we longed to be whenever our various duties made it possible for us to have a free evening or weekend. It was a haven of peace, comfort and happiness. Dad was as much in his element as my Mother. If she was the hostess with the mostest, he was her accomplished consort. I had thought that my father was coming south to become a gentleman of leisure. Not a bit of it. In his different way he was almost as busy as Mother. When Nye and I or any of our friends arrived at the local station it was Dad who would be there to greet us. Fortunately there was little or no traffic on the narrow lane between the cottage and the station, for although he liked to drive he was, apart from myself, probably the most erratic driver on the roads. The one thing he did not care for, and never had, was gardening. He liked to quote a favourite saying among Fifeshire colliers – a house without a garden is worth a pound on the rent. He knew, of course, that there was no need for him to tax his strength unduly, since there were other willing hands ready to help us subdue our wilderness of a garden.

One weekend Nye and I observed senior American officers stop their car to ask Dad, who was in the garden, if he would direct them to an American camp somewhere in the vicinity. My pedantic Scots father pointed to the crossroads in the lane outside, where a signpost had been removed during the early days when the possibility of a German invasion had to be taken into account. 'Now why,' he said, 'do you suppose that signpost was removed?' Nye, all Welsh smiles and charm, hastened to the rescue of the stranded Americans. We had reached a time when we were bamboozling ourselves and our allies, not any potential enemy invaders, by those missing signposts.

When America came into the war, John Balderston returned to England and, one weekend, brought Burgess Meredith to the cottage with him. They thought it would film well, and were on the look out for the kind of setting that would give American soldiers due to arrive soon some notion of the English countryside and the ways of the English rural population. My mother was perfect as the lady of the old thatched cottage, but my slender father was no good. We had to find her a more bucolic-looking husband. Farmer Benham was brought in to play the part, and we enjoyed explaining to Ma that if she wanted to be a film star she must not quibble about such a small matter as changing her husband.

When the film was made the Americans kindly invited the local station staff, the Benhams, and all the other people who had helped them, to a private showing in London. Burgess Meredith was staying at the home from home for visiting American VIPs, that is, the Connaught Hotel. One day I arrived to have lunch with him, but when he saw me his face fell. 'Where's Ma?' he said. He had been looking forward to me bringing her with me. Benn Levy, one of her many admirers, wrote about her (in a foreword to *This Great Journey*) as we all felt about her:

'Ma Lee', whom I shall love and remember always, was everything she didn't know she was; in particular, a mighty influence. She, who claimed nothing, who saw herself (if indeed she ever stopped to look at herself at all) as a kind of dutiful nanny ministering to a clutch of boisterous, combative, argumentative giants, all outsize knights in shining armour who no doubt knew what they were about and could count on her support, if not her attention, loomed over and dimmed the lot of them; not only her own gay assertive family but the most eminent of their friends. Somehow one's eye was forever drawn to the background which Ma Lee contentedly supposed she inhabited, drawn there and fascinated and touched by that rarest form of greatness, a being without ego.

Because she exuded sanity in a dotty world, she was truly the mother-figure: we could not be frightened when she was there. There was no dark, no nightmares. She concentrated on the trivia which are the daily stuff of living and on the loving-kindness which so rarely blesses it. Within the orbit of that dear Scottish dumpling; chuckling, resilient, selfless, alert, uniquely uncompetitive and unacquisitive, her broad Fifeshire accent often barely intelligible, lay indestructible warmth and security and reassurance. By contrast the clamant turbulence of the highly masculine world about her, where I was so much at home, seemed somehow pitiful and immature, though not of course to her; Cabinet Ministers seemed prancing idiot-children. What she was no man could be. Hers was superlatively the feminine contribution, hers was the power and unclaimed glory, the feminism that feminists had turned their backs upon.

14. Churchill Leads the Coalition Government

Winston Churchill, like Lloyd George, was no hero in the mining areas before the Second World War. Miners have long memories: they had not forgotten the troops brought in against them in 1910, his role during the 1926 lockout and much else besides. But it was a relief, an immense relief, to all of us when he took Chamberlain's place in May 1940. Churchill would fight. But you cannot separate military strategy from war aims, and India became a bone of contention between Nye and Churchill right from the start. Our sympathies were with Nehru and the Congress Movement. Churchill preferred to gaol the Congress leaders rather than invite them to fight by our side as free men. He was determined to hold on to the brightest jewel in the Imperial crown, whatever the cost.

Churchill's speeches in Parliament and over the radio, at a time when the Germans might well have landed on English soil, eloquently echoed and underlined the national resolve to go down fighting rather than surrender. We were not France: there would be no suing for peace. Churchill was not speaking for everyone, for there were influential elements who thought we could not win and therefore should come to terms with Hitler. That made Churchill's romantic, heroic stand all the more crucial. But his weakness was that he would not tolerate criticism of any kind. He would have gagged the press and reduced Parliament to impotent sycophancy if he had been given his way.

When I resigned from the Ministry of Aircraft Production I was invited to join the staff of the *Daily Mirror*. Under the energetic, erratic control of Guy Bartholomew, the *Mirror* slogan had become 'Forward with the People'. I was urged not to waste my time writing for a socialist weekly that no one read. I could have my own column with a mass audience for whatever I cared to write. There would be no censorship. At this same time Frank Owen was merrily at work as editor of the *Evening Standard*.

Bartholomew lost his nerve when the Government threatened to close his paper if he did not keep strictly in line. Frank Owen did not lose his nerve; he fought back. Nye and others fought along with him to maintain reasonable freedom to criticize the Government even in wartime. We wanted no one-man dictatorship. We were all too conscious of Churchill's shortcomings as well as his strengths. Then Ernest Bevin came along with proposals which aroused the hostility of the miners. Another long-drawn-out battle had to be fought. At one point there was a strike in the Welsh coalfields. Ernest Bevin, as Minister of Labour, tried and failed to come to terms with the men. Where Ernest Bevin failed, Nye succeeded. It was all a matter of whether you approached working people in a mood of respect and comradeship, or tried to dragoon them. Sheep don't make good soldiers either on the military or industrial field.

Nye was not so successful on another mission. When there was the fear that the Germans might try to land in Ireland, all the conventional diplomatic channels had tried and failed to persuade De Valera, the Irish Prime Minister, to allow a garrison of British troops to be stationed there. As a last resort, Dick Stokes, Labour MP and a devout Catholic, along with Nye who was known to have admired Michael Collins and to have friends among the Sinn Feiners, were despatched to Dublin to see what they could do. When Nye returned he gave us all a hilarious account of their reception by De Valera.

The Irish Prime Minister was courteous and hospitable until they came to the serious purpose of their mission. He would tolerate no British troops on Irish soil. What if the Germans attempted to land? He would fight the Germans just as hard as he would fight the British. 'I shall take a gun myself,' and then, red in the face, almost apoplectic with rage, he made it clear that they had failed like everyone else to pierce his fervent isolationism.

At this time Ilsa often came to the cottage at the weekends. In London she was doing a job that ideally suited her temperament and gifts: she was one of those who received and helped to look after Jewish refugees from Germany. Being German, there was no language barrier. Being sensitive and sympathetic, this non-Jewish young woman won the confidence and affection of all those she was helping to look after, many of them in a distraught state of mind. But we saw nothing of Horace. That bold fellow was serving in a tank regiment in North Africa. At a time when we had little good news to cheer us, his letters were handed around from Wales to the cottage and back again. We would sometimes be helpless with laughter when reading of his exploits. Horace was a kind of Charlie Chaplin figure, getting into all kinds of scrapes, but of course, no fool. When Montgomery on one occasion came on a tour of inspection, Horace and the rest of his tank crew had to step forward, stand to attention, while Monty congratulated them on the smartness of their equipment. Unfortunately when the tanks had to move forward, Horace and his mates were stranded. Their tank would not move. This was the sort of thing that just would happen to Horace.

But there were other voices reaching us from North Africa. Front-line fighting officers, faced with having to lead the men in their charge against an enemy much better equipped, got in touch with Nye and others who had voiced in Parliament and elsewhere concern about their plight. Eventually, after immense pressure, a back-bench all-party committee of MPs was set up to investigate the complaints that were coming in thick and fast. Nye was chairman and as such had to report the findings of the committee to Parliament. Churchill was furious. He was temperamentally incapable of listening to criticism even when backed by unanswerable hard facts. Instead he vented his spleen on Nye. The chairman of the all-party committee was branded 'a squalid nuisance'.

In the years immediately after the war Field-Marshal Montgomery, who was a trustee of St Paul's Boys' School, invited Nye to dinner to ask for his help in getting their playing-fields restored to the pupils. They had been taken over for food-growing purposes. It may be the Field-Marshal felt he had to walk warily in approaching Nye. As far as I know the two men were virtually strangers to one another. But there was no need for him to beat about the bush. Straight away Nye said, of course, the boys should have their fields back. It was all nonsense still holding on to them. At some point in the evening they got round to talking about the battle of Alamein. Nye, in the quick, disconcerting way he sometimes had in conversation, asked the blunt question, 'Field-Marshal, why didn't you just send Rommel a postcard?' Montgomery, far from flaring up in outraged indignation, replied quietly, 'Because, Minister, we needed a victory.' Both men knew precisely what they were talking about. Nye came home that evening much impressed by Montgomery.

No one who may read what I am writing must take the meaning of that conversation to be that lives were thrown away at Alamein that might have been saved. The opposite is true. The war had been going dangerously, tragically badly until then. Public morale was low. The victory at Alamein was the shot in the arm so desperately needed. As Nye explained to me, Rommel's supply lines were so over-extended that he could have been beaten without Monty joining battle when he did – but a quick victory was the over-riding need of the hour.

In the autumn of 1941 I found myself once more off to the United States of America. Don't come back, Nye said flippantly, until you have brought America into the war. At this time, from coast to coast, America was swarming with British and German agents. On the way out we stopped off in neutral Portugal. In the splendid hotel in Estoril where we British lot put up, Germans were also staying. No one was allowed to wear uniform while there, but the great central table in the dining-room was reserved for the Germans and their ladies. We sat at modest side tables. It was a great joy therefore, on the return journey, to find that the careful Portuguese had decided we were going to be the winning side. The Germans now sat at the side tables. We were ceremoniously conducted to the prestigious table in the centre.

It was Brendan Bracken, then Minister of Information, who asked me to go to America, but it was Sir Stafford Cripps who gave me my instructions. First of all, I could have any extra clothes coupons I might require; I was going on a propaganda tour, but there was no need for me to arrive in rags and tatters. I said I did not need extra coupons– my pride was involved. I reckoned I had a couple of good costumes (we did not talk of 'suits' then) and a couple of evening dresses that would see me through. I would be met on arrival, and as soon as I reached Washington I must contact Cripps's friend, Dean Acheson. In Detroit Walter Reuther and his brother Victor would look after me. In Minnesota someone called Hubert Humphrey, who in later years I was to know so well, but at that time had not yet met, would be expecting me. In Hollywood, my friend John Balderston, a member of the pro-British White Committee, would make my arrangements.

No doubt the reason I had been asked to go to America was that I had a story to tell. I had been around the East End of London as well as in factories all over the country during the Battle of Britain. This was vivid, first-hand, intensely human material. The other consideration was that I had quite a few influential friends among liberals and trade union leaders, and would be invited to address audiences barred to official diplomats. Walter Reuther, for instance, was passionately anti-fascist. His German democratic socialist father had left Germany when he was eleven years of age. His three sons shared his socialist views, but had to adapt them to the American scene.

Before the Japanese attack brought America into the war,

Walter already had worked out plans for switching car production to armament production. I thought it would be counter-productive when he invited me to meet the men coming off the night shift in one of Detroit's largest car plants. But when in Rome – apparently it was common practice for union leaders to talk to the men in their canteen, where many of them went for light refreshments before going home. They listened to me quietly and courteously but at question time one blurted out, 'You are all right, but we don't like your Tory toffs.' I got this refrain again and again. A fellow-feeling for working people facing all the hardships and horrors of war, but a strong antipathy towards self-assured, patronizing, born-to-rule, public school products. Considering the heroic war record of some of the 'public school products' that was grossly unfair. I am simply reporting the general feeling in the car plants towards those they called our 'upper classes'.

The only one of my friends on the American left who was adamant in his opposition to American aid for Britain was Norman Thomas. Knowing his affection and admiration for Stafford Cripps, I asked, 'So you would like to see Britain and all of us over there, including your friend Stafford, defeated by Nazi storm-troopers?' That he said would be a far lesser evil than America entering the war. To be fair to him, he believed that if America was put on a wartime footing, it would degenerate into just as ugly a dictatorship as Nazi Germany. Anyhow at meetings large and small, public and private, I did what I could to win sympathy for our beleaguered country. Once I reached Hollywood, in spite of all the love and comfort which Marion and John Balderston gave me I was devoured with impatience to be home again. When would I be given a place on a plane? You cannot live on bread alone, not even on rump steaks and zabaglione. All I wanted was to be back in bomb-blasted London, not hanging around Hollywood.

When the Japanese attacked Pearl Harbor I was paying a fleeting visit to friends living further down the coast. John

Strachey's divorced wife, Esther, was now married to Chester
Arthur, who liked to joke about being a descendant of the
most obscure of former American Presidents. One of the most
delightful of their friends was Jimmy. He was leader of the
vegetable-growing Japanese community on the West Coast.
One evening when I was crossing the garden to the
high-domed library which was the centre of their home,
Esther stopped me. 'Don't go near the library,' she said.
'Jimmy is in there with Chester.' This lively, likeable, highly
intelligent young Japanese leader had come to his friends in a
mood of total despair. All the hard work he had put in to
build up good relations between his people and other
Americans was now shattered. He lay on the library sofa
under the window, sobbing his heart out – and Jimmy was no
coward, no weakling. He was simply overwhelmed by the
immensity of the disaster he now had to cope with.

When at last a place was found for me on a plane that would
take me home, I had interesting travelling companions. Now
that America was in the war, top business personnel had to be
rushed over to England to make plans for the feeding of the
American troops who would soon be stationed on our side of
the Atlantic. At one point I sensed a great deal of restlessness
in the plane. After Estoril the men were quietly, discreetly,
shedding their civilian clothes and getting into uniform – our
saviours wanted to arrive looking like saviours. But what I was
totally unprepared for was the warmth of the congratulations
showered on me once we were safely on English soil. I was a
heroine. I had behaved with the cool sang-froid in face of
danger that was what made us British what we were. My
astonished self then learned that part of the restlessness among
the men – I was the only woman passenger – was that we were
being tailed by a German plane. As I am, always have been,
and always will be quite moronic about machinery – cars,
planes, what you will – I had been completely unaware of
what was happening. In order not to embarrass the men as
they changed into uniform I had been quietly reading, or
pretending to read.

Apparently good conduct marks had been given me for my American efforts. One by-product was that I was invited on a number of occasions to become a member of the popular wartime 'Brains Trust'. This was Churchill's doing. Theoretically he was not supposed to interfere in these matters, but of course he interfered in everything. The irony of our domestic situation was that here was I, in high favour, while Nye was branded 'a squalid nuisance'. Our point of view was identical. We were not pacifists. We were dedicated to helping the men and women in the fighting forces in every way we could, most of all helping them to secure the best possible planes and tanks. We were equally dedicated in our desire to win the war for a better future, not a return to the past. If I had been a Member of Parliament during the war years, I would have been just as much an outcast as Nye. I agreed with his hard, often lonely fight, on one critical issue after another. We were each doing all we could in our different ways to promote both military victory and preparations for a civilized aftermath.

While still in America I learned that Nye, in addition to his other responsibilities, had become unpaid editor of *Tribune*. Pat Strauss, who had taken her young children to friends in America for safety, was staying in the New York hotel I returned to after each of my propaganda expeditions. We were together in her room when the New York Sunday papers arrived and my mail from home. Among the vast conglomeration of glossy magazines and newsprint a poor little grey mouse emerged. It was Nye's *Tribune* printed on grey wartime paper, but the letter accompanying it was spilling over with enthusiasm and pride. As usual, Nye could do nothing by halves. He went often to El Vino's, the Fleet Street pub frequented by journalists, and there persuaded illustrious employees of the Establishment press to salve their consciences by making unpaid contributions to *Tribune* – not under their own names, of course. Another contributor was George Orwell. *Tribune* was the only paper that gave him complete freedom to write as he pleased.

Later on I was to blot my copy-book by standing as an

Independent candidate in a by-election in Bristol Central, while the war was still on. This was in 1943, at a time when the combined Russian, American and British forces had made the defeat of Hitler absolutely beyond question. There was ferment in the factories and in the Services, as men and women turned their thoughts to what was going to be the pattern of their lives when the war ended. Memories of the 'hard-faced businessmen' who took over after the First World War made them resolve that it was going to be different this time. The ILP was pacifist and becoming increasingly irrelevant. Dick Acland was chairman of the Common Wealth Party, whose policy was 'fight on both fronts – against Hitler and against Tory reactionaries'. Churchill as war leader, fine. Churchill as chairman of the Tory Party, the friend of King Victor Emmanuel in Italy, of King George in Greece, the leader reluctant to accept that it was Tito and the Communist partisans who were doing the fighting on our side in Yugoslavia, the leader who tried to gag both press and Parliament: that Churchill was wholly unacceptable. He would try to drag us back to an imperial past that had gone for ever. Churchill was too cocooned by sycophants, too much a prisoner of his own romantic temperament, to know what was really going on. Nye never doubted that if we could prise Ernest Bevin and Clem Attlee away from their subservience to Churchill and persuade the rank and file of the Labour Party into rejecting any form of coalition after the war, there would be a resounding Labour victory.

When asked if I would stand as a Common Wealth candidate in Bristol Central I refused. Then I was asked if I would be prepared to stand as an Independent with Common Wealth support. That was the most enjoyable election I ever fought. Against me I had a Tory candidate and an ILP candidate. For me I had Dick Acland's idealistic troops and also the great majority of the members of the Bristol Central Labour Party. They knew perfectly well that although Nye, Stafford Cripps, and quite a few other Labour MPs could not support me openly, they were entirely on my side.

It was then I met Mervyn Stockwood for the first time. He was Vicar of St Matthew's, a close friend of Stafford, his local Member of Parliament, and knew Stafford's mind as well as I did. Mervyn, who became chairman of my election committee, wore a long flowing black cloak in those days. He was with me on the night before the poll. We had no loud-speaker equipment then, all we had was a barrel-organ that we trundled from street to street to alert the surrounding populace that we were in the area. As the evening wore on Mervyn's speeches grew shorter and shorter. A vote for Jennie Lee was a vote on the side of righteousness. A vote against her was a vote for the devil. Of course these are not the words he used, but that was the gist of it. Under my breath, I was thinking, 'Please, Mervyn, put in a few conditional clauses.'

Another of my flamboyant supporters was Rebecca Sieff. Rebecca was chairman of an organization called 'Women for Westminster'. She had more than once asked me to join, but I invariably said, 'No, Becky. I shall always vote on policy issues, not on the sex of the candidate.' The by-election in Bristol was Becky's great moment. She came hurrying to my aid, bringing all her women with her. The next development was that the candidate chosen by the Tories was a woman, the widow of the Tory Member whose death as a serving soldier had caused the by-election. Nothing deterred, Becky turned up at my committee rooms, but of course a much larger contingent of these middle-class ladies turned up to support the Tory candidate.

Becky was born before her time. With every fibre of her being she resented the restrictions imposed on her because of her sex. Her husband, Israel Sieff, and her brother, Simon Marks, were off together on the great adventure of building up the Marks and Spencer empire, but Becky was excluded from their business world. Husband and brother loved her and she loved them, but they were men of their time; they accepted the Victorian and Jewish conventions where women were concerned. Becky never surrendered to those male-dominated conventions. She kept on fighting, and she has a distinguished place in that galaxy of brave women who fought so hard and endured so much in the long hard struggle for political, social and economic equality. She could be awkward, talk out of turn, shout to be heard when she found soft words led nowhere. This was her response to the frustrations that entangled her. With Nye and with me, there was never any of this defiant behaviour. There was no need. She would be relaxed, her true lovable, rational self, for she knew we accepted her not as her husband's wife or her brother's sister, but as a person in her own right.

Perhaps the light-hearted atmosphere of this campaign was due to the enormous relief of believing that the war was nearly over and we could now look ahead. Our meetings were crowded and enthusiastic. There was only one snag; Bristol Central had been heavily bombed. Well-to-do business people could return to cast their double votes for the Tory candidate on polling day, but working people who had lived there, many of whom would no doubt have supported me, were scattered far and wide. So we did not win. The Labour Party bosses pursued their usual routine: they began expelling the rebel local leaders who had defied the Party truce and supported me, but we were not too much dismayed. We were quite sure, whatever temporary setbacks we might face, that the tides were flowing our way.

After Hitler invaded Russia and Sir Stafford Cripps returned to London and reported that the Germans would cut through Russian resistance like a hot knife through butter, I knew he was wrong. The Russians would fight. It would not be just formal resistance enforced on people whipped into obedience by their military high command.

Stafford had great purity, dedication, and was a devastatingly brilliant barrister. But as British Ambassador to Russia he was a hopeless misfit. He was in a world he knew nothing about, and the Russian leaders did not give him their confidence. I was no expert, but in 1930 and 1932 I had travelled from Moscow and Leningrad to Georgia and farther afield. I had met all kinds of Russians. In 1936 I had talked to the headmaster in charge of the school where Stalin's children were being educated. I remembered what he had said. In the early years of the Revolution there was anarchy in the schools, but by 1936 there was strict discipline. When I entered a classroom with him the children rose to attention in perfect silence and order. No Prussian academy could have been more disciplined. This distinguished headmaster, a friend and confidant of Lenin's widow, said to me, 'Remember, we are going to have to fight. The entire capitalist world is hostile to us. With this outweighing every other consideration, we must stress discipline, patriotism, and the qualities and skills that will be needed for our survival.'

I put a damp cloth round my head and wrote without stopping until I completed a pamphlet entitled *Russia, Our Ally*. It was published by Allen Lane in record time and sold well. In writing it, I remembered the young fellows drilling in the Donbass. I remembered waitresses in Moscow practising parachute-jumping in their spare time. I had no military expertise. All I was sure about was that the Russian people, not just the Russian Government, would fight to the last drop of their blood. What we had to do was to help them withstand the onslaught of the full force of the German military machine.

There were those in high places in England who thought it would be excellent if the Germans and Russians just about exterminated one another. We could then saunter in with a walking-stick to easy victories. There were military leaders who, preoccupied with other theatres of war, knew little and cared less about the Russian front. But throughout Britain the demand was growing for a Second Front to ease the terrible punishment the Russians were having to stand up to. We Second Fronters were a mixed lot. Inside the Cabinet, Max Beaverbrook was almost alone in pressing for adequate aid to Russia. His newspapers reflected his point of view. The *Evening Standard* was edited by Frank Owen, then by Michael Foot. Others of us contributed. The left in the Labour Party, odd Liberals, the Communist Party, and at times even members of the ILP, were pressing for a Second Front. Churchill was under even greater pressure from President Roosevelt and his military advisers led by General Marshall, but we knew little of this at the time.

Another active element in this campaign were influential Jewish families. They were frenetically concerned to defeat Hitler. He must not be allowed to win in Russia, then turn his forces against a hopelessly weakened Britain. One of the most militant of the Jewish advocates campaigning for aid to Russia was my friend, Rebecca Sieff. One evening Michael Foot, Frank Owen, Nye, myself and some others were dining with Israel and Becky at Brook House. This was when Nye knew for certain that he was being spied upon. When one member of the company, who professed to share our criticisms of the way the war was being conducted, left the room, Nye followed him into the men's cloakroom. Clutching him by the scruff of the neck, he forced a confession. The man in question, who had great charm and had made himself so agreeable to everyone when visiting our cottage, was being paid by M15 or some other secret service outfit, to report Nye's every movement. Nye had begun to be suspicious of him before then, but it clinched matters when he said he had been abroad for a few weeks. In what capacity? In whose service?

As the war drew to a close we had to make a hard decision. We were living almost two hours from London by road, and we could not afford a flat in London as well as the cottage. I had rejoined the Labour Party and was parliamentary candidate in a constituency I ought certainly to win when the General Election came. We had no choice. We would have to sell the cottage and find a home in central London. Lane End was the first real home of his own Nye had ever had. As a child he had had good parents and now he helped to maintain a house in Tredegar for his widowed mother. But the cottage was different. He had put his heart as well as his muscle into transforming a rural slum into a fairy-tale home.

This was the time in our lives when I at last learned not to listen to the impossible things he so often said, not to what

was on the tip of his tongue, but to what was in his spirit.
That was no mean feat, for part of me was a literal-minded
Scot who liked to feel solid ground under her feet. But what
was to be done about someone so vulnerable, so trusting when
once he had given you his heart? Archie and I could fool Nye
any time we liked, and often enjoyed the fun of doing so.

I don't know what might have happened if we had had to
face the strains of the 1945–50 Parliament while I was still
restless and uncertain and, incredible though it may sound to
those who knew only the external Nye, when only a saint
would have put up with me. I would be off to New York,
Moscow, Vienna, Berlin, pursuing my own interests and
leaving him to fend for himself. We never quarrelled about
private, domestic matters. I could do as I pleased. I could
have my own way. But there were times when he had an
infuriating habit of looking at me with what I called his Mona
Lisa smile, and saying, 'I shall win in the end.' He did. I
would have been a fool not to have come to understand that he
had a better mind than I had, a more creative, far-reaching
intelligence. And he had an unfailing sense of humour, which
I did not always have. Also, although he was working
underground before his fourteenth birthday, he was better
educated. It was not the clever Edinburgh graduate who wrote
the thesis on Kant's Categorical Imperative that was praised
by Mr P. W. Dodd, Senior Tutor at Jesus College, Oxford, as
the best thing on Kant he had read for years. Nye wrote this
for Archie Lush around 1927, when both of them were
thinking of becoming Oxford students. Archie made it. Nye
had neither the time nor the means to accompany him. But
they studied together. Nye was avidly interested in philosophy. Archie found it his most daunting subject.

A little later it was Nye, not me, who first won the
friendship of Michael Ayrton, Felix Topolski, Henry Moore,
Graham Sutherland, Jacob Epstein and others among the most
gifted artists of his generation. The artists became my friends
too. But I was completely out of my depth when Solly
Zuckerman, Cyril Joad, J. D. Bernal and others such as they

came to Cliveden Place to spend a mutually enjoyable evening discussing scientific and philosophical problems I neither knew nor cared much about.

15. The Move to London

Nye had neither the time nor the heart to make arrangements for the sale of the cottages and to find suitable accommodation in London. All this had to be left to me. It was still wartime, so I had a wide choice, for very many houses had been abandoned. My favourite hunting-ground was around Sloane Square as I wanted us to be near the House of Commons, but not too near. Ultimately I settled for 23 Cliveden Place. It was large enough to give my parents a sitting-room and two bedrooms, Nye and I a sitting-room and two bedrooms, a small study, a small garden behind, and a dining-room and kitchen quarters. We bought a twelve-year remainder lease for £180 a year, and I reckoned that my overheads were £6 a week, rates included. This same residence now costs a fortune. At the same time a Newbury agent put the cottages on the market for an asking price of £3,000.

One evening, when we were with Becky and Israel Sieff at Brook House, all hell was let loose. German bombers had begun intensive night raids on London. Judith, their young married daughter, and Sarah, her baby, were with them; they had to be got out of reach of the German planes. We invited them to have Dad's cottage as Kay Griffith and baby Nicola were now living with relatives in another part of the country. That is how Israel came to know and to love Lane End. He bought the property for Judith, but the last thing she was interested in at that time of her life was an old country cottage. Nor was it exactly Becky's scene. She too had other interests.

One day after we had moved to London, Israel visited the cottage and found it damp, dismal and deserted. He spent the night sleeping in a damp bed, fully clothed, overcoat and all. When he first said that if we really were moving to London, he would like to buy the cottage, I warned him that it was not as simple as it looked. I had refused to sell it to a retired army major, for I thought it would have been a cruelty to do so: he would not have been able to afford to maintain it. The combined labour of my parents, Nye and myself, Joice, her brother, her father occasionally or some other local help and willing weekend gardeners among our friends, meant that we had all the comfort we could wish for, but it was not a one-man job. Israel definitely did not want a large country house. He had had all that. Since we had no choice but to sell, it was a comfort to see it pass into the care of someone who had fallen in love with it and would lavish not just cash but his own personal supervision in keeping it as it should be. When Israel took over, for quite a time he himself was the cook at the weekends, Nye providing skilled assistance if we happened to be visiting.

Being an unstoppable empire-builder, Israel acquired lots of surrounding farm land and took his farming seriously, but the cottage remained essentially unchanged. I loved to lie back on a comfortable sofa in front of the log fire, listening to the two of them wandering off into magic regions all their own. They would talk about history, philosophy, religion, poetry, but never on a pedestrian level. It was the far, outer reaches of man's quest for understanding that fascinated them – what Nye called the mystery at the heart of life. The Celt and the Jew were well matched. They knew how to escape from mundane cares and responsibilities into this private world, and when the talking stopped, Israel would find a Mozart, Bach, Handel, Beethoven record, or any other of the great classics they both enjoyed so much and so would end a tranquil, contented evening.

Nye never became reconciled to living in London, even though we had found a comfortable and conveniently located house. I too missed the old cottage but not as much as he did; I enjoyed the challenge of planning 23 Cliveden Place in such a way that my father could have his private fireside, we could have ours, and room would still be left for office space.

The ground floor with the French window in the rear and steps leading down to the garden would, I decided, be just right for my parents. That left the L-shaped room on the floor above as a sitting-room for Nye and me. But I had reckoned without my mother. She thought this was a daft arrangement and was not prepared to put up with it. Dad's sitting-room was going to be the little back-room on the same floor as her kitchen, with a window looking out on the garden. My sensible mother had her way. There was a lift from the kitchen to the ground floor, so she said we could have that as our dining-room and sit talking there all night if we wished without being in anyone's way. Meaning by 'anyone', of course, herself.

I looked at the small back-room. There was no wall I could knock down, so I was deprived of my favourite pastime, but at least I could tear out the ugly gas fire embedded in a Victorian surround, and replace it with the largest open coal fire in London. I am afraid at that time 'air pollution' was not in my thoughts. While we were still using the small back-room as our dining-room, its worst feature was the iron bars across the window. One evening I arrived home after an evening meeting to find six or seven men around our refectory table, which we had managed to squeeze into it. I recognized Michael Foot, Frank Owen, Wilfrid Macartney, but not the others. Nye's way of introducing me was to say to one of the strangers, 'Jennie hates these window bars. You are a professional. Are they any good?' A slender man with a gold filling in a front tooth, glided rather than walked from the table, went to the floor above, and on returning said, 'Useless. No self-respecting burglar would waste his time on them.'

Nye's burglar guest was an Irishman with an incredibly brave war record. He had enlisted with the Germans, claiming that he hated the English, and was keen to see Hitler marching through London. His name was Eddie Chapman. He was in fact working for the British Government. The Germans on checking his record found it stood up to what he had told them of having been dragged up in the back streets of a seaport town, unemployed, turning to burglary, being caught and gaoled. That evening when he came to our home he and his friends were asking Nye's help to overcome defence regulations, which were preventing him from publishing a book about his adventures. Given time, I usually found Nye's behaviour quite reasonable, but he did enjoy springing surprises on me.

Alas for all my fine plans. When we moved into London we thought the bombing phase was over; instead we had to contend with the doodle bugs. My parents were sent off to safety, living in the country with old Lochgelly neighbours. Nye and I camped in the basement, sleeping in the back-room, using the kitchen as a dining-room and pretty well abandoning the rest of the house.

Our American friends, the Reuther brothers, wrote to say that one of their pals, Jack McElhone, had not waited for America to come into the war. He had joined the Canadian Air Force and was now due in London. When Jack called on us, Nye, hospitable as always, brought out his one bottle of vintage claret and a special French cheese that Hubert Griffith had brought us from France. Afterwards when we came to know Jack well, we found that he disliked wine and fancy cheeses, but ate and drank manfully not to give offence to his host. We came to love Jack, as did his many friends in America. Always when on leave he hastened to Cliveden Place like a homing pigeon. My last memory of him is seeing Nye and him sprawling on our sitting-room floor with an excited Jack spreading around them his proposed lay-out for the paper he was going to edit for the automobile workers' union when the war was over. A few weeks later I got a letter from him which did not disguise just how exhausted he was. He had been one of those used in bombing raids over Germany, he was due for leave, but on the last evening of his spell of duties he was shot down. Always when his friends meet our first thoughts turn to Jack.

Towards the end of 1944 I had applied for membership of the Labour Party, and in December 1944 I received a letter from Mr G.R. Shepherd, Labour Party National Agent, informing me that the National Executive Committee had decided to offer no objection to me becoming a member. It was not exactly an enthusiastic welcome. The statement submitted to the NEC by the National Agent after interviewing me reads as follows:

Miss Jennie Lee

(a) Agreed that the conditions surrounding the departure of the Independent Labour Party from the Labour Party were dead, and were no longer a guide to her political views.

(b) She indicated that her severance from the ILP arose out of the war issue. In her view the military defeat of Hitler is vital.

(c) She agreed that she had written articles in the American Press, chiefly the *New Republic*, but that whilst there may have been criticism of Labour therein, there was no wickedness in it.

(d) She indicated that Labour's declaration to fight the next election as an independent Party had been the chief impulse in the steps she had taken to seek membership. She felt she understood the Party case for the General Election, and so far as she knew it she certainly approved of it. Her view was that in the Election, the rival policies of the Conservative and Labour Parties should be sharply defined and kept free from 'splinter' issues.

(e) She was unconnected with any other Political Organization. Her loyalty to the Labour Party would be full and generous. She had no personal aims to achieve. Her activities would be devoted to supporting the broad Policy of the Party.

In that 1944 atmosphere the pre-war divisions had become irrelevant. It was either Labour Party or Tory Party, a Labour Goverment or a Tory Government. As soon as it became known that I had rejoined the Party, various constituencies, including three winnable ones, Slough, Aberdeen and Cannock, invited me to go before the committee that would select their General Election candidate. I did not hesitate. I thought of Cannock as a mining constituency. I would feel at home there. Of course it was a vast county constituency with strong Conservative support in the rural areas, but it was the mining areas and the vote of the miners which would count for most in selecting a candidate.

The Cannock agent at that time was Jack Evans, formerly a Rhondda miner, forced to leave the pits for health reasons. The chairman was Arthur Hampton, whose deeply committed socialist faith remained undimmed throughout the whole of his life. He was a Methodist in his youth, was teetotal, and had had to struggle through every kind of hardship. Cyril Hotchkiss, a most likeable schoolmaster, was treasurer. I called him 'sinful Cyril', for he was a good mixer around the working men's clubs. Arthur and I were not beer drinkers, and I had had no experience in Scotland of going into drinking places to meet people, so I would tell Cyril, 'In you go and don't forget you have to drink for three of us.' During the war years he had been a leader of the Home Guard, and had many friends in the clubs.

When the date of the selection conference approached, I decided it was a waste of time for me to go forward. Hector Hughes, a quaint little lawyer, later a Member of Parliament for Aberdeen, had persuaded the local miners' agent to have him adopted as the official miners' candidate. He was the only nominee invited to address the miners' executive committee. Frank Beswick (later Lord Beswick), then a young Air Force officer, was flown over from the Far East and was sponsored by the Co-operative Party. The Transport and General Workers considered they had most right to the seat as the previous Member of Parliament had been one of their members. All three promised to meet election expenses and to make handsome contributions to constituency funds between elections. I could make no offer of financial support of any kind. But Jack Evans and Arthur Hampton said, 'You are going to go forward. You will lose on the first ballot and win on the second.' They were reckoning that three right-wing candidates would divide the right-wing vote, then only one of them would be in the ring to contest the vacancy with me in the second round.

I won on the first count. I had not been a member of the official Party from 1932 to 1944, but what did that matter? I had at all times been part of the broader Labour movement. The miners' delegates paid not the slightest heed to the instructions that had been given to them to vote for Hector Hughes.

I was proud, excited and grateful to have so great a trust given me. Soon I was hearing all about the battles the older people had fought long ago and how, along with a younger generation, they were now looking forward to reaping the fruits of their early sacrifices. We were on our way. And we were a great team. I stayed with Frank Rowley, an idealistic schoolmaster, who, along with his wife Millie, did wonderful work in his spare time helping boys in that deprived area to enjoy camping and all the comradeship and worthwhile values that went with it. Most of all I remember standing at the top of the main street in the mining village of Hednesford when Jack Phillips, another local Labour leader, pointing to a pit in the valley below said, 'That is where Churchill brought the troops.' For a moment I thought he was talking about some recent wartime event. No, it was a bitter recollection of 1910. As I have said, miners have long memories. I admired the fine head with its mop of white hair and the eyes of an Old Testament prophet as Jack pointed down the hill. There were so many more, dear to me, though I do not list them all. They were true believers. They knew what they were fighting for and loved what they knew.

Some years later when Jack Evans moved to another job his place was taken by Alfred Allen, who, before qualifying as an agent, had worked for many years as a railway signalman. I was again in luck. I knew that when Nye, myself, both or either of us, were involved in internal party controversies, I need not worry about my constituency position. Every Member of Parliament knows just how much it means to have a staunch man on the spot guarding your rear. Alfred and I never once quarrelled either about political or personal matters, but it was a well-seasoned joke between us that always when a General Election was looming, I would say to him, 'Now, remember Alf, anything that goes wrong is your fault. You take all the blame. And everything that goes well is my doing. I get all the credit.'

When the result of the General Election was declared on 26 July 1945, Nye's forecast of how both industrial workers and returning soldiers would vote proved correct. If Ernest Bevin and Clement Attlee had had their way, there would have been no Labour victory. We would have been a minor party in a coalition government, trailing behind Churchill's triumphant chariot.

Nye had at long last been elected a member of the Labour Party's National Executive Committee. At the Party Conference preceding the Election, speaking for the first time from the platform, he said:

> We at this time are completely united. There are no differences between us now, and any memories of past differences we shall erase from our minds and from our hearts, because we have before us the greatest opportunity this nation has ever provided for a Party. It is in no pure Party spirit that we are going into this election. We know that in us, and in us alone, lies the economic salvation of this country and the opportunity of providing a great example to the world.

Such was his faith.

16. Aneurin Bevan, Minister of Health and Housing

Nye had no way of knowing whether or not he would be invited by Attlee to join his Government. All he was clear about was that it would be nothing or a senior Cabinet post: he was not prepared to be an office boy carrying out policies he had taken no part in shaping. Ernest Bevin is supposed to have encouraged Attlee to give Nye a senior Government post, but at the same time, when someone said that Nye was his own worst enemy, Bevin is supposed to have retorted, 'Not while I am alive.' You can pay your money and take your choice. Maybe the calculation was that the loud-mouthed demagogue would find himself unequal to a constructive task and so be finally disposed of. That is all speculation; whatever the motives, Attlee did send for Nye. He was appointed Minister of Health and Housing.

Nye was proud of his strong physique. But he had to pay a price for those six years' hard manual labour underground and his love of climbing the Welsh hills. When as a Member of Parliament and later a Cabinet Minister, he had to lead a more sedentary life, he began to have trouble with his shoulder muscles. John Buchan, a physiotherapist and a family friend, would come in first thing in the morning and massage his shoulders when they were painful. Sir William Douglas, the Permanent Secretary at the Ministry of Health, was also one of John's patients. When Nye was appointed, Sir William said to John, 'I have let it be known that I am not prepared to serve under that man.' Some time later when John reminded him what he had said, he replied that this was the best Minister he had ever worked for. John was vastly amused. Sir

William of course did not know he was one of Nye's close friends.

Never once during the 1945–50 Government, when Nye had to fight all comers in order to establish the Health Service, did he come home in the evening and complain about his permanent officials. On the contrary he was full of gratitude to them and was worried only by the strains he was imposing on them. But he would let off steam in the privacy of his home by damning and blasting some of his Labour colleagues. Herbert Morrison, in particular, kept interfering with him and was especially hostile to his decision to take control of local authority hospitals as well as privately endowed ones. The degree of trust, indeed affection, that came to be established at the Ministry between Nye and the great company of men and women from top-rank civil servants to doorkeepers, who worked loyally and without stint to help him through every crisis, is reflected in a letter I received from Sir Charles Trevelyan's oldest daughter, Pauline, many years later, that is on 15 April 1977. She was thanking me for sending her a copy of Michael Foot's biography of Nye and went on to write about Sir John Hawton. Here are Pauline's own words:

Dear Jennie,

I was so very glad to have your letter, and thank you so much for sending me this new issue of this fine book about Nye. I remember him so well. I did not before know what an extraordinary personal story his is, from a start with no advantages in the worldly sense, to a position where his great strength of personality could have full scope.

When I was a member of the Waterways Board, my Chairman was Sir John Hawton, who was head of the Health Division of the Ministry when Nye took over. Sir John soon discovered that I had known his Minister and he was never tired of talking about him – that rather staid, shy, very senior civil servant was simply 'bowled off his feet' by Nye's vigorous aliveness and determination, and still talked of him with adoration, saying there was no one like him – as indeed there wasn't.

In easier times it might have been quite reasonable for one Minister to be in charge of both Health and Housing. In the circumstances following the Second World War that was no longer so. After four years of arduous non-stop concentration on the problems of both sections of his Ministry, Nye drafted a report to the Prime Minister setting out plans for their separation. But in the meantime he had to get ahead as best he could on both fronts.

Immediately after the war, such labour and materials as were available were urgently needed to repair bomb damage to docks and factories as well as to private homes. Ernest Bevin refused to release from the Services ahead of their turn men who were badly needed in the building trade, insisting on no favouritism – first in, first out. That was quite right, but every rule, however good, now and again needs to be set aside. During the war Churchill had promised that the 'homes for heroes' which did not materialize after the First World War this time would be produced. There was a public clamour for houses and an innocent belief that Lord Portal's promise of 500,000 steel houses was something solid to build on. Nothing could have illustrated more glaringly just how remote the Portals and Churchills were from the plain realities of the steel situation. If those houses had been built there would have been no steel for the repair of damaged factories or the building of new ones, or for any other national need. Nye said privately at the time that it would have been better to build no houses in the first year or two after the war. That would have given time for the orderly switch back from war to peace work in the factories, for the assembly of the hundreds of diverse parts that go to the making of a house, and quicker progress would in the end have been made than by the improvised methods he was forced to adopt. But you could not have that kind of planning in a democracy. The public were not prepared to wait.

On the information supplied by his senior officials, Nye gave the House of Commons a much more optimistic estimate of the number of houses that would be needed to meet all housing needs than in fact turned out to be the case. Maybe the beginning of his rapport with his officials was that neither in Parliament nor by the kind of snide leak to the press that some Ministers did not hesitate to use, did he try to excuse himself by blaming his advisers. The sheer physical strain of getting around the country, in order to visit building projects on the site, was quite something. He was on excellent terms with his official driver, who was a man after his own heart. They both enjoyed fast driving. One evening, on coming home after a long day's journey, Nye told me laughingly how as they were driving along at top speed his driver had said to him, 'What was on that sign-post, Minister?' 'Paint, you bugger, paint,' was Nye's reply. But another evening he came home grief-stricken. His driver had died of a sudden heart attack. Had he been worked too hard?

One of his most senior officials had a nervous breakdown. Had his work load been just too much? Nye himself had a serious illness during this period. An ordinary bout of flu developed into pneumonia. His doctor friend, Sir Daniel Davies, attended to him devotedly, John Buchan, aided by my mother, nursed him during the day, and I was night nurse. This was another time when I prayed to the God I did not believe existed. Listening to Nye's breathing during the night, I began to fear that this was not just pneumonia. Was Nye too to be the victim of the pneumoconiosis that killed so many miners, including his father, death coming after a long painful illness? Although working underground for six years only, the conditions in the pits where he had worked had been such that he left with the symptoms of pneumoconiosis already there. I prayed, 'Please God, not that, not that. I shall never complain about anything for the rest of my life if only Nye is spared that kind of suffering.'

Nye was soon well again and from first to last during his years as a Minister he was a reformed character. No more lying in late in the mornings, and wide awake reading or talking or listening to music at midnight and into the early hours of the following day. His vitality was always highest in the evening, but he disciplined himself to be up, bathed, breakfasted (and, most unusual for him, eating a proper breakfast) then off to his office by 9 a.m. at the latest.

Three years after the end of the war, in spite of all the dislocations caused by the shortages of labour and materials, Sir William Douglas, Permanent Secretary, and Sir John Wrigley, Deputy Secretary, in charge of Housing, were well pleased with the way the housing programme was progressing. In l948, 284,230 houses, permanent and temporary, had been built. The following year they estimated that they could exceed 300,000, and that without cutting standards, as Tory politicians who did not themselves live in council houses kept nagging them to do. Then came a blinding blow: a Cabinet instruction to cut back on the housing programme. In l949 the number of completions was reduced to 2l7,000. Even that did not satisfy the Prime Minister and the Treasury Ministers. Nye was ordered to reduce the annual output to something under 200,000 a year, and must on no account exceed 200,000. What to do? Resign? There were several major Cabinet policies Nye did not agree with, covering international as well as domestic issues. The agony in that kind of situation of deciding what best to do has to be experienced to be fully realized. Could you best help all you cared about by resigning, or would that merely hasten the collapse of the Government? Ultimately when Nye did resign it was not over any one issue. It was the cumulative effect of years of in-fighting inside the Cabinet. The public of course knew little or nothing of all this.

It has often been quoted, but it is not an invention – it is indeed true – that Sir John Wrigley said to Nye, 'Minister, if we build more than 200,000 houses, I'll be sacked by the Chancellor, and if we build less, I'll be sacked by you.' The Government was going through a period of severe economic crisis. It was no part of Nye's case that no cuts needed to be made; his argument was that the Cabinet had got its priorities wrong. There were other areas of public expenditure which could have been cut without the damage to public morale and to the Government's standing in the country caused by those housing cuts. Health and housing are not urgent matters for those with ample incomes enabling them to buy homes and employ private doctors. But they were at the heart of the needs of the great majority of families.

Why was a Labour Government so blind? Why did Hugh Dalton, on becoming Minister of Housing, deride Nye's insistence on having two lavatories in the three-bedroomed type of council house designed for mixed families? Did he not know that with father coming home from work and the children coming home from school, how much it helped mother if they did not always have to clamber upstairs, father maybe with work-soiled clothes, and the children with muddy boots? Or how much it mattered if there was sickness in the family, or maybe an elderly parent to be cared for as well as the children? Dalton by birth and upbringing belonged to a privileged world. He had not sympathy nor imagination enough to bridge the gap. A reduction in housing standards would mean more houses for the same amount of cash and materials, and that would win approval. He would be acclaimed a successful Minister. So Dalton paved the way for Harold Macmillan and no one in fairness ought to withhold admiration for the whole-hearted, intensive rejoicing of the Tory press and Tory Government that they were building the 300,000 houses a year that Nye's colleagues had prevented him from building.

On the lighter side of things, Nye was delighted by the ease with which he won Cabinet consent to introduce legislation to enable local authorities to spend up to sixpence in the pound on cultural activities. This measure was not at the centre of power politics, and anyhow it was permissive, not compulsory. Members of the Cabinet who knew little and cared less about the artists' world and the artists' problems, were satisfied with an arrangement which meant that councils were not bound to spend as much as a brass farthing on the arts if they did not wish to do so. Another helpful pointer to plans for a brighter future was Labour's decision to provide funds for the Festival of Britain.

Stress of work meant that Nye had little time for his favourite leisure-time pursuits, but we did not entirely drown in official despatch boxes. We could still sometimes escape and there was always a warm welcome from our friends. Alfred Hecht, who liked describing himself as a picture frame-maker, was indeed a picture frame-maker, but in addition he had the gift of recognizing genius long before the general public came to recognize it. In his home we spent happy carefree evenings with artist friends, some of whose early promise came to nothing, while others, among them Henry Moore, Graham Sutherland, John Piper and Francis Bacon, were to reach the highest pinnacles of their profession.

Then we had our own private artist. When first we moved to Cliveden Place, the back basement room had bare white walls, a layer of paint having been hastily applied to cover up the ravages of war damage. Jane Lane, a young art student who was brought along by friends, asked if she might paint a frieze around the walls. We were using this small back-room next to the kitchen as a dining-room at the time, so I said, 'Jane, go ahead, if you have in mind to paint something easy to live with, but I don't want anything too strident.' I became suspicious when Private Howard Samuel began visiting us rather frequently. Jane had a rare Rossetti-type of beauty. Howard was obviously enraptured. One day I said to her, 'Jane, don't hurt Howard. Don't flirt too much with him.' A few days later they came upstairs to my sitting-room, hand in hand, to announce they were engaged. I like to recall that happy time when none of us could know the tragedies that ill-health was later to bring them.

Again and again attempts were made to 'frame' Nye. I had to be constantly on my guard. One attempt nearly came off when a woman who had all the hallmarks of the crudest type of prostitute threw her arms around his neck as he was walking along the Embankment late at night. It was a put-up

job. There was the instant flash of cameras. Nye just managed
to fight his way out of the trap. I knew about this incident
only when he asked me to go walking with him the next
evening. I too had had a long hard day and was sprawling
comfortably on my favourite sofa in front of a glowing fire. I
got sleepy in the evenings and had not Nye's need to go
walking after spending the day imprisoned in Parliament, or
in his Department, or in his car. I had not even noticed that
he had begun to carry a stout stick if he felt he must stretch
his legs in the evening.

At that time Betty, our young secretary, worked half-time
for us and half-time for George Orwell. Every morning I
would throw on a dressing-gown and go quietly downstairs to
open the post before she arrived. I wanted to spare both Nye
and her the horror of reading obscenely abusive letters and
opening the packets of filth that came through our letter-box.
There are all kinds of ways of fighting the class war! The press
was responsible for most of these excesses. They would take
one phrase from an hour-long speech, quote it out of context,
then go to town in a merry old game of abuse and
misrepresentation. 'Lower than vermin' was one such that was
made to work overtime. Nye was totally uninhibited in his
relations with all manner of people. His friends were those he
liked, his intimate friends those he loved. They came in all
shapes and sizes, with no regard to class, colour or religion.
Beggars or princes, rich or poor, black or white, saints or
sinners – he had them all. If the gentlemen of the press had
wanted to tell the truth about his attitude to people, they
knew where to find it. He had published a pamphlet entitled
Why Not Trust the Tories? The opening sentence in chapter six
reads as follows:

Do I think that Tories, considered as men and women, are worse
than other people? I answer at once: of course I don't. A Tory,
considered as a private individual, is neither better nor worse than
anyone else.

In an impassioned speech, recalling the hardships and

humiliations imposed on poor people by the between-war
Tory Governments, he indeed used the phrase 'lower than
vermin'. But it was the policy-makers of the Tory Party, not
the half of the nation that voted Tory, he was attacking, and
that was perfectly clear from the context.

As security officer for Nye there were serious pitfalls I had
to look out for, but we got a bit of fun as well out of some of
the goings-on. Coping with Mother, for instance. She had not
a clue about rationing. She did not believe in it and while we
lived in the country eggs, chickens and garden produce were
easily available. True, we were strictly rationed for tea, sugar,
butter and other such items, but that was nothing compared
with London austerities. One day when she came in from
shopping, she dumped her basket on the kitchen table and
was obviously in a most unusual mood of high indignation.
'What's wrong, Ma?' I asked. 'That butcher,' she said. 'The
exact rations. He should be gaoled.' All she cared about was
feeding her family. To my horror I found she had formed an
unholy alliance with our Italian friend, René de Meo of the
Pheasantry Club. He was just as amoral, just as free from any
sense of sin as my mother. I had to stop their illegal traffic
right away. On the day when there was a small back-page
paragraph in one of the papers, reporting that the Junior
Carlton Club had been fined for black-marketing, I heard
René's voice downstairs, shouting 'Mama, Mama.' He had
brought her a substantial piece of meat.

I had visions of the blazing front-page headlines if we had
been caught black-marketing. 'Ma,' I said, 'this is illegal and
if you are caught and sent to gaol, we will not bail you out.'
To René I said, 'Please take it back, dear. I know how kindly
meant this is, but Nye above all people must keep strictly to
the letter of the law.' Let me add that I was not being prissy.
It was not a 'holier than thou' exercise. I simply knew too
much about how he was being spied upon, the trip-wires that
were set for him.

No one need envy the wives of Prime Ministers and senior
Cabinet Ministers for, irrespective of party, they have much

to contend with. They are expected to tag along behind their husbands, remain awake, even remember not to look bored, as they sit hour after hour on conference platforms or in public halls, and hear the same speech for the hundredth time. I was spared all that. Nye looked after his constituency. I looked after mine. At election times he paid one ceremonial visit to Cannock and had a heart-warming reception. I did not go even once to Ebbw Vale. What would have been the point of it? In addition to Cannock I spoke in surrounding marginals at election times as that made sense. But Ebbw Vale had not the slightest need of outside help.

I could cope with parliamentary and constituency duties, but the social chores Ministers and their wives were expected to wade through was something I could not take. I liked a party. Nye and I could give a good party and enjoy a party in the relaxed atmosphere of the home of a friend, but the frozen-cod type of entertainment where the guests were solemnly seated around, say, an Embassy table, each lady with a gentleman on either side, the sexes carefully invited in even numbers, and the ladies sent out of the room towards the end of the meal, the hostess then acting as lavatory attendant, was something I could not take. I found it, quite simply, outrageously ill-mannered. When Frank Cousins, general secretary of the Transport and General Workers' Union, left the security of his trade union office to become a Cabinet Minister, he had Nance, his wife, to contend with. Writing to me on 1 July 1958 on other matters, my friend Nance included the following:

It's wonderful being married to a man like Frank. He is completely ignorant of protocol so just ignores it. The first time we dined with the Yugoslavs, the hostess rose and collected the ladies and when we had left the Ambassador said 'Now we can talk'. So Frank said: 'Not without Nance. She'd never forgive me, and she is fairly intelligent, you know, she'll understand what you have to say.' So, much to the surprise of the three Yugoslav ladies, in trooped the men and we had a wonderful evening. When we dined the second time we all left the table together.

As a footnote Nance added, 'Ask Lady Megan if she would like to borrow Frank next time she goes.' The reference to Megan Lloyd George arose from the fact that there was a lot of grumbling among women, some of them Ministers or Members of Parliament in their own right, and yet they were so conditioned that they just could not break free from the upper-class, male-dominated rituals which relegated women to the position of tame poodles taken out on a lead by their husbands.

Protocol practices are not one of the great burning issues of world politics, and practices are changing, but you have to be at the heart of that world to know just how slowly, how reluctantly. Nye was completely on my side. We detested this kind of evening, and avoided it if we could. When invited to a dinner at the Yugoslav Embassy in the early days of the 1945–50 Government, I thought I would be safe enough in a Communist Embassy from what I considered insulting behaviour. Not so. When I found myself dismissed from the table, I made for the cloakrooms, collected my coat and left the building. I had not gone far when Nye caught up with me. Foolish? You may think so, but don't forget external modes of social behaviour are not fortuitous. They reflect and underpin social and sexual relationships.

One occasion I did enjoy was the first time I accompanied Nye to a very grand Buckingham Palace reception. It was a wonderful comedy of manners. When we all lined up to be presented to the Queen, George Tomlinson, our good-natured Minister of Education, was just behind us. George was having a bit of trouble with his hired evening outfit. It was bulging in the wrong places. Nye wore a well-fitting dark suit, an immaculate white shirt and a light-grey silk tie. They were his own. He too had his sticking points and would not have dreamed of submitting to the indignity of wearing hired clothes.

The next day the press gave the world the important news that he had turned up at the Palace wearing a blue suit and brown boots (brown boots, I ask you), the purpose being to convey the impression that he had been deliberately uncouth and discourteous to the Queen. I, on the other hand, was reported as wearing a glittering evening dress that must have cost at least one hundred guineas. How true that was; if I had paid for it, the price would have been about that. It had been made for me as a labour of love by my clever Viennese friend, Trude, and was cut from two scarlet and gold Behari saris that were presents from Indian friends.

The only time we attended an official dinner at 10 Downing Street after the 1951 defeat of the Labour Government was when Mr Harold Macmillan, as Prime Minister, was entertaining President Léopold Senghor of Senegal. When Nye showed me the invitation I said I thought we should accept. We were wholly on the side of the emerging African nations. The dinner in honour of Senghor was a very special occasion. We did not so much as mention to one another my dislike of the way those dinners are usually conducted, and I took it for granted that on this occasion I would just have to put up with it. To my surprise, when the ladies had left the dining-room and were seated around a pleasant fire in a room separated from it by a longish between-room, Edwina Mountbatten, that most lovable and enlightened of women, got up from the rug in front of the fire where she was sitting, and said: 'Quick, there's Nye.' She was on her feet and leading the rest of us towards the men, while I hardly knew what was happening, since I was sitting on a sofa with my back to the room where the men had appeared.

Nye, incorrigible as ever, at the end of the dinner had said why not join the ladies, or language to that effect. Monstrously rude of him. He should have waited for his host to give the lead. But that was Nye! And everyone seemed to enjoy an unusually relaxed dinner party.

I have always had good women friends as well as men friends. An evening when one or two of us can let our hair down together is very enjoyable. Men too enjoy being on their own sometimes. But if it is a mixed company, then let women take their place as part of the company, not just as appendages to their male partners. To a certain extent in the year 1980 I am shooting at a dead duck. No, not quite dead. Primitive tribal customs die hard.

17. My Return to Westminster, 1945

I felt diffident and ill at ease when I returned to the House of Commons in 1945. I did not speak with the same fluency as I had done in the 1929–31 Parliament. Any time Nye had a difficult speech to make, I would be in the Chamber, half looking forward to it, half apprehensive. It was always a relief when it was safely over. Nye, on the other hand, hated to be present if I were speaking. Why? Because he was nervous for me and protective. It was the old male chauvinist pig showing through his rational self. No man, as every one of our women friends will testify, was more completely on our side in every claim we could make for equal status, equal rights, equal opportunities, but emotionally, where I was concerned, he simply did not want me exposed to hurt or strain of any kind. This nannying was completely misplaced, as in many ways I was tougher than he was. But our rational selves and emotional selves don't always move along parallel lines; more often they criss-cross, leading to misunderstandings that can be disastrous, or again merely add an extra bit of spice to life. There was no rivalry between us – if there had been our whole relationship would have gone up in smoke. By 1945 we had been together long enough to have won through to secure mutual trust and dependence. Nye's happiness and well-being meant more to me than my own. My happiness and well-being meant more to Nye than his own. Not that there were not moments of intolerable strain when I felt I was being suffocated, when I almost went under. I shall speak about those a little later on.

My first responsibility in the new Parliament was to my constituency. The letters that came pouring down to

Westminster were promptly dealt with, but the new fashion of holding what were called 'surgeries', where constituents could bring their problems to their 'political' doctor, did not work well in a large county constituency. I did what I could; fortunately I had grown up in a county constituency and knew that each village had its own distinctive needs and personality. A visit to one part of the area meant nothing to the people living in another part, each had to have its own meed of attention. I thought of the occasion in the 1929–31 Parliament when James Maxton, seeing me sitting at a desk drowning in a sea of anguished letters from North Lanark constituents, tapped me on the shoulder and said, 'You had better make up your mind whether you are going to be a Member of Parliament or a bloody welfare worker.' Easier said than done. Each MP has to work out a pattern of behaviour suited to his or her special circumstances.

Nye took a cavalier attitude towards his constituency. They would have liked him to spend much more time there. 'You must pay the price of your success,' was his answer to them. Of course he would have loved to have spent more weekends in Wales; he could have climbed his beloved Welsh hills and enjoyed a battle of wits with Archie and other friends as well as attending constituency functions. Instead he would be off to crowded, exhausting meetings in Liverpool, Glasgow, Birmingham – the insistent requests came in from everywhere. This was not Nye's idea of an enjoyable weekend, but it had to be done. The Labour movement needed teachers. It had to be educated. It needed to know, in the language of Cromwell, both how to fight and what it was fighting for. So we each divided our time and strength as best we could among those various conflicting claims. And we still kept home life happy and secure.

My special interests were education, housing, commonwealth and foreign affairs. On one occasion I bearded Ernest Bevin in his den. He listened to me most courteously as I explained how deeply I and others felt about the rumour that the Ruhr steelworks were going to be given back to the

Krupps family; my plea was that this great industrial complex should remain a public trust. But of course his Foreign Office officials saw to it that he kept to a conservative line of policy. Whether it was the future of the Ruhr, waging the Cold War against Russia, fighting against the emergence of an independent Israel or, with the exception of India, almost any other international issue at that time, he was easily led, for he had no real quarrel with his officials.

Nye insisted on putting his point of view inside the Cabinet on both domestic and foreign affairs. In public he respected the doctrine of collective Cabinet responsibility and held strictly to it, but in private you would find us giving a party in our home to Ruth and Seretse Khama when official Labour was treating them badly, or to Cheddi Jagan and Linden Forbes Burnham, at that time working in double harness, when they came to London and got the cold shoulder from the right-wing leadership of the Party. Our ties with Israeli friends were especially close. Friendly, worldly-wise advisers would ask Nye, 'Why do you go out of your way to antagonize Cabinet colleagues? Stick to your last. Save your strength for health and housing.' But Nye could not accept that concept of the duties of a senior Minister. If he accepted collective responsibility, then he must be free to put his point of view, however unpopular, before the final decisions were made. His strength lay not in the Cabinet nor in the Parliamentary Labour Party. In both those areas the right wing was firmly in control. But in the constituencies, at the grass roots, it was a different matter. He was now a member of the Executive of the Party and any candidates seeking election to the constituency section who were known to share his point of view had a good chance of being elected.

I would have liked to have become a member of the governing body of the Party, but I held back. If I stood at this time and had been elected, that would have meant one place less for other friends whose support Nye needed. Also all kinds of other activities were crowding in on me. The one that meant most was an invitation to visit Vienna. It was still early days, Austria was under Allied military occupation, but a provisional Government had been set up in which those of our socialist friends who had fought against Hitler played a leading part. In April 1946 the National Executive Committee of the Labour Party invited Vice-Chancellor Dr Adolf Schärf and Dr Bruno Pittermann, MP, to visit London as their guests. When Parliament rose at the end of July I was invited to visit Vienna. Before, during and after the war, both Nye and I had been closely associated with Austrian socialists and had helped them in any way we could. Before leaving, knowing the bare-bone poverty I would find throughout Austria I begged, borrowed, did everything but steal, until I had filled a large sack with tinned meats, cigarettes and everything else I thought would be useful. The only mistake I made was including lipsticks. I thought these would help to cheer up women friends during this grim time, but I had not remembered the puritan streak in the Austrian socialist movement.

I had no difficulty in getting through the Customs with my over-weight luggage. Everything was under military control. The Customs men knew I was not a trader and the British Government had provided me with all the necessary clearance papers, Service personnel saw me safely through Italy and on to Vienna. Before we crossed into Austria I could not resist buying some extra goods to take to my friends, which I packed in the boot and under the seat of the car as I did not intend to declare them and risk being held up by fussy control officers at the frontier. I had no difficulty with the private who was driving the car; he came from Glasgow, knew me, and was game for anything. But what about the officer who had been sent to accompany me? He was obviously no socialist, came from a New Zealand farming family and looked a very proper, conventional conservative serving man. But there are times and circumstances when we all step out of character. He let me do my little bit of law-breaking. Once in Vienna I was installed in the Sacher hotel, the headquarters of our top military brass. I knew the contents of my sack would be welcome, but I certainly had not realized what the hotel staff were prepared to do for a packet of cigarettes. I smoked slightly but had never before seen the desperate craving of the true nicotine addicts.

One of our wartime agents there was Eric Gedye, for many years *The Times* correspondent, author of *Fallen Bastions*, and an old friend I was glad to meet again. He gave a party for some of our military people, along with some Austrians. I was escorted to his flat by one of our senior officers; as we paused in the doorway and looked in, he said, 'Quite a gathering of old boys!' What he meant was that every Austrian in the room had taken his life in his hands working with British Intelligence. Afterwards I learnt that this was the first time these Austrians had spent an evening with their British allies in an easy-going social atmosphere. I spent long strenuous days going around Vienna with a young Austrian socialist, one of those with an impeccable anti-fascist record, acting as my guide. The first evening, when we returned tired and hungry to the Sacher hotel, I invited him to have supper with me. This, I was told, I could not do. He was an Austrian. Apparently no distinction was being made between pro-fascist and anti-fascist Austrians, military regulations classified them all alike, all enemy aliens. I blew the roof off. I at once contacted our Ambassador, who gave me anything but a warm welcome. But, however reluctantly, he did help. Before I left I had returned the hospitality of Austrian friends by giving a dinner for them in the Sacher hotel. This was a much-needed breakthrough from stifling immediate post-war military regulations. War is hard enough on those who face its hazards with the backing of their own Government, but our Austrian allies in those war years had to take their stand knowing they would be denounced as traitors to their country and punished as such if caught by the Nazis.

While I was in Vienna, Nye, Mumpitz and Trude travelled to Ascona and were waiting for me there. In the most depressing pre-war and early wartime days, Mumpitz would sometimes reminisce about this holiday village he had known and loved so much, talking most of all about his companions of those days. 'We shall go there,' Nye would comfortingly say to him, 'as soon as the war is over.' So there they were in the summer of 1946 and arrangements had been made for my safe convoy from Vienna to Venice, then on to Ascona. The glamour of Venice was marred for me by the ugliness of the approach and a vast Coca-Cola sign monopolizing the skyline, but once there delight in the beauty I had read about and visualized all returned.

I was now handed over to the Italian authorities and after a sight-seeing tour, a splendid supper in an upstairs dining-room in St Mark's Square and a sound night's sleep, I was ready to move on. My hosts were the city fathers, almost all of whom had been Communist partisans. They provided transport and several companions who, as we crossed the mountainous roads leading to Switzerland, told me of some of their wartime exploits.

Everything had been organized with military precision. Nye was at the waterfront waiting for me when I arrived, but it was not the blissful return we had wanted for Mumpitz. There were too many ghosts. Only one of his old friends was living in the vicinity and it rained and it rained and it rained. Then Nye was outraged that I had given his precious watch to the New Zealand officer who had been so kind to me. I wanted some way of thanking him and as he greatly admired this watch I said, 'Let's swap.' I had never any feeling for complicated mechanical gadgets but ought to have remembered that Nye valued it. It would have been understandable if he had lost his temper and been generally disagreeable. Maybe it was my contrite looks that softened him. But, all the same, I was not let off lightly. He paced up and down our bedroom floor, a habit he had when agitated or thinking hard over some problem, talking as well as walking as he explored every angle of the matter to which he was giving his mind and imagination. 'Oh!' was his opening gambit, 'Oh! So you have reached the stage when you have to buy yourself a gigolo.' That was only the beginning. Anyone listening to this address of welcome might have wondered just what was happening. But to know that you would have had to see Nye as well as hear him. His eyes were sparkling with mischief. He was enjoying himself hugely – at my expense. Of course it was all a game between us. He was as pleased to have me back again as I was to be with him. He knew perfectly well that my relations with the helpful New Zealander were formal and decorous. The days were over when he could not be sure of me when I went off round the world, or even if I would so much as return.

A happy sequel to that Austrian visit was the reception I was able to arrange for eighty Austrians in September 1948. Senior British and Austrian Ministers did not need me or anyone else to arrange their visits to one another, but there was a second level of Members of Parliament, mayors and others, who were left out of these top-level exchanges. I originated the idea and, as is so often the case, as titular head got most of the credit. But it was Joan Bourne, Woman Organizer of the London Labour Party at that time, who did the real hard work. Joan like myself could be a controversial figure, but the beatitude for both of us was that in this project we were received with open arms everywhere – right, left and centre. Herbert Morrison, Aneurin Bevan – it was all one. Would they give a talk to our Austrian guests? Willingly. Would the London County Council give them a reception? Of course. This was a new experience for me and a marvellous one. Nearly all my political life I had been blackballed by the Labour Party Establishment. But we all knew what our Austrian comrades had been through in the war years; we were at one in the warmth of our welcome to them.

It would never have occurred to me to contact the Port of London Authority, the River Police, the London Fire Brigade. These were some of Joan's bright ideas. Everywhere we found friends tumbling over themselves to be helpful. The Port of London Authority arranged a trip down the Thames, refreshments thoughtfully provided; the Fire Brigade gave a special display of fire-fighting, the River Police co-operating.

Joan was encouraged to take all the time she needed, irrespective of her other duties, especially in finding the right kind of hospitality for our guests. Thirty went off to Glasgow. I had not a moment's worry about them. I knew the warm hospitable nature of my own people beneath their sometimes gruff exterior. Fifty Austrian guests were conducted on arrival to a hall off Oxford Street, and introduced to fifty London families who had offered hospitality, most of them found for us by the London Labour Women's committees. Most of the Austrians did not speak English and most of the English did not speak Austrian, but what did it matter? There was a happy, chaotic scramble as all got sorted out, and many of the friendships begun then have survived to this day.

Nye's contribution was to pack me into his official car along with Herr Leopold Millwisch, the charming leader of the group who, when he arrived in London, had only an iron hook where his right hand had been. We wanted him to return with the best artificial hand our hospitals could provide. Nye had arranged for us to go to Roehampton Hospital. Those of us who have survived the hazards of war unscathed too often do not even begin to realize the price others have paid. The first thing that struck me about this wonderful hospital was the cheerfulness in the air: officers, and other ranks, all learning to use artificial limbs. I am quite sure the ordinary decent Britisher would have been happy to present our Austrian guest with an artificial hand. But we were taking no chances. We knew what unpleasantness some corners of the gutter press could cause. We were careful to pay the bill ourselves.

Another pleasant memory of the 1945–50 period was when we journeyed through Italy from Rome to Naples, then over to Capri, as the guests of Professor Fanfani, who at that time was Minister of Health in the Italian Government. He had paid an official visit to London as Nye's guest, and this was the usual exchange of diplomatic courtesies. Although we were travelling in Italy in hot August weather, we survived the hospitality of a dozen local dignitaries, and responded to invitations to taste the new wines as we moved south without either of us having so much as a headache. That was quite a survival test. Some of the accompanying entourage, both English and Italian, did not do so well. One had just to be careful without seeming to be. Nye was expert at that kind of self-imposed discipline, and had a strong head. I was not so good, and did not have a strong head. A few evenings before leaving London we had attended a Jack Hylton theatre first night and the supper afterwards was too much for me. That put me on my guard. I promised myself that I was not going to spoil our Italian holiday by eating or drinking anything, however hard pressed to do so, that I could not cope with.

We left Rome in great good form. What made the journey so companionable was that both Ministers had a car provided for them, the rest of the company travelling in a large comfortable bus. We were soon playing musical chairs between cars and bus, more often in the bus than the car. In that way we got to know one another, no stiff-necked formality. At one point in the journey we arrived at a hotel where a much-relieved proprietor had just said goodbye to Winston Churchill and his wife, and a largish company of their friends. The poor Italian had had nightmares as he feared the two parties would collide with unspeakable consequences. How little he knew our English ways. Instead of the rough-house he dreaded, there he was presenting me with a bouquet of flowers and a note from Mrs Churchill wishing us a happy holiday. Still more amazing, he had been given a copy of the latest volume of Churchill's war memoirs to present to Nye. Winston's companions may have had a bit of trouble with him before he was persuaded to 'play the game' as he was in a very morose mood at that time, but anyhow there we were, giving a splendid demonstration of solidarity when outside our own country.

The most memorable part of that stay in Italy was when the official visit was over and we were free to go on to Formia to spend a few days with our Chelsea friend, René de Meo. We saw more of the realities of the Italian situation during this private visit than when courteously cushioned and surrounded by our Italian Government hosts. Formia was then a quiet seaside village. René's older brother was a priest in a village high in the hills on the opposite side of the highway, and we were looking forward to visiting him. René, in a mischievous mood, played a trick on his brother. Instead of waiting for the evening when we had been invited to supper, he drove up with us one day when we were not expected. Of course Nye and I did not know this. When we arrived the priest was unshaven and looked embarrassed. He at once gave an order for the church bells to be rung. In a matter of minutes as we walked together outside the church, we saw a plump elderly village woman hurrying towards us. Nye turned to the priest and said 'Perpetua?' They both burst out laughing. The miracle is how they communicated with one another, but they did. Nye knew no Italian. The priest knew no English. René's English was far from perfect, but there they were enjoying a glass of wine together while 'Perpetua' prepared a succulent Italian supper. Afterwards Father de Meo produced a cigar for Nye and himself, along with most excellent brandy.

He was a quite unexpected type of priest. He told us that as oldest son he was drafted into the Church, but plainly his true vocation was looking after the social welfare of his congregation without being too fussy about fine points of doctrine. These villages on the hills between Rome and Naples had been razed to the ground by Allied bombers, and most of the remaining population were living in makeshift shelters among the debris of their former homes. But it was not the Allies who had pilfered everything of value from both church and homes; Moorish troops under fascist leaders were the marauders.

Before we returned to London we called on Father de Meo to say goodbye. He had had a valuable collection of ancient Roman coins, but these had been looted. All the same, he presented Nye with one of the very few that had escaped the Moors. Then I was presented with a tiny square of white lace. Now it was our turn. What little souvenir could we send from

London? The priest was fond of music and had played some of his favourite gramophone records to us. We thought some records available in London, but not in Italy at that time, would give him pleasure, or maybe a box of cigars, but before we could say anything I saw a look exchanged between the priest and the local schoolmaster. They knew exactly what they wanted – calcium. A load of calcium, enough for all the children in the area. Many of the children were suffering from rickets and other health problems caused by malnutrition.

POCKET CARTOON
by OSBERT LANCASTER

"Hi, Mister, you swappa da free spectacles for da feelthy pictures, yes?"

Nye said, certainly, he would see they had what they so much needed as soon as he could arrange matters. What do we do next? A British Minister of Health could not press a button, summon a civil servant and order the despatch of calcium to Italy, although they obviously thought this was how things were done. Instead, once back in London, we got hold of American friends who organized the whole thing for us through an American relief agency. The appalling background to this story is that funds had been allocated for first-aid in this area but had vanished. Some corrupt intermediaries had stolen the lot.

Another experience that had Nye hopping mad was when we visited Naples and found that private luxury buildings, including a huge cinema, were in course of construction, while the desperate needs of homeless people were being ignored. That was Italy. In one mood you found it adorable and basked in its warmth and beauty. Then there was the other side. A kind of bottomless callousness.

18. The Struggle to Establish the Health Service

Every member of the 1945–50 Cabinet was under severe strain. Each wanted to do a good job and no one, with the possible exception of Ernest Bevin, could have all his or her own way. In the gloomy circumstances of 1947 a 'get rid of Attlee' conspiracy began. The first I knew about it was when I heard George Brown in the division lobby whispering at the top of his voice that it was high time Attlee was replaced by Bevin. Then, the day Parliament rose for the summer recess, Sir Stafford Cripps sent an urgent message asking Nye and me to have tea with him and Lady Cripps. Obviously this was not just a polite social invitation. We had no choice. We had to go and, as we anticipated, Stafford was in a highly emotional mood. It was a matter of life and death importance to get rid of Attlee. Bevin should take his place and he, Stafford, would take responsibility for the Treasury. It was clear that Cripps thought it would be a still better plan if he himself became Prime Minister; but first Bevin was to be asked. Both these men, with Herbert Morrison, Hugh Dalton and others, had had tentative exchanges of views. Nye was courteous but quite definite. He would not even agree to think it over. He said he did not believe in palace revolutions.

The outcome of all this was that Attlee remained Prime Minister, Stafford became Chancellor of the Exchequer, and Ernest Bevin remained at the Foreign Office. Just as Stafford fancied himself as Prime Minister, so too did Herbert Morrison. Bevin, on reflection, apparently came to the conclusion that he would be well advised to remain the most powerful member of the Cabinet with Attlee, who was very much under his influence, preferable as Prime Minister to any possible alternative.

Though every Minister was harshly affected by the 1947 economic crisis, Nye was singled out by the press for special treatment. At a time when he was locked in endless stormy negotiations with the British Medical Association, the violence of the attacks on him frightened some of his colleagues. They urged that more concessions be given to his critics. While cold feet under the Cabinet table were making life difficult for Nye in private, hot-heads, led by the Socialist Medical Association, were lambasting him in public. There must be no concessions – a full-time salaried staff, no private beds – the socialist dream, the whole dream, and nothing but the dream. Nye in private made the same comment about the demands of Dr Stark Murray and his Socialist Medical Association colleagues as he had made about the I L P when it insisted on disaffiliating from the Labour Party – pure but impotent. Sometimes he swore under his breath at the importunities of the purists, but with no real grudge against them. In his philosophical moments he would say it was a good thing he was being pressed by the Socialist Medical Association to make no concessions, as this helped to balance the much more powerful right-wing pressure groups he had to contend with at the same time. He sought always what he called 'the principle of action'. What, he would ask himself, is the maximum I can hope to achieve in these particular circumstances?

An invaluable friend when all this hectic activity was going on was Sir Daniel Davies. To understand the relationship between these two, let me describe the evening when Nye and I went along to Wimpole Street to have an informal supper with Dan and Vera, his charming, devoted wife. They were in the process of moving into a prestigious Wimpole Street establishment, and when Vera opened the door Dan was wandering around carrying a crystal chandelier and trying to decide where it should go. With a smile and a wink he said to Nye, 'Living above the shop, boy bach.' They were two small urchins again in neighbouring Welsh villages. Dan was a total romantic about all things Welsh, and as a doctor just as romantic. He enjoyed earning good fees charged to his well-to-do patients, and also enjoyed giving free service to poor people. He did not agree with Nye's Health Service proposals, but it was round his hospitable table that Nye came to know the heads of the Royal Colleges and other influential medical men. With total privacy, the gentlemen of the press a thousand miles away, they could talk quietly and sensibly to one another. Inadvertently the crude caricatures of Nye in the press rebounded to his advantage. He was so unlike the uncouth, loud-voiced demagogue the press had led leading members of the medical profession to expect that relations changed quite quickly from hostility and suspicion to a willingness to co-operate.

Overcoming the fears of the ordinary GP was a much harder and longer task, but in the end the Health Service survived all opposition and became law. Nye was not worried at this stage by its imperfections. 'Let it begin,' he would say. 'No future Government will dare undo it. The flaws can be put right as the public learns to use and value it.'

I took no part in the work of the Ministry of Health. That was not my line of country. But in the evenings Nye needed time to 'unwind', to damn and blast if it had been a particularly frustrating day, to rejoice if he felt he had made

"B.M.A. OR NO B.M.A., HE SAYS HIS SCHEME IS GOING ON"

worthwhile progress. So I was kept well informed. Housing was different. I rather fancied myself as an architect *manqué*. I had enjoyed designing a two-bedroomed cottage for my parents with all modern conveniences inside, but on the outside, its rough bricks painted white and its red tiles giving no offence to its nearest neighbour, the old thatched cottage. Better still, I enjoyed pulling down walls in an old house and making a complete transformation. So I readily accepted an invitation to become a member of the Housing Advisory Committee. The first friend I made on the Committee was Mr Laing, the elderly, deeply religious head of the great building firm of his name. He had come to Nye as soon as Nye was appointed to say that he agreed that council houses to rent for people who could not afford to buy should be given a high priority. This was an important breakthrough for Nye.

Another member of that Committee was Lady Reading. Nye and she had come to know one another when he opposed a government proposal to disband the WVS at the end of the war; he knew there was valuable work they could do that he wanted done, especially helping to meet and settle refugee families. They became good friends. One day when I arrived at the Ministry in the middle of the morning to attend a Housing Advisory Committee meeting, I went into Nye's private room just as Lady Reading was leaving. I have forgotten what difficult, contentious matter was coming before our Committee that morning. Lady Reading, in her WVS uniform, was an imposing figure. All I heard of the conversation between them was Nye's final remark as she left for the committee room, 'In you go, Stella, and give them hell.'

Although I took no part in the work of the Health Ministry, I called there for Nye one day and found an Admiral in the room with him. An Admiral? I am not quite sure of that, but he was certainly a retired high-ranking naval officer. The press had given him the impression that as a voluntary worker he would no longer be allowed to have anything to do with the local hospital which was his special care, and he had come to plead with Nye not to interfere with it. As he was leaving he stood to attention, saluted and left with his head held high. Nye had explained that he would be needed as much as ever, that as Minister he would be dependent on voluntary workers of his fine quality to make the Health Service all it should be.

Another encounter at that time is a joy to recall. One Sunday morning I asked Nye to drive me to St Teresa's, a small Catholic hospital in Wimbledon. I was taking flowers to my friend Joan Bourne, who was being nursed there, and intended just to hop in and out quickly while Nye remained outside in the car. But one of the nurses recognized him and immediately there was a general flurry. Sister Agnes, the matron and Mother Superior, insisted he must come inside. This eager, little grey bird of a woman led the way up a flight of stone stairs, Nye followed, and I was immediately behind him. At one point she turned round, looked at Nye and said, 'You know, Minister, you are the most hated man in Great Britain.' Then, after a slight pause, '*and* the most loved'. She truly believed that God had sent Nye to her in answer to her prayers. She badly needed twenty more beds for she had only thirty, and fifty was the minimum number required before she could qualify as a teaching as well as a nursing hospital. Until then she had applied in vain. First thing on Monday morning Nye called for the file where her application was set out. The hospital was on contract to the Ministry as it looked after Health Service patients. Nye, like everyone else, had fallen for Sister Agnes. He simply could not wait to grant her request. He would brook no delay.

There are two things I do not wish to do. One is to claim that Nye was always right and that anyone who disagreed with him was always wrong. In matters of great moment, right or wrong depends largely on the point of the political compass from which events are viewed. One of Nye's favourite quotations was, 'This is my truth; now tell me yours.' But since I am in a better position than anyone else to know not only what Nye did, but the motives that guided his every political thought and act, what I do seek to do is to give a true picture of Nye in the round, a three-dimensional figure, the private as well as the public man.

The other thing I am not seeking to do is to give a detailed account of all that had to be done to establish the Health Service. *In Place of Fear* was first published in 1952, while every nuance of the struggle was fresh in his mind. There Nye gives, in his own words, a fairly full account of what was done, and how and why. Michael Foot, in his biography of Nye, gives a blow-by-blow account, not only of the means Nye used to establish the Health Service, but also of many other battles he fought inside the Cabinet. From first to last Nye tried unceasingly to prevent the Labour Government from making a number of mistakes that he earnestly believed were fatal, both for our own country's future welfare and for the contribution we at that time could have made to the easing of world tensions.

He feared the consequences of allowing Russia and America, the two super powers, to carve up the world between them. That kind of polarization could only lead to a modern version of the religious wars of the Middle Ages. Communists would be ready to crucify capitalists and capitalists would be ready to torture Communists, by every diabolical means they could devise. This was all the more unnecessary as neither pure undiluted Communism nor pure undiluted capitalism is a viable way of running a modern economy. Whatever their theories, in practice each has to make adjustments to the methods used by the other. Hence Nye's much quoted phrase, 'the commanding heights of the economy.' Let the State bring order out of the anarchy of unrestrained private enterprise by taking over industries essential for a planned economy, such as coal, steel, transport and such like, but leave ample margins for private individuals and groups of individuals to make their contribution. Total nationalization is not compatible with a democratic, constitutional, parliamentary system. Even assuming it to be desirable, or even possible, it could be enforced only by a rigid dictatorship with all the dullness as well as cruelty that accompanies dictatorships, whether of the extreme right or extreme left.

Could we, in Britain, progress towards a tolerant democratic form of socialism by peaceful constitutional means? Nye was not prepared to give a dogmatic reply to that question. He knew too well the strength of the opposition that would have to be overcome. But he did believe that we were blessed among nations in that our history gave us at least a sporting chance of avoiding the horrors of civil war, the inescapable destiny of less fortunate people in many parts of the world. Nor did he see a democratic socialist approach as an easy option between hide-bound Toryism and hide-bound Communism. In his own words:

Democratic Socialism is not a middle way between capitalism and Communism. If it were merely that it would be doomed to failure from the start. It cannot live by borrowed vitality. Its driving power must derive from its own principles and the energy released by them. It is based on the conviction that free men can use free institutions to solve the social and economic problems of the day, if they are given a chance to do so.

This comes from *In Place of Fear*. In a later chapter on this same theme, he added:

Democratic Socialism is a child of modern society and so of relativist philosophy. It seeks the truth in any given situation, knowing all the time that if this be pushed too far it falls into error. It struggles against the evils that flow from private property, yet realizes that all forms of private property are not necessarily evil. Its chief enemy is vacillation, for it must achieve passion in action in the pursuit of qualified judgements. It must know how to enjoy the struggle, whilst recognizing that progress is not an elimination of struggle, but rather a change in its terms.

No one reading the screaming headlines to be found in almost every newspaper during those years, denouncing Nye as a ranting, ambition-crazed, Communist fellow-traveller, was given even a hint of what he in fact believed in and fought for.

Nye was not anti-American. No one with his good mind

THE RIVALS

and warm sympathies could reject an entire nation. But he was always alert to the fact that America was not all of a piece: you could never be sure which of its various contending elements would be in control at any given time. A John Foster Dulles? A McCarthy? A General Marshall? A General MacArthur? And how far did the President of the United States prevail and how far the formidable Washington pressure lobbies? Most decidedly Nye was not prepared to acquiesce in the indignity of seeing his own country's diplomacy reduced to sycophantic acceptance of all things American.

He was not anti-American. But he was, if you like, pro-British. He had faith in the qualities of his own people if only they were given sane and courageous leadership measuring up to the needs of the times.

There were powerful Cold War crusaders in all the capitalist powers of the West. Communism had to be rooted out of the body politic. It was a foul disease. It was heresy. To the stake with the heretics! In America, everyone from Washington to Hollywood who showed even the slightest sympathy with liberal ideas was dubbed Communist. This was the age of John Foster Dulles and McCarthy. Everything said and done in America was scanned and analysed in detail by Stalin's Russia. The more bloody-minded the mood of the West, the more bloody-minded the mood of the Soviet Union. In this gruesome, doom-laden atmosphere, Nehru, then at the height of his powers, was a beneficent influence. Nehru's India, like Tito's Yugoslavia, wanted to distance itself from Russia, but was equally resistant to becoming the creature of Dulles's America.

Nye was in close touch with both Nehru and Tito, and at one time acted as an intermediary between them. All three thought in terms of a third force of non-aligned countries, and there were others ready to join them. In France the Socialist Party was split, as in Britain. So too in Italy. The most clear-headed and wisest French statesman was Mendès-France. Another link forged there was with *L'Express*, the Parisian paper edited by Jean-Jacques Servan-Schreiber, which promoted the views of Mendès-France. I am now anticipating some developments. Everything did not happen in the years 1951 and 1952. It was a continuing process. Inside the United States there were also many who shared our views. A constant stream of American friends were received happily, indeed lovingly, in our home. Ned Russell, at that time London editor of the *New York Herald Tribune*, and his charming, warm-hearted wife, Mary, were among our dearest friends. As Bill Shirer, Maurice Hindus, Edgar Mowrer, Vincent Sheean, Louis Fischer, Walter Lippmann, Ed Murrow, John Gunther or Walter Duranty either passed through London, or for a time were stationed here, we never failed to meet. That does not mean we always agreed. But we enjoyed exchanging views with our American friends, whether from the newspaper world, Hollywood, trade unions or the business community, as much as they enjoyed Nye's far-ranging, stimulating comments on all the great problems of the day.

American contacts were many and easily accessible. Parallel Russian contacts were just not available unless on a limited formal Embassy basis: the Russian bear was crouching in its corner and licking its war wounds. Just how devastating these wounds were was something that neither our economic experts nor our defence chiefs were able or willing to grasp. Nye hammered away, in season and out of season, on the contrast between Russia's 30 million ton steel output and the Western Allies' 140 million ton steel output. Russia was in no condition to advance across Europe as some feared. She could even have been prevented, in Nye's view, from establishing herself in the eastern section of Berlin. We had held the line for Tito's Yugoslavia by a firm declaration that if Stalin invaded we would be militarily involved. The Yugoslavs are a brave people, they would have fought to the last man. But it is ludicrous to imagine that the sheer weight of Soviet arms and numbers would not have won in the end if Stalin had calculated he could have had it all his own way.

From the same premise Nye urged that Allied tanks should drive through to Berlin, preventing the Russians from cutting off the German capital from the Western zone. Was he right? Was he wrong? I am in no position to give an expert answer to that question, but it was his firm conviction that the Russians would have had to concede Berlin to the Allies. Armies march on their stomachs. They also need transport and arms. That takes us back to Nye's awareness of the ruined state of Russian industry at that time compared with America, where never a bomb had fallen, and Britain with its defence factories in fairly good working order.

Alas, Nye's voice, and that of those associated with him,

was strong in the constituencies, but frenziedly shouted down in the Parliamentary Labour Party, the National Executive and the TUC. Illness had forced Stafford Cripps to resign, Hugh Gaitskell became Chancellor, Ernest Bevin died. But Arthur Deakin, secretary of the Transport and General Workers' Union, Tom Williamson, secretary of the General and Municipal Workers' Union, and Will Lawther, secretary of the National Union of Mineworkers, continued Bevin's policies with, if possible, even greater gusto.

At this critical time Attlee became ill. Nye had finished his job in the Ministry of Health and Housing; these had now become two separate departments. When Attlee invited him to become Minister of Labour he asked to be given time to think it over. He would have liked to have been entrusted with the Foreign Office, but that was out of the question. Even if Attlee himself had favoured that proposal he could not have got his way. He was the prisoner, sometimes willingly, sometimes reluctantly, of the right wing of the Party, with Deakin, Williamson and Lawther jangling their money-bags and quite blatantly reminding the Cabinet, the NEC and the Parliamentary Labour Party that he who pays the piper calls the tune. Nye had several discussions with Attlee, in which he made it clear that the Ministry of Labour would not be acceptable to him unless in addition to departmental duties he could take part in determining economic policies and help to solve production problems. Attlee agreed and wrote the following note to Nye on 16 January 1951:

10 Downing Street
Whitehall

My dear Nye,

I have been considering how best to meet the point you raised as to indicating the increased share that you will have on the economic side after the change-over. We do not, of course, indicate in the official announcements of appointments membership of government committees, but we do frequently give such news to the Press.

I think that the point could be made by background given to the Press to the effect that the Minister of Labour, apart from his purely

218 My Life with Nye

departmental duties, is, of course, one of the Ministers intimately concerned with economic and production problems. In his new office Mr Bevan will be brought closely in touch with the whole range of joint activities on the economic and planning side. Will this be all right by you?

Yours ever,
CLEM

In addition Nye had every reason to believe that he would have the Prime Minister's support in resisting the pressures inside the Cabinet, led by Hugh Gaitskell, in favour of imposing health charges. This, above all, was Nye's sticking-point.

He could have resigned in 1945 because of his disagreement with the Cabinet's decision to accept the impossibly onerous terms imposed by the United States as a condition of granting Britain a loan. He could have resigned over Bevin's policy towards Israel. Or over German rearmament, or the proposed £4,700 million three-year defence programme imposed by the United States when the Korean War was at its height. Again and again he had to weigh carefully what best to do. To resign while up to his eyebrows in the struggle to establish the Health Service and to get on with house-building was impossible. It would have been counter-productive, and any electoral set-backs would have been blamed on an incompetent Minister who had funked his responsibilities.

Nor did he wish to resign over health charges. He thought he could get his way without doing so, as he had made absolutely clear to his Cabinet colleagues that he could not remain a member of the Government if charges were imposed. The right to impose a prescription charge if need be at some future time had been carried in the Cabinet against his strenuous opposition, but he believed he could leave it at that. He could not believe that the majority of his colleagues cared so much about this issue that they would defy the clearly expressed views of both Labour and trade union conferences, not just isolated rank-and-file members.

Nye was proved wrong. He underestimated the venom of

the right-wing opposition he had to face, and also the pressures on Gaitskell to make use of this golden opportunity to destroy the acknowledged leader of the left of the party.

There was a strict rule in Nye's Ministry that any unsolicited gifts sent to him should be promptly returned. On one occasion, and only one, an exception was made. Nye brought home a letter containing a white silk handkerchief with crochet round the edge. The hanky was for me. The letter was from an elderly Lancashire lady, unmarried, who had worked in the cotton mills from the age of twelve. She was overwhelmed with gratitude for the dentures and reading glasses she had received, free of charge. The last sentence in her letter read, 'Dear God, reform thy world beginning with me,' but the words that hurt most were, 'Now I can go into any company.' The life-long struggle against poverty which these words revealed is what made all the striving worth while.

An added complication at this time that we could have well done without was an attempt by Lord Kemsley to bankrupt Michael Foot and myself. Among other consequences that would have meant we could not have remained Members of Parliament. This had the most improbable beginning: on 2 March 1950 the *Evening Standard* carried the headline 'Fuchs and Strachey. A great new crisis. War Minister now involved in MI5 efficiency probe'.

John Strachey was not one of my favourite people, but I was as indignant as Michael when he was subjected to this dastardly, totally unfounded attack. *Tribune* came to his defence with one of Michael's most hard-hitting articles. The heading was 'Lower Than Kemsley', meaning that the Beaverbrook Press had degraded decent journalistic standards even more than Kemsley. The cynical worldly-wise Beaverbrook sat back to enjoy the fun. It was Kemsley who sued. We fought him from the lower courts right up to the Court of Appeal and on to the House of Lords. In our family, the joke, rather a sick joke so far as I was concerned, was that our total modest savings were in my name. That had been my idea in order to protect Nye in case in a rash moment he said

something that involved him in a costly libel action. Lord
Kemsley engaged a formidable team of lawyers led by Sir
Walter Monckton, KC. Our good fortune was that Gerald
Gardiner, KC, in later years to become Lord Chancellor, was
persuaded to act on our behalf.

As Michael and I struggled on through this long-drawn-out
legal battle, Nye insisted that we must finish what we had
begun. We must not allow ourselves to be intimidated even
though the legal costs were mounting heavens high. It was a
tense moment when Lord and Lady Kemsley, Michael and
myself appeared before the judges in the Lords to hear what
proved to be the essential decision in our favour. I was half
stunned with relief.

19. Once More into the Wilderness

Once established in the Ministry of Labour, Nye was eager to seize the opportunities his new Department offered. How best could he advance the cause of industrial democracy? How make clear that men's hearts and minds as well as their hands had to be involved if we were to have a buoyant, expanding economy? How to separate economic and industrial planning from outmoded Treasury methods, which belonged to old-time pastoral societies where the changing seasons conditioned production and consumption? A modern industrial community obeyed different rhythms.

Nye would have enjoyed his new Department if he had not become involved in the renewal of Cabinet dissensions that he thought had been amicably settled. His understanding with the Prime Minister was that no health charges would be imposed. His further understanding was that he and Harold Wilson, then President of the Board of Trade, would not resign over the proposed £4,700 million defence expenditure for the next three years, although they both made it clear that this figure was a nonsense. Time, Nye was certain, would prove them right; this money, although allocated by the Chancellor and his Treasury officials, would not and could not be spent, for it was a sum that far exceeded our industrial potential. Hugh Gaitskell could make his respectful bow to our American allies. Nye would have preferred the Americans to have been told the truth, to have been given an honest account of Britain's defence capacity. We needed America's friendship. But had America no need of friends? Of course it had. And was telling lies the best basis for any alliance?

Hugh Gaitskell was still not satisfied. He had threatened to resign if he did not have his own way over defence promises. He followed this up by again threatening to resign if health charges were not imposed. The Prime Minister, a sick man at the time, was faced with threats of resignation from two of his Ministers. Gaitskell had all the big battalions on his side. The trade union bosses had contemptuously abandoned their former support of Herbert Morrison, considering, quite rightly from their point of view, that they needed a younger and abler man to impose their dictates. Insistence on health charges was a golden opportunity for forcing the resignation of the acknowledged leader of the left. Attlee had no real choice. He was the prisoner of the right wing of the Party, sometimes willingly, sometimes reluctantly. He could not afford to antagonize the majority of his Cabinet, Parliamentary Party and the TUC bosses by honouring his understanding with Nye. His own position was not so secure; there had already been one attempt at a palace revolution and there could be others. Indeed there were others. When against his will he was later on forced to resign to make way for Gaitskell he most certainly 'did not go quietly into the night'.

Nye would not have resigned if Attlee could have persuaded Gaitskell to drop his insistence on imposing health charges. This is something that has puzzled some commentators. Why swallow the £4,700 million defence estimate and jib at accepting a £23 million cut in the Health Service? The answer quite simply was that one was a fiction: it would not happen. The other was an immediate, inescapable reality. Nye predicted, and unhappily was proved right that once charges were imposed on any part of the Health Service, further charges would follow. He was also vindicated in his insistence that we could not possibly expand armament production to the tune of £4,700 million in the following three years. But what had logic, what had objective reality to do with those violently contested issues? Very little. Nye and those who shared his views had to he trampled under foot. The sooner they were expelled from the Party the better.

Harold Wilson, the President of the Board of Trade, John

Freeman, the Junior Minister but the driving force in the Ministry of Supply, and John Strachey, the Minister of War, met at our home to discuss what best to do. They shared Nye's indignation over the folly of imposing health charges, and felt even more strongly the insanity of promising an arms programme we could not carry out even by borrowing money from America to pay for it. Why should not each country contribute according to its resources? That is how the argument ran. Nye made clear that as he had stated publicly as well as in the Cabinet that he could not remain a member of the Government if health charges were imposed, he intended to resign, but he asked his friends not to do so. He had an educational job to do that would absorb all his energies, but he did not want the split in the Party to be deepened by other resignations. Wilson and Freeman said they had had enough. They too would resign and make clear their reasons for doing so. John Strachey sat squirming by our sitting-room fireside enjoying exquisite thrills, but he had no intention of resigning.

It is one thing to recount the external facts of a past political situation. It is quite another to convey the passionate emotions involved. It was a power struggle. Nye made one of his worst parliamentary speeches, from the point of view of his immediate audience, when he stated his reasons for resigning. He made plain his frustrations not just with the treatment being meted out to the Health Service, but with a long list of other disagreements going back through his whole period as a Cabinet Minister. If he had talked with the tongues of angels, he still would have made no impact on that particular audience at that particular time. He knew that. Also he was nervously exhausted. But, as was his way, he was soon on his feet again and giving long careful thought to what must next be done to sustain the socialist faith he lived by and that he believed was being dangerously eroded. The question he was now asking himself was this: how long could he go on with six of the seven constituency seats on the NEC held by his supporters, but always outvoted by the twelve trade union seats and the five women's seats which were controlled by the block trade union votes? He was not prepared to be confined inside a cosy play-pen. That was not serious business, that was mere dilettantism. Local Labour Party workers and local trade unionists did not live in separate worlds, they were the same people; so he decided he must challenge the union bosses right at the centre of their power.

Should he leave Parliament and take over the leadership of the Miners' Union? Will Lawther, then President, was due to retire. If Nye stood he would win. After careful thought he decided to keep his power base in his constituency, where his hold was secure, and stand for the Treasurership of the Party. That meant surrendering his safe seat on the NEC as a constituency member, and facing certain defeat in the contest for the Treasurership. Hugh Gaitskell was the chosen champion of the union bosses. 'I will lose first time round, second time, but I will win in the end.' That was Nye's prediction, and he was proved right. But these were three years of bitter struggle and endless hard labour. Some of his closest colleagues disagreed with his plan of action. Dick Crossman wrote to him telling him to be satisfied with the victory he had achieved in the constituencies. I don't think a single one of his supporters agreed with the harsh punishment he was meting out to himself. I hated to see him defeated, humiliated, out-manoeuvred, and would have settled for a less taxing life. One of the gibes against him was that he had no real grass-root support in the trade union movement, that he was just a self-indulgent mischief-maker. He was determined to prove that he had more rank-and-file support than his opponents and, in the end, by his own unshakable faith in the policies he advocated, he succeeded in doing so.

This was a hard time privately as well as publicly. At home it was clear that my father's strength was ebbing away. Every evening, however late the hour, he waited expectantly for Nye, who never disappointed the 'gaffer', as he called him. I usually went straight upstairs to our bedroom on the floor above, leaving the two of them to talk. Then one morning

Nye carried Dad, who had become as light as a child, down to his sitting-room, where we had prepared a bed for him. To use Dad's language, he was now back in the land of the living. He had Mother's kitchen on the same floor; the treasured radiogram we had bought him for his seventieth birthday within reach of his hand; a cheerful coal fire on the other side of the room; Smokey, his Siamese cat, and two budgerigars Margaret Delargy had given him, within easy sight and touch.

All our friends made for Dad's sitting-room, so he did not lack company. He was no longer able to visit Scotland, but Scotland came to him. Walter Beveridge, the son of my mother's bridesmaid and favourite cousin, came quite often to London as a senior member of the Transport and General Workers' Union. Instead of staying in the hotel arranged for conference delegates, he stayed at Cliveden Place. Walter at that time was an attractive black-haired, blue-eyed Scotsman in his mid forties. He and I were good friends. Just how remote members belonging to the same Party can be from one another in outlook and life-styles was brought home to me one evening when I invited Walter to have dinner with me in the Harcourt Room of the House of Commons.

We had a table for two looking out on to the terrace. At one moment we were holding hands across the table, and Walter was gazing into my eyes and saying earnestly: 'Ye will noo!' Ye will noo!' This romantic idyll was interrupted by a hefty Scotsman clamping his hand on Walter's shoulder and saying in a voice of thunder, 'Ye will be at King's Cross the necht.' It was not a statement; it was a command. Neither of us had noticed that at a large round table at the opposite side of the dining-room a number of other members of the Transport and General Workers' delegation were having dinner. Apparently they had decided that Brother Beveridge had fallen into the clutches of a scarlet woman, and even worse a hated member of the left wing of the Party. This was not just plain pardonable sin. It smelt of treachery. What in fact we were discussing in this intimate fashion was the coming marriage of Walter's pretty young daughter. He was most anxious that Nye, my mother and I should travel north to attend the wedding. I on my side was explaining that Nye was so overwhelmed with urgent work in his Department that we might not be able to get away, but we would be there if it were humanly possible. At this point Walter was holding my hand and saying, 'Ye will noo!' On the sleeper to Scotland that night he had a lot of explaining to do!

Another favourite visitor from our home village in Scotland was a member of the executive of the Post Office Workers' Union, and in due course its President. But it was not union affairs my parents were eager to know about. Jenny Duncan brought us all the news of old friends and neighbours. Then when Archie Lush arrived from Wales it was carnival time. Wicked Archie introduced my teetotal father to an evening tipple they enjoyed together, consisting of rum and orange. His unfailing sense of fun lightened for a time the shadow of Dad's illness.

My father was obviously happier now he was back among us all instead of being isolated in an upstairs bedroom. But there was no sign of recovery. One evening when I got back from the Commons after a 10 p.m. vote, my mother, looking very sad, said, 'Your Da's asking for you.' My heart turned over. I knew this was the end. He was propped up on his pillows, quite peaceful, no pain, and he talked to me quietly and naturally. There had been a long estrangement between us. After Nye's warning, when he first came south, I had carefully avoided arguing with him, and he had come in time to pay me back in my own coin by refusing to argue with me. 'Anyway you choose or fancy' was his curt rejoinder if I asked his opinion about anything. I did not realize it then, but obviously he had resented being treated by me as a kind of sacred cow. But maybe it was just as well. We were very like one another. A quick flash point of temper, a caustic tongue, but no sulking, no festering resentments. Now we were talking to one another again without any kind of restraint. When he heard us coming home in the evening and asked for me, Nye, with his unfailing sensitivity, left us alone. I did not so much as take Dad's hand in mine. There was no fond embracing, or easy endearments. That was not our Scottish way. But no bond could have been closer. He died peacefully.

When that moment came, I saw again the amused, sparkling eyes of my young father as he stood in the doorway before going out to an evening meeting. He would pause to look in at my brother and myself sprawling on the rug in front of the fire with our story-books and toys around us. Looking back all those years, I now know just how much it meant to him to see us, lying there, contented and secure. Sometimes before going out he would simply look in for a moment, saying nothing at all, or there might be a teasing 'Well, Lady Jane?' That was his name for me.

After my father's death my mother was sometimes alone in the evening until Nye and I returned from the House of Commons. That worried me, even though good friends called frequently to keep her company. Hugh and Margaret Delargy were favourite visitors. Shortly after my father's death, fireworks dropped through the letter-box set fire to the hall carpet. Fortunately Margaret Delargy was with my mother and when the smell of burning reached her sitting-room they were able to contain the fire before it got out of control. Years later Margaret told me that when she said to my mother that she would walk round to the police station and report the incident if she did not mind being left alone, my mother replied, 'I was ne'er a cooward.'

This kind of attack on defenceless old people, invalids and children enraged me more than anything else. Nye and I were fair game. We were in the ring. But could our families not be left in peace? Alas, as we know from Ireland, indeed from all over the world, that kind of immunity is never given. Our enemies know too well where we are most vulnerable.

In 1951 when Parliament rose for the summer recess we had accepted an invitation to spend the month of August in Yugoslavia. No holiday was ever so timely. We both needed to get away, to see new places, new people, to make new and stimulating political contacts. The Yugoslav leaders were very

"Don't look now Tito, I think we're being followed."

different from the Soviet leaders we had met. They were more
relaxed, argued openly and in depth with one another and had
a delightful sense of humour. Could we hope that the Communist dictatorship of the wartime period would mellow into a
parliamentary democracy? Not of course while Stalin was
trying every possible form of coercion in an effort to mould
the social and economic life of the Yugoslavs to suit his con-
venience. But in time? That seemed to us more than likely.
These proud, independent people would not want either to
impose or be imposed upon by suffocating forms of author-
itarianism, once they could safely advance to a freer type of
society. Indeed, Milovan Djilas, Deputy Prime Minister and
our host, seemed to us to have reacted so violently against his
earlier devotion to Stalin that he was in danger of exaggerating
the virtues of the Western world.

Nye took part in all the discussions and with no holds barred. It was all very enjoyable. Above all Nye loved Djilas's
homeland. We climbed the mountains of Montenegro, arguing
about everything under the sun, Djilas's halting English
helped out by Vladimir Dedijer, who spoke fluent English.
The affinity between Nye and Milovan was not, as some
thought, based on political agreements. It was a matter of

temperament. They were both poets, romantics, unrestrainable individualists, stormy, unpredictable mountain types. It was arranged that the following summer we would return, not as official government guests but on a private visit, and that we did.

When we first met Tito, he was standing in front of a magnificently carved wooden cupboard in his main reception room. When I admired it, he opened the top drawer of his desk and smilingly produced an American magazine and a key. The magazine had a picture of this very room with Tito posed in front of the cupboard. The key had been sent by the former owner of the house, which of course had been confiscated by the partisans. The message accompanying the key read, 'Since you have my cupboard, you may as well have the key.' Somebody, obviously, had a wry sense of humour!

Then there was the evening on the island of Brioni, when Tito was coming to have dinner with us in the hotel where we were staying along with Djilas, Dedijer, Boris Kidrik, Edvard Kardelj and Aleksander Ranković. At a neighbouring holiday hotel a loud band violated the night air. Its quality was appalling and Nye, the perfect guest, made his views known in no uncertain terms. Far from any sign of indignation, the Yugoslavs around the table seemed to be enjoying a good joke. Vladimir Dedijer then said, 'Nye, here is what we want you to do. When Tito comes along this evening, will you say again just what you have been saying?' In those early days members of leading orchestras were chosen from musicians with sound partisan records; it was the same with football teams. But it was time now to break from these wartime restrictions. We had arrived when this argument was in full swing. All went according to plan. Towards the end of a good dinner, and after several toasts in slivovitz and strong local wine, Nye did his stuff. Tito was easily tuned in to the prevailing mood of his senior colleagues.

Another incident that meant little to me at the time gives the key to the later conflicts that led to Djilas's expulsion from his party, then to long years of imprisonment. We were visit-

ing the charming Adriatic resort of Dubrovnik. Vladimir Dedijer accompanied us everywhere so there was no language
barrier. Djilas had invited one of his friends, a partisan
general, and his pretty young actress wife to dine with us.
On arrival I took the young lady up to my bedroom and
at once she produced a packet of cigarettes and began to
smoke. She was obviously a 'flighty' youngster with not the
slightest interest in politics, and completely out of sympathy
with puritanical partisan standards. I learned their marriage
had met with stern disapproval in government circles, some
of the wives of leading partisans being particularly censorious. Djilas took a light-hearted view of the whole affair and
said that the trouble with the old battle-axes was that they
were jealous of her youth and beauty.

These comments got around. So far as our Montenegran
friend was concerned, himself a recklessly brave partisan
general, discretion was most certainly not the better part of
valour. The furore caused by the publication of *The New
Order*, the book in which he condemned what he called the
growth of a new privileged class, was given an additional emotional dimension by the remarks he had been known to make
about the wives of some of his most important colleagues.

The following summer when we were again in Yugoslavia,
spirited arguments were going on, but *The New Order* had not
yet been published. Disagreements had not so far disrupted
personal friendships. Indeed when Nye sent Djilas a Christmas
present of smoked salmon which came from Alistair Forbes,
John Mackie's brother-in-law, who was a keen fisherman, in
December 1953, Djilas wrote to say that he was expecting
Tito to dinner very soon and was saving the salmon for that
special occasion. How could we have foreseen that Nye would
be writing to Tito on 1 February 1954, after having heard that
Djilas had been stripped of all his public offices and the same
fate might be in store for Vladimir Dedijer.

On 22 February Tito sent a reassuring reply about Vladimir
and said that Nye had no need to worry about his friend
Djilas, although 'the destructive character of his writings ab-

out our realities has hurt his friends and collaborators of long
standing in a revolutionary cause'. I suppose the hope was that
Djilas would come to heel, would make his peace. Instead he
went his long, hard, lonely way. This was his truth. He could
no other. We never deserted him. We tried to have him freed,
or at least to have his rigorous gaol conditions softened to
house arrest, but all to no avail. Politics, as Nye so often said,
is a blood sport.

At this time – 1954 – Nye too was again under fire, the feroc-
ity of the attack leaving no doubt that if his Tory opponents
could have had him hung, drawn and quartered, they would
have done so with relish. What was it all about? We had been
invited to visit Israel as the guests of the Israeli Government on
a nine-day visit, beginning 4 January 1954. At that time, Sar-
dar Panikkar, the distinguished Indian historian, was Indian
Ambassador in Egypt. He was an old friend we met frequently
in London, so we happily accepted his invitation to stay with
him in Cairo before going on to Israel. He knew how much we
wanted to see better relations between Egypt and Israel. It was
an ideal arrangement for us as we could meet people with
varying political views without being in any way beholden to
the Egyptian Government. Dick Crossman, who had made
friends with Egypt's up and coming man, Colonel Nasser,
gave us typewritten impressions of the various Egyptian leaders.

General Neguib, to whom I took a fancy, was confined to
bed with flu, but we were kindly invited to visit him. As we
left his bedside, he clasped my hand and said, 'Tell your
Israeli friends that there will never be war between Egypt and
Israel.' Alas, alas, events proved him tragically wrong, but
that was clearly his wish. I was not so taken with the much
more prim, formal manner of his chief lieutenant, Colonel
Nasser, but he too talked the language of peace between nations so that they could get on with the task of dealing with
their acute poverty problems at home.

From Egypt we crossed through Jordan and there, too,
were received with every kindness and courtesy. What I recall

with great sadness is how the high hopes of dedicated social workers on both the Jordan and Israeli side came to nothing. We visited community centres for homeless adolescent boys in both countries. They were being fed, housed, educated, and given agricultural training to fit them to earn their living later on. We carried good wishes from one community to the other. The community leaders were friends who knew all about the work each was doing.

In Israel the red carpet was down for us. We had many friends and saw much that we wanted to see, especially the achievements of the kibbutz movement, with Yigal Allon as our guide. So what was all the fuss about? Why was Nye branded in the British press as a traitor to his country, a man who was unworthy to be a Privy Councillor, and much else of a similar kind?

The innocent cause of all the uproar was our *L'Express* friends in Paris. Nye was writing a weekly article for *L'Express* which they liked so much that Karol Kewes, then a leading member of the staff, suggested it ought to be syndicated. This they arranged. After the offending article had appeared in half a dozen different countries it was published in General Neguib's *El Gonmhouria*. Its theme was that it was useless for any imperial power to garrison troops in the middle of a hostile population. Better to withdraw while there was still time to do so on friendly terms. This was one of Nye's

more philosophical pieces. I ought to know as each week he dictated his copy at top speed, then trusted to me to deal with too involved sentences, split infinitives or any statement that could expose him to an unpremeditated scrap with official Labour. This article appeared at a most sensitive time in our relations with Egypt and the Tories fastened on it as yet another example of Nye's lack of patriotism.

20. To the Stake with the Heretic

When Nye, in November 1952, decided to allow himself to be nominated for membership of the Shadow Cabinet, he tried to persuade me that he must demonstrate that he was ready to take his share of the work of the front bench, the gibe against him being that all he wanted was power without responsibility. I taunted him with his masochistic tendencies. I was not serious of course. Nye loved the pleasant things of life when they came his way and knew how to enjoy them, but he would not buy ease by abandoning any course of action that he felt it was his duty to pursue. I now see, as I did not at the time, how confusing those two sides of him must have been to those who knew him only slightly, or not at all. This was no austere Stafford Cripps, no grim-faced Savonarola. One of his favourite quotations was, 'Oh God, why did you make your world so beautiful and the life of man so short?'

Against the advice of most of his friends he handed himself over, to be bound and gagged, by the right wing of the Party. No one could stop him. He saw the dangers of a further widening of the breach between the local parties and their representatives in Parliament and wanted to do what he could to ease matters. 'Build Labour Unity' was the front-page headline in *Tribune* on 17 October 1952. But far from welcoming his good-will gesture, when the votes for the twelve Shadow Cabinet places were announced, it was clear that the majority of Labour MPs were in no mood to meet him half-way. He came twelfth in the list. No other candidate sharing his views was elected.

About this time a cordial invitation came to Nye to visit India in January of the following year. I urged him to accept.

This, I hoped, would give him a much needed change of scene and he would also be in congenial company. The visit renewed and consolidated an old friendship with Nehru which went back to his wartime opposition to Churchill's repressive Indian policies and to our pre-war support of the Congress Party. But it started badly. He was in great pain all the way there because something had gone wrong with the injections he received before leaving, and one arm was badly swollen and unusable. This meant that instead of enjoying the few quiet weeks I had looked forward to, in which I could relax at home and see to all manner of things that had been neglected during the political storms of 1952, I was worrying about him. At last the letter arrived I had been waiting for. The pain-racked sleepless air journey was behind him. The arm was improving. He could now enjoy the company of his Indian friends in their own fabulous land.

It was a relief to him to get away for a few short weeks from the nightmare politics of John Foster Dulles, who was dragging not only the Tory Establishment, but also the section of the Labour Party led by Deakin and Gaitskell, along the suicidal road of a 'holy war' against Russia, against China and against Indo-China. Mendès-France in France, Nehru in India, Tito in Yugoslavia, Nye in Britain, and valiant American allies, men of the calibre of Walter Reuther, Hubert Humphrey, Ed Murrow and Walter Lippmann were not prepared to accept the leadership of John Foster Dulles.

Nye was in Delhi when he received news of the death of Stalin. Writing to me from the President's house on 6 March, his comment was, 'I am incapable of any reaction about it. He has been dead so long.' What he meant was that he had written off Stalin just as totally as he had written off John Foster Dulles. He was waiting for the more civilized elements with whom he was in contact in both countries to wrest control from their dinosaurs.

At this moment Winston Churchill, old and ill though he was, showed more imaginative understanding of the new possibilities opened up by Stalin's death than did Labour's

Shadow Cabinet. Nye pleaded in vain for the Party to take the initiative in proposing new high-level talks aimed at reducing international tensions. As his memoirs later disclosed, Churchill had to overcome considerable resistance in his own Cabinet before he got his way. Alas, a further deterioration of his health led to the cancellation of the crucial conference that was to be held in Bermuda and, alas again, far from regretting this lost opportunity, the American 'holy warriors' made no secret of their satisfaction at the way events turned out. No one reading the wartime, and post-war, memoirs of those with first-hand knowledge of all those tortuous twists and turns can indulge in easy optimism abou the future of mankind. 'We are balanced on a knife edge,' Nye often said. More and more, although not lessening in any degree his vigilance in fighting against Tory attacks on the domestic front, his chief preoccupation became how best to avoid the consequences of a world divided into two hostile blocs, unwilling to concede to the other even the right to exist.

Nye returned from India in a more hopeful mood than when he left. A third non-aligned force in the world was beginning to gather momentum. To the last days of his life, this is what he fought for. Friendship with America, yes; friendship with Soviet Russia, yes; but blind subservience to either was something to be rejected by every country that retained any semblance of dignity and honoured the aspirations of ordinary men and women everywhere. Old-fashioned European imperialists had had their day. What was now essential was to prevent their American successors who now called the tune from driving us into a nuclear war. The hysterical nature of their fears of a future in which they would no longer be able to lord it over the great majority of their fellow men made them capable of even that final madness.

In April 1954 John Foster Dulles came to London to pressure the British Government into agreeing to join America in armed intervention to prevent the defeat of the French in Indo-China. Sir Anthony Eden makes this perfectly clear in his memoirs. Churchill, writing later also declares that, 'what we were being asked to do was to assist in misleading Congress into approving a military operation, which in itself would be ineffective, and might bring the world to the verge of a major war'. In private, Churchill and Eden were trying to avoid a definite commitment in support of this horrendous proposition. In France, Mendès-France was taking his political life in his hands in unequivocal opposition to Dulles. If ever there was a moment when the leaders of the Labour Party should have spoken out loud and clear, this was it.

But Attlee failed to do so. He could have strengthened, not weakened, Eden's hand if he had made quite clear that Labour was in total opposition to Dulles. It was left to Nye to take the same stand as his American, Indian and French friends were taking. He broke all the rules by which the parliamentary game is played by striding to the despatch box after Attlee sat down and making the declaration that Attlee ought to have made. Now, once more, the hounds were at his heels. What did the possibility of a third world war matter compared with the enormity of a member of the Shadow Cabinet snubbing his leader by doing his job for him? In an article in the *Daily Mirror* on 2 April Nye had set out his point of view in urgent, explicit terms. But he had not been heeded. Nye resigned from the Shadow Cabinet. Harold Wilson took his place. John Freeman wrote to Nye urging him not to cut himself off from the weekly lunch meetings in Vincent Square because of 'Dick's folly and Harold's ambition'. The uproar in the press and in the Parliamentary Labour Party caused by Nye's cavalier behaviour in speaking out of turn was not allowed to die down. Instead eager hands piled high the faggots ready for the final act.

The climax came early in the following year. In a Commons Defence Debate on 2 March, Nye made a dramatic intervention in a debate on nuclear weapons, how they might be used, and who might use them first. Certainly he did not set out with any intention to challenge the Party leadership, but he was determined to raise the debate to the level of world events. In the exchanges he had with Churchill and Attlee, that is what he sought to do. However, the Party leadership presented the event in an entirely different light – as a direct challenge to Attlee. The Shadow Cabinet took the lead in proposing the withdrawal of the whip in circumstances calculated to lead to his expulsion from the Party altogether. This time there must be no mistake. The death sentence must be pronounced and promptly executed. On the arithmetic of the situation there could be no escape. The National Executive Committee had been given their orders. The block vote of the big unions controlled the trade union members and the five women members. Nye himself accepted that nothing he could say or do at this stage could prevent his expulsion. He had been near the brink several times before, but now all was set to push him over the precipice. It was always a sign of mounting tension when the great meetings in Nye's constituency went beyond singing the 'Red Flag' or the 'Internationale' and with whole-hearted fervour turned to their own Welsh songs and hymns. There was no question about his hold over his constituency. Even with an official Labour Party candidate in the field, he felt he could hold his seat. But what after that? Nye leading a splinter party? Nye repeating the mistake the ILP had made? Most certainly not. His concern was to damp down any such thought in the minds of some of his supporters. Often he would say, 'What this great blundering Labour movement with its trade union base cannot be persuaded to do, cannot be done.' He planned to continue his educational work in Parliament, in *Tribune*, and in public meetings. It was the awareness of Deakin and his henchmen of the growing support for Nye in the unions that added to the frenzy of their expulsion campaign. This was their moment. They could not afford to delay.

Then the whole applecart was unexpectedly turned upside down. One of the five women members of the NEC, Mrs Jean Mann, although she was dependent, like the other women members, on the block votes controlled by the union bosses, voted against Nye's expulsion. Why? I imagine from mixed motives. She knew from her constituency reactions, the mood generally in the west of Scotland and the shifts beginning to surface in the unions, that there would be blood on the moon if Nye were expelled. To expel him would be an act of wanton irresponsibility. However much Nye might try to minimize the effect, there were explosive rank-and-file elements that would be difficult to control. Nye had antagonized Jean by telling her to 'contain her bile' when she made distracting interruptions at a private Party meeting when he was making a most difficult speech to a hostile audience. It was very silly of Nye to make enemies of several women in the Party by not remembering that a little bit of soft soap can go a long way. But you cannot have everything. That was Nye! From my schoolgirl days when Jean had stayed with my parents as a visiting I L P propagandist, we had been on friendly terms. That too may have been an element in the situation. Anyhow, whatever her motives, she saved the day. By fourteen votes to thirteen the expulsion vote was rejected.

In the hectic political atmosphere of 1954 Nye added a bit

of additional fuel to the implacable hostility shown towards him by leading right-wing members of the Labour Party. He had a car accident and did the most foolish thing anyone can do. Instead of waiting patiently for the arrival of the police he sped on his way. He was anxious to get home. My mother was alone that evening and he did not want her alarmed by press men telephoning to inform her he had had an accident. His concern for her was very genuine and no doubt influenced him, but just as strong would be his natural impatience. I say 'would be', for when I returned home the following day and learnt what had happened, I did not discuss the accident with him. What would have been the point? Most certainly, if I had been with him, I would have prevented him behaving so inexcusably. But reproaching him after the event would not have helped matters. All I knew was that at a dangerous corner where a side road met the main road into London, his car crashed into a bus. It was the car, not the bus that took the main shock. No one was injured.

Denis Healey, making a bitter attack on Nye in the American *New Republic* because of his intervention in the parliamentary exchanges following Anthony Eden's statement on South-East Asia, could not forbear from adding, just for good measure, that Nye had been fined £50 for a motoring offence and that failure to stop after an accident could well be his political epitaph.

There were times when Nye's fast driving made me feel like Mary Pickford hanging on to the edge of a cliff, but during all the years we were together, we never had an accident. He loved speed but he was a superb driver. Once at an NEC meeting when the solid trade union vote was massed as usual against him, he cried out in exasperation, 'Can't I be allowed to be right just once?' In regard to his driving offence he might equally well have asked, 'Can't I be forgiven for being wrong just once?' Unfortunately I was in America when he had to go through the ordeal of a jubilant press in full cry against him during the trial. It was only afterwards that I learnt just how searing it had all been. But again, I did not discuss it with him. What would have been the use? He knew he had blundered, but he had suffered quite enough without a nagging wife coming home to prolong the agony. That was not our way.

The gap between Aneurin Bevan and Hugh Gaitskell was unbridgeable. Both believed, fervently believed, that what they stood for was in the best interests of their party and their country. But they had grown up in different worlds, and from their political experiences they drew very different conclusions. Hugh Gaitskell dreaded a Communist take-over of the Labour movement, and wildly exaggerated the extent of Communist Party influence. Everyone left of centre was suspect in his eyes. He genuinely believed that most of those in the party associated with Nye were either undercover Communists or fellow-travellers. He is on record as having denounced Nye as a fellow-traveller, and one sixth, later modified to one tenth, of the delegates to the Annual Conference of the Party were branded by him in this same blindly biased fashion.

Part of the irony of the situation was that he was just as authoritarian as the leaders of the Communist Party. Each wanted total control. Each wanted those who disagreed with them eliminated. It was never a question of live and let live. Gaitskell supported every attempt to expel Nye from the party and not just Nye. Let Stafford Cripps go, George Strauss, John Freeman, Harold Wilson, Charles Trevelyan. Off with their heads was his motto. Another extraordinary feature of this impossible situation was that well-to-do members of the party could dine with one another in their private homes or in discreet restaurants – no one could prevent them doing so. This was not conspiracy: this was just a civilized exchanging of views. But woe betide members of the party who did not have convenient homes near the House of Commons. Where could they meet? Obviously in a room in the House of Commons. But that was forbidden; this type of get-together was denounced as a party within a party, as a dangerous intrigue to undermine the authority of the party leaders.

The same abrasive attitude was shown towards *Tribune*, the weekly paper that some of us managed to keep going by just about killing ourselves. I shall describe how hard it was, particularly on Michael Foot and myself, a little later. What was our crime? What were we trying to do? We were seeking to put our point of view on both domestic and foreign affairs before the public in general, and the activists in the constituency parties in particular. No other journal would do this for us. We were eager to win support just as Hugh Gaitskell and those who agreed with him were eager to win support. The difference was that that the Tory press, regarding the right wing of the Labour Party as no serious threat, gave its members an easy ride. We on the left, Nye in particular, were depicted as devils, complete with horns and a tail. All we asked was that both sides of the argument should be heard, not just one side.

Gaitskell was not prepared to tolerate even one small weekly journal that dared to disagree with official policy. We could state our point of view in the private meetings of the Parliamentary Labour Party in a room in the House of Commons, but once the vote was taken, there must be no further public discussion. This of course was death by suffocation for some of us. Part of the trouble was the double-dealing of quite a few of our parliamentary colleagues. They spoke one language in their constituencies and voted quite differently in our private meetings. They could always shelter behind the plea that they had to accept the will of the majority without revealing that they themselves had helped to create that majority. Nye detested secret diplomacy. Let the issues be freely discussed in a spirit of live and let live. Allow rank-and-file members to hear the arguments, not just the conclusions.

When our meetings were banned we opened them to any member of the Parliamentary Party who cared to come along and take part. But even that was not enough; we were still forbidden to meet. All that was left was to retreat to Dick

Crossman's home in Vincent Square, but our numbers, about sixty of us, were too unwieldy for regular, serious, weekly discussion sessions there. The authoritarian attitude of the Party forced us not only to meet in secret, which we did not want to do, but also forced us to exclude most of our close associates from these meetings. Only the six members of the constituency section of the NEC, along with Michael Foot, Bill Mallalieu and myself representing *Tribune*, and John Freeman the *New Statesman*, met for regular lunch-time discussions in Vincent Square. It was heroic of Anne, Dick's charming, devoted wife, to put up with us all, week after week. It was Anne who had to do the shopping, prepare the sandwiches and salads and coffee, then serve us in her demure, efficient manner. This was the only way we were able to meet.

Another contentious issue was the *Tribune* Brains Trusts. What were they? What was their purpose? There could be no secrecy charge here. We were only too anxious to have the general public attend our meetings, ask questions at the end and, hopefully, contribute to a collection for *Tribune*. This was badly needed. Jack Hylton had joined Howard Samuel in making generous donations to the paper, but never enough. The trouble was that we had virtually no revenue from advertisements. What we were seeking to do was to maintain a lively exchange of views at all party levels, believing that by free discussion the vitality of the whole working-class movement could best be sustained. Of course when a General Election was due we closed ranks. From 1944 onwards when Nye became a member of the NEC, he was always one of the small committee who drafted the election manifesto.

What could be more reasonable? Who would want the two great parties in the State to be monolithic? Who can genuinely argue that that kind of rigid bureaucratic control enlivens the political scene? If you suppress free discussion, you disenfranchise the rank and file. Theirs not to reason why, theirs but to do or die is a fit philosophy for conspiratorial Communist or fascist movements, but a poison draught for those who believe in a lively, participating democratic party.

In the 1945 Parliament Hugh Gaitskell regarded some of the ablest of the new Members as Communist infiltrators bent on undermining parliamentary democracy. Donald Bruce, Will Griffiths, Hugh Delargy, Stephen Swingler, Tom Driberg, Frank Bowles, Barbara Castle, Harold Davies, Bill Mallalieu, Ian Mikardo, Geoffrey Bing, Leslie Hale, John Baird, Michael Foot, and many others who were looked on with suspicion, were just as reluctant to foment civil war as Nye and I were. But some of them were intellectually sceptical that the formidable vested interests of capitalist society would permit a Labour Government to do more than play around with a few mild reforms. Because Nye too had a question-mark over whether or not we could achieve socialism in Britain by parliamentary means, he held their confidence. Along with him they were willing to have a go, to exert their very considerable ability in an attempt to make Parliament a genuine forum which heard and answered the needs of a restless, challenging, post-war working class. What Hugh Gaitskell totally failed to comprehend was that Nye, by his vigorous but realistic pursuit of socialism by parliamentary means, was doing more to prevent the growth of Communist influence than any other man in public life. The leaders of the Communist Party knew the score. Destroy the left inside the Labour Party and a sizeable section of the working class will turn in desperation to them. That was their belief and motivated all their actions.

This fear of Communist infiltration spilt over into foreign affairs. Ernest Bevin behaved towards the Soviet Union as if it were a breakaway branch of the Transport and General Workers' Union. He did not have to pressure his candidate for party leadership to follow his lead. Hugh Gaitskell was right there, completely in accord with Bevin's views. What we were saddled with was a foreign policy based on the belief that America could do no wrong and Russia could do nothing right. Nye saw this as a deadly, self-defeating distortion of the problems crowding in on us from all over the world. He knew more about Communist philosophy and practice than Hugh and feared it less. He knew there was not the slightest danger of Britain falling under a Communist dictatorship, provided democratic socialists showed as robust a faith in their creed as Communists and capitalists did in theirs.

Through all the turmoil of political events Nye never abandoned his dream of getting away from the hot-house atmosphere of central London. Ideally he longed for a home in the Welsh mountains, but that was not possible. We had to be near enough to London to enable us to keep constant contact with our parliamentary duties. Nye had also to be to the west of London in order to shorten the distance to his constituency, because he liked to travel there by car. I was the world's worst driver and was content to keep contact with my Midlands constituency by rail.

A number of our friends were on the look-out for the kind of cottage we were hoping to find. Then out of the blue a farmer friend, John Mackie, invited us to visit another farmer friend, Tony Harman, who had told him of a small farm for sale on the top of the Chilterns. At first I demurred. This property had fifty acres attached to it, as well as the farmhouse and expansive farm buildings that had at one time belonged to a much larger farm. Our life was complicated enough without adding the hazards of amateur farming. We could of course buy the lot, sell the fields and cottages, keeping only the house and garden, but that was simply not on. It would mean we would have strangers breathing down our necks and easy access for the press right to our door, when what above all we both needed so badly was a home where we could be truly private. But the price was tempting: £9,000 for the lot. Anyhow there was no harm in looking.

When Nye saw Asheridge Farm I am sure he decided without a moment's hesitation that he had found what he was looking for. The farm manager and cowman could continue undisturbed in their cottages. The fifty acres could continue to be used as grazing land for the small Jersey herd we had also had to buy, then a pig and poultry unit would be added to make the whole enterprise viable. That was a practical possibility then, although most certainly not now. John Mackie said he would see to things for us. Without his encouragement and help it would have been madness for us to embark on this kind of venture.

There was no central heating in the farmhouse. That had to be seen to at once. I did not fancy facing the rigours of winter on the top of the Chilterns in a bleakly cold farmhouse and, still more important, Mother had reached an age when she needed warmth. I was delighted when Nye went off to China and Japan via Moscow as a member of an NEC delegation. Now Mother and I would be left in peace to tackle all that had to be seen to in the house and garden.

The garden had been lovingly cared for by the previous owner, so it was just a matter of finding a local handyman to help with maintenance. The house was a more difficult proposition. The front door opened on to a largish room, with a 'ye olde English fireplace'; the kind where you have to duck under a low front to reach a narrow left-hand bench in the alcove. But above the fireplace there was a great oak beam level with my eyes which, I reckoned, could help me make a complete transformation. As in our first cottage, we would have to take the risk of meddling with the supporting structure. Thankfully all went well. A local builder decided it was a reasonable risk to raise the front to the level of the beam. Now we could have a spacious fireplace with room to accommodate an even more generous log fire than at Brimpton Common.

'But, Winston, it's not even original'

When the wintry weather set in we made the belated discovery that the central heating pipes we had installed in the attic were not lagged and the roof was not lined. So there we were up in the attic shovelling out the melting snow. But we were still young enough and strong enough to make light of all those teething troubles.

Nye was now an enthusiastic farmer. Some silly newspapers informed their readers that he was planning his retreat from active politics, tired and defeated. The opposite was the truth. Now that he could sleep in country air and wander around the countryside unmolested, all his old optimism and joy in life came flooding back. I was glad our home was now in the country, but before we had time to get used to the new freedom this gave us we made the shattering discovery that my mother was suffering from cancer, which had reached such an advanced stage that all we could do was see that she was kept as happy and as free from pain as modern medicine could devise. We had an assortment of tablets prescribed for her and we saw to it that these were given with due care.

Such were her reticent Scottish ways that I had never seen my mother undressed during the day, and in bed she wore a demure long-sleeved, high-necked nightgown. One of her breasts had a deep suppurating wound. This she had hidden from us, but when Dr Wise, the efficient local Health Service doctor with whom we had registered, called to examine her for what we thought was nothing more serious than a severe flu cold, she was unable to prevent him discovering the state of her breast. When the doctor came downstairs we went together into our small ground-floor study. I screamed hysterically, and I am not a screaming type, on hearing of my mother's condition. Grief, fear and above all, a terrible sense of guilt overwhelmed me. As Nye held me to him to calm me I can hear his sad voice saying, 'Life will never be the same for us again. Ma leaves too many gracious memories.'

Grandmother Greig had died of cancer after a long, painful illness. My mother, her daughter, had nursed her devotedly, so knew every nuance of her suffering. So all that life now held for my mother was a future of suffering with no hope of recovery. That is how I felt and thought at that moment. During the last years of my father's life a doctor was often in our home, but my mother had hidden her breast from him as well as from us. We must not be worried. That was all she cared about. Did she suspect cancer? I do not know. But the wonderful thing was that she lived for another eight years, most of the time happy and cheerful as ever with almost no pain. I scolded her when I went upstairs once the doctor left and I had got control of myself. Nye and I had agreed that we must not alarm her unnecessarily. So, as I have said, I went upstairs and gave her a good scolding for not having her breast seen to long before now. It was an abscess and it must now be properly treated. I think she believed us. In the last years of her life her memory switched off and on and nothing in her state of health corresponded with what she thought cancer entailed – that is, endless unrelieved suffering.

21. International Bridge-Building

In January 1955 I escaped for a short time from the tortuous, protracted witch-hunting of the previous year. When first I was invited to visit India I had declined because of anxiety about my mother's health. But there she was, as active as ever, giving no outward sign of the terminal cancer I had dreaded so much. Another part of my reluctance was the thought of all the poverty, illiteracy and disease which was the lot of the great mass of the Indian population. In my imagination the very sun was blotted out by the human misery beneath it. When the invitation was renewed, Nye wisely insisted on me going, the more so as he knew I would return with a more balanced picture and, most of all, because he knew I had been under so much strain that I needed to get away from both public and domestic responsibilities for a few weeks.

In India I was a privileged guest, meeting old friends and making new ones. At that time Mr S. K. Dey was the able administrator of community projects. He arranged for me to visit villages and outlying places where the so-called 'dirty hand' experiment was the order of the day. The theory behind all this was that young men would volunteer to live and work in the villages, teaching not so much by what they said as by what they did. If they could convince the rural people that their way of planting and harvesting gave better results than older, time-hallowed ways, it was confidently believed that a valuable increase in food production could be achieved.

I was also the victim of my friend Pandit Nehru's passion for industrialization at that time. He insisted I visit several huge steel works, all of which was wasted on me as I was incapable of understanding the various industrial processes I was shown. That was my weakness, my laziness if you like; all the same I have never been able to understand some of the denigration of Nehru long after his death because he realized that villages needed roads, electricity, deep wells: they could not live by ploughing and spinning alone. Pure undiluted Gandhism seemed to me pure undiluted nonsense. India had somehow to build its industrial infra-structure linking towns and villages together, as well as giving a proper place to cottage industries.

Then there was the morning when Rajkumari Amrit Kaur, Minister of Health, called to take Lady Mountbatten, a much loved and valued friend of India, to a newly built village hospital that was not attracting either sufficient staff or sufficient patients. Off they went, in full nursing regalia, to serve in the hospital and hoping by their patronage and example to weaken caste prejudices. Rajkumari, a princess by birth who had spent many years in gaol during the struggle for Independence, was tiny in stature, but impressive in her determination to attract money and urgently needed hospital equipment from Western sympathizers. Nye and she became great friends when he was Minister of Health. I enjoyed seeing her stamp her little foot and look up at him, saying imperiously, 'But Nye, I must have it, I must have it.' It was a case, if you like, in the early post-war years of the poor helping the poor. But in relative terms we were rich, not poor. Nye did his best, being careful to avoid publicity where possible, for there were always a few Fleet Street vultures around, ready to pounce and make mischief, even out of the most innocent transactions.

I visited factories, colleges and hospitals from Delhi to Madras, but time was also arranged to allow for visits to villages high in the Himalayas, to the Taj Mahal, and to many other of India's timeless treasures. One Saturday I arrived in Calcutta on a bleakly cold wet evening. As I saw men, women and children cowering into the shelter of a high wall, I prayed that I would never again talk glibly about how much easier it was for poor people in a warm climate. But the following day there was a bright blue sky overhead and the pavements were populated by a colourful crowd of humanity that would be any painter's dream. They were in lively, friendly mood, one man shaving, another having his hair cut, children playing happily together, the broad pavement being treated as their bedroom, bathroom and drawing-room, as indeed it was. How can we even begin to bridge the gap between the Western world and what we now call the developing nations?

That evening in Calcutta, the Governor, with whom I was staying, was just beginning to recover from an illness. His only guests were Lady Edwina Mountbatten and myself. When we joined him and his family for dinner I was asked if I preferred Indian or English food. I was about to say Indian as I thought that would give less trouble, also I liked Indian food. But before I could do so, Lady Mountbatten told the attendant, 'We shall both have English food.' Then she quietly explained to me that there were two sets of cooks in the kitchen, dating from the days of the British Raj. That had been the arrangement in order to ensure a choice of Indian or European dishes. Both groups were still in the kitchen, for with India's vast unemployment problem dismissal would have been stark tragedy. No alternative jobs were available.

This changing India, which in so many respects was not changing, was endlessly fascinating. In Delhi on Independence Day the President gave a ceremonial garden party. He had invited VIPs of various kinds, including representatives from all the Embassies. The garden was a splendid spectacle, the scarlet uniforms of tall soldiers stationed at various points, rivalling the brilliance of the flowers. Three trumpeters in scarlet uniforms appeared on the balcony of the presidential palace. Startled by all this pomp and circumstance I said teasingly to Nehru, 'If this does not impress you natives, nothing will.' 'Jennie,' he said, 'we promised to retain them after the take-over.' 'I hope you never part with them,' I thought, for after all they were harmless enough and we all like a bit of colourful pageantry.

While we were joking, the crowds stood aside, including the Prime Minister, to make way for the President. That was the climax of the scene. A small figure, clad only in a dhoti, advanced along the pathway that had been respectfully cleared for him. Though the British Raj had departed, all the outer framework was still there, but it was the modest figure who looked the very embodiment of Gandhi and all he had fought for who symbolized the new reality.

I was always curious about other parts of the world and made friends easily with people whose race, religion and colour of skin were different from mine. But let's face it, who were those Indians, Africans, Chinese, Russians, Europeans and Israelis I came to know? Without exception, members of the educated elite of their respective countries. The foreign students I met, mainly at ILP conferences and summer schools, returned to their countries to vanish in the power struggles there or to emerge as their countries' leaders. They too were the privileged few who found the means to come to Britain to study in our colleges and universities. But even this limited level of contact was not to be belittled. We interacted on one another and were nourished by the same poets, philosophers, economists and novelists.

Nehru was sometimes disparagingly called the 'brown Englishman'. All his life, unembittered by the arrogance of the British Raj and the years he and his family and friends spent in British gaols, the best of our culture was an essential part of him. He was a poet and a dreamer. So too was Tagore. In the last years of their lives they had to fight against pessimism and depression as so much of what they had lived for failed to materialize, but that does not undo all the good they did.

It is a mistake to assume that men and women who have not been taught to read or write have a low intelligence, or that those who have had all that conventional education can give are as a consequence sensitive and intelligent. I did not have to go to India to learn these elementary facts. I was schooled in the Fifeshire coalfields and had ample opportunity to compare the knowledge and intelligence of some of our local peo-

ple with that of the students I met in Edinburgh. Again there
is an elitist element here, for I am talking of the natural leaders who emerged in the coalfields. We need the special ones
who will help the rest of us forward. All that is wrong with the
world I grew up in and that still exists is that the gathering
ground is too narrow. The best in education should be available for every child, so that each may find his or her true level
and in so doing enrich their country as well as their own private lives. We have a long way to go before we come anywhere
near that goal, for education is not simply assembling children
into classrooms. It embraces their total environment, most of
all the type of home they return to when school hours are
over.

It is a crude caricature of the kind of socialism Nye and I
believed in to imagine we sought to reduce everyone and
everything to a drab uniformity. Nye was fond of quoting the
following passage from *The Motives of Proteus* by José E.
Rodó, his favourite South American author:

Democracy alone can conciliate equality at the outset with an ine-
quality at the end which gives full scope for the best and most apt to
work towards the good of the whole. So considered, democracy becomes a struggle not to reduce all to the lowest common level, but to
raise all towards the highest degree of possible culture. Democracy in
this sense retains within itself an imprescriptible element of aristocracy, which lies in establishing the superiority of the best with the consent of all; but on that basis it becomes essential that the qualities
regarded as superior are really the best, and not merely qualities im-
mobilized in a special class or caste, and protected by special pri-
vileges. The only aristocracy possible on a democratic basis is one of
morality and culture.

I returned home to a quite cheerful atmosphere as Western
relations with the Soviet Union were less tense, the situation
in the Far East less menacing and Khrushchev, now in power,
was giving every sign of seeking to meet Anthony Eden half-
way in renewed efforts to edge away from escalating armament
expenditure. When the General Election came the Tories held
all the winning cards. It was Eden, not Attlee, who had been

taking the initiative in peace moves. On the domestic front we were told that we could look forward to an age of affluence under beneficient Tory leadership.

The Tory majority over Labour in Parliament increased from seventeen to fifty-nine. The Party was in the doldrums. Arthur Deakin had died during the election campaign. Attlee was once again appointed Leader and Herbert Morrison Deputy Leader. It was Nye who, at the Parliamentary meeting, moved that Attlee and Morrison should be re-elected unopposed. He did so because he felt that the Party needed time for its wounds to heal. A highly orchestrated campaign led by Herbert Morrison claimed that Nye's vermin speech had cost Labour the election. The truth was that Labour had lost its way. In the Election it had nothing distinctive to say, the soothing syrup it offered put its supporters to sleep and middle-of-the-road voters were not impressed by Labour's promises to manage the capitalist system better than the capitalists.

In the autumn, when delegates gathered in Margate for the Annual Conference, Nye was no longer in such an accommodating mood. The Party, he declared, ardently desired unity, but:

> Unity must be achieved on the basis of policies that will inspire the Party to fight and not by slurring over the issues that divide us. The Labour Party must have as its aim the establishment of a socialist society. Otherwise it will have no significance in the life of the nation.

Conference delegates responded with thunderous applause. There was no doubt about the mood of the Party's rank and file, but when the result of the contest for the Treasurership of the Party was announced Hugh Gaitskell, for the second year running, had an overwhelming victory.

Six weeks later Attlee was forced to resign as Party Leader. He did so with the utmost reluctance; his hand was forced and he made no secret of the fact. Herbert Morrison was also pushed aside. When the Parliamentary Party met to elect a new Leader he received only 40 votes, less than the 70 votes Nye received. Hugh Gaitskell was elected Leader with 157 votes. All the time, a noisy outcry was maintained about 'a party within a party', about a sinister Bevanite conspiracy. It should have been plain for all to see that the so-called Bevanites were at sixes and sevens. It was the right wing that had successfully organized 'a party within a party'.

After the General Election Nye had again become a member of the Shadow Cabinet. A year after the Margate Conference at the 1956 Annual Conference in Blackpool, when the result of the contest for the Treasurership was announced, he was once more a member of the NEC. His supporters had romped home in the constituency section and he had become Party Treasurer. But in his fight to rally support in the unions it was still narrow margins. He received 3,029,000 votes; the defeated candidate, George Brown, received 2,755,000 votes. George was a member of the Transport and General Workers' Union, and received its support. Many assumed that the issue had been decided in Nye's favour because Frank Cousins had succeeded Deakin as Secretary of the Transport and General Workers' Union, but that year Frank was too new to the job to be able to disentangle himself from the commitments made by his predecessor.

When the Blackpool Conference greeted Nye's reversal of fortune with prolonged and hilarious cheering, only I could know just how much the struggle of the past three years had cost him in nervous wear and tear. Nye hated acrimony. He loved good fellowship. If his aim in life had been personal advancement, if he had chosen to disarm his critics by abandoning his principles, the leadership of the Party was his for the taking. Sam Watson, the influential leader of the Durham Miner's Union, had a personal liking for Nye and was one of many friends who again and again tried to persuade him to change his views. But Nye knew that the end was a summation of the means. The idea that he should pretend to accept policies that he believed would emasculate the Labour movement at home and make it of little or no account in foreign affairs, was anathema to him.

And let me at once add that it would give an entirely false

picture of those fierce internal struggles for the soul of the
Labour movement if full justice was not done to Hugh Gaitskell, Nye's most formidable rival. Just as much as Nye he was
fighting for what he believed in. If he had been a mere career
politician he would have been infinitely less effective.

To return to 1955, as the Christmas parliamentary recess
approached, we were both looking forward to spending at
least part of it quietly at home. Members of Parliament are
expected to visit their constituencies when the Commons is
not sitting and at other times the House can be a demanding
place. Short excursions to various parts of the world stand out
in the memory, but they are not the daily bread of our existence. One of our problems was synchronizing the times when
we might be at home together, and the times when we were
off on our various engagements; but we decided nothing
should prevent us spending this Christmas at Asheridge. We
were now comfortably settled, with Ma still showing no outward sign of her illness. We were careful to see that she was
given the various medicines prescribed to keep her free from
pain; we told no one about the cancer problem. None of our
friends guessed we had this private anxiety.

Nye relished every moment of that Christmas at Asheridge.
Would 1956, I wondered, be a less traumatic year? I was hoping so. Instead we went headlong into the Suez debacle and
the heroic, doomed uprisings in Poland and Hungary. Eden
succeeded in uniting right, left and centre of the Labour Party
in opposition to him, with the American Government and the
United Nations equally vociferous in condemning his madness. He was forced to call a halt to his military adventures,
but not before he had dealt a deadly blow to our national self-
esteem. It was typical of Nye that, instead of accepting the
prevailing mood of defeatism, he tried to point the way once
more to what he was convinced was our true role in the world.
'I do not take the view,' he said in the House of Commons on
19 December, 'that Great Britain is a second-class power. On
the contrary, I take the view that this country is a depository
of probably more concentrated experience and skill than any

other country in the world . . . What we have to seek are new ways of inspiring and igniting the minds of mankind. We can do so.'

Nye had no doubt about what these new ways should be. He was incapable of looking at the quelling of the Polish and Hungarian uprisings and the Suez fiasco as isolated incidents. Concerted British, French and Israeli military advances against Egypt were a powerful weapon in the hands of the hawks in the Kremlin against those of their colleagues who were looking for signs that they could trust the peaceful intentions of Western capitalism. One of the most dangerous delusions anyone could harbour at that time, or indeed, at any time, was that there were divided counsels in London and Washington as to how best to conduct world affairs, but that no corresponding controversies were raging in Moscow. The leaders in the Kremlin, far from being monolithic in outlook, were debating among themselves just as seriously as their opposite numbers in the West. An awareness of this influenced all Nye's thinking. Khrushchev and others who were keen to improve relations with the West and to work towards detente were given a deadly blow by the Suez affair. After Suez the Kremlin hawks were not prepared to take any risks in dealing with unrest in any part of Eastern Europe. And what price Western moral indignation after our behaviour in the Middle East? One of the most saddening and discouraging features of this whole period was how little effort was made to find a way out of a financially, as well as militarily ruinous situation.

Harold Macmillan succeeded Eden as Prime Minister early in 1957. He was a better demagogue than Eden. The author of *The Middle Way* and the much quoted 'winds of change' speech understood the lives and aspirations of ordinary men and women better than his predecessor, but there was no basic change in our foreign policy; he gave unqualified support to the so-called Eisenhower doctrine, which was America's offer of aid, including military aid, to every country in the Middle and Far East that declared its allegiance to the West and hostility to Russia. That was another act of provocation, strengthening the hands of the hawks in the Kremlin. But maybe most clearly of all, the crass one-sidedness of British diplomacy was shown in its response to the letters sent by Marshal Bulganin to Anthony Eden and Guy Mollet in September and October 1956. These were private letters, not published until April of the following year. Their purpose was to urge Britain and France not to attempt to seize the Suez Canal by force, as this would lead to the destruction of the Canal and of adjacent oil fields and pipe lines. Any such move, Bulganin declared, would end in failure, and as Soviet interests were involved Russia could not stand aside. In common sanity one would have thought that responsible capitalist statesmen would have been able to restrain their hostility to Communism, at least to the extent of talking to the Russians, seeking to find out their positive alternative suggestions and how far these might be acceptable.

This blind clinging to our American big brother highlighted once more how difficult it was for Aneurin Bevan and Hugh Gaitskell to come to terms. Hugh declared in favour of the Eisenhower doctrine, while Nye maintained his contacts with the non-aligned statesmen who in various parts of the world were seeking to cool East West rivalries and fears. Visiting India again in April 1957, he found hostility to Britain's high-handed ignoring of Indian interests in the Middle East and much more besides so intense that Nehru did not believe it was going to be possible to prevent both Houses of the Indian Parliament severing all connections with the Commonwealth. At Westminster, on many crucial occasions, the views expressed by Nye cannot be ignored by any serious student of politics, but in my judgement his speech to Indian Members of both Houses of Parliament at this most dangerous moment in our relationship was the greatest oratorical *tour de force* of his career. Nehru was grateful to him for giving him a breathing space. The immediate, all too real danger of India leaving the Commonwealth was averted. India was a tonic, but when

Nye's thoughts turned homewards his mood darkened. On 11 April he wrote to me:

The more I reflect on Gaitskell the more gloomy I become and the more I dread the ordeal before me if ever he becomes Prime Minister. With that power and authority in his possession it will be difficult to brake his reactionary impulses and compel him to make concessions early enough. Even the thought of the effort needed to influence him to the right courses makes my spirit sink. It is true that Gaitskell will give in in the last resort, but only after the Party suffers damage and leaving the leaders exhausted by wholly unnecessary private exertions.

That letter gives the key to Nye's dilemma as, during the rest of his life, he struggled with the problem of how best to maximize Britain's influence in a world where holy crusaders, on both sides of the Iron Curtain, remained irreconcilable. He held that it was madness to say to the Russians that we expected them to agree to a united Germany which would be free to join either East or West and free to rearm. All the weight of Western capitalism had come down on the side of assisting Dr Adenauer to victory over his Social Democratic opponents in Germany. It was a mockery to say Germany would be free to choose. The cards were firmly stacked in favour of Adenauer. How could any sane man or woman expect the Russian leaders to regard the activities of the West as a serious effort towards cooling the torrid international temperature? On the contrary, they saw it as the ruthless pursuit of class-war interests that could all too easily escalate into the final horror of nuclear war.

In some moods Nye was close to despair. 'We have not much time,' he would say again and again. Then the opportunities opened up to him as a member of the National Executive and, still more, as Shadow Foreign Secretary, brought him round to cautious optimism. He was meeting all the leading political figures in America, Russia and Europe. He was consolidating old friendships and making new ones. During 1957 he spent a considerable amount of time travelling from capital to capital. After attending the French Socialist Conference at Toulouse he was glad to renew acquaintance with Mendès-France in Paris, for the two men had much more in common than Nye had with the abysmally reactionary French Socialist Party leaders. A little later the Socialist International Conference in Vienna was a heartening affair. All condemned France's hostility to Algeria's struggle for independence. All agreed that a serious effort should be made to probe the Russian proposals for disengagemnt in Europe.

I was with Nye on the two most important journeys he made that summer. We went first to Poland, then on to Russia. The Poles were polite, but distant when we arrived. Before we left, Nye had won their good will and all formalities melted away. As usual, Nye was outspoken in his criticisms of much that he saw. 'Small but good' was the joke of the year. This was how a Polish wit had described a monstrous, tasteless centre of 'culture and recreation' built in Warsaw by the Russians. The phrase caught on: it was a kind of password. On our last evening our hosts invited us to dine with them in a chateau some miles from Warsaw. It had all the charm and elegance the Russian-built centre lacked. 'Small but good,' they smilingly said, this time meaning it. When we asked questions about some of the fine paintings the chateau contained, our Polish friends laughed as they told us they were strangers there themselves. This was the first time they had been in possession of the chateau. The pro-Stalinist wing of the Polish leadership had been replaced by more liberal elements under Gomulka's leadership, and use of the chateau was a privilege that belonged to the ruling clique. This was not anything like a revolutionary change, but it was certainly an encouraging step forward.

By far the most important occasion that summer was meeting Khrushchev in his Crimean holiday home. It seemed that new winds were also beginning to blow through the Kremlin corridors of power. Stalin must have humiliated Khrushchev in ways he could never forgive, and this lent bite to his outspoken condemnation of his former leader. We were able to talk together at length and in perfect privacy; Nye, Khrush-chev, myself, and a superb interpreter sat together in a shady corner of their garden overlooking the Black Sea. During those conversations I wondered if the Russian leader was as much of a rough-neck as he appeared to be, or was it that he found it good politics to stress his proletarian origins? I ask because of his keen concentrated attention as we discussed one aspect after another of outstanding issues between East and West. He was well schooled in Marxist economics and philosophy, and he was also well briefed not only about Nye's activities but, to my surprise, about mine as well. He knew that I had expressed strong views on the subject of public ownership at the Labour Party Conference, and that I had helped to influence the vote on nuclear disarmament at a private meeting of the Parliamentary Labour Party while Nye was in India. The Soviet Intelligence Service apparently followed in minute detail every nuance of the British political scene. In Khrushchev's own words, said with obvious pride, 'Not so much as a sparrow hops from branch to branch without us knowing about it.'

Then there was Madame Khrushchev, gentle and court-eous, and most certainly not just her husband's shadow. She appeared in public with Khrushchev more than any previous leader's wife had done. As I walked with her in the garden we made friendly noises to one another in my halting French and her rather better French. When she pulled a rose and graciously gave it to me, it meant something quite different from all those mechanized beribboned bouquets that are part of the stock in trade of international diplomatic exchanges.

We had lunch on a large balcony overlooking the garden. The only other guests were a daughter and son-in-law and Mikhail Sholokhov, the author of *And Quiet Flows the Don*. The morning discussions went well, and by lunchtime Khrushchev was in a rumbustious, playful mood. An enormous bottle of champagne was produced but none of the Russians could open it. When Nye made a teasing remark, Khrushchev challenged him to see what he could do. Without a moment's hesitation Nye rose from the table and opened the bottle by pressing it in the hinges of a strong, elaborately carved wooden door between the balcony and the dining-room. 'Superior Western technique,' Nye happily quipped. This was pretty rough behaviour, but everyone laughed and applauded. They apparently enjoyed meeting an emissary from the 'capitalist West' who could meet them in play as well as in argument. When Suslov, Communist Party Secretary and leading theoretician, shortly afterwards led a delegation to London, he said to me at a reception in the Russian Embassy that Khrushchev had asked him to give his regards to 'General Lee'. I at once retorted, 'And please give mine to Corporal Khrushchev.' That we could joke together did not mean that either side had lowered its guard, but at least we were showing signs of a common humanity.

22. The Strains Are Too Much for Me

My most distasteful task in 1957 was for the second time allowing myself to be nominated for the Women's Section of the NEC. I considered it an anachronism. I wanted it abolished. But until at least three of the five women members were on the left of the party, there was no possibility of persuading the right-wing trade union leaders to do what many of us thought was eminently fair and sensible; that is, we sought to add those five places to the seven constituency places, which would have given the local party workers the same representation as the unions. The Leader of the Opposition and Deputy Leader would continue to be chosen by the Parliamentary Labour Party and the Treasurer by the votes of both unions and constituencies. I knew that I would not win easily or quickly, but it would have been cowardly of me to expect Lena Jeger and others to face this kind of ordeal if I myself was not prepared to do so.

The mounting political strains of that year could not have come at a worse time. Our home life was losing its old easy-going comfort, for my mother now had to be helped more than she realized. Her bright spirit was undimmed, but her strength was failing. I struggled on as best I could. But a family tragedy, added to all else, brought me to the brink of a complete nervous breakdown. My brother had left for Australia in 1925 when he was barely eighteen. He returned in 1946 a broken man. We knew all about his frequent periods of unemployment, and when his cables for financial help came we responded whatever the sacrifice. We knew his wife had to go out to work to help keep the home going and provide for their three children. But we had no suspicion that their difficulties were anything more complicated than bad luck in the struggle for survival in a tough country.

When war broke out my brother joined the Australian Army, and in his letters home gave the impression that he had done so from love of Britain and detestation of all that Hitler stood for. The truth was that he had by then undermined his health and morale by drink and drugs. At one point his wife wrote saying he had agreed to brain surgery, and she had signed the requisite papers. The next news was a letter from her warning us that he had left the hospital and found a job as a steward on a ship bound for Britain.

I still did not grasp the full hopelessness of the situation. I was still seeing the gentle, fair-haired, blue-eyed, witty younger brother I had adored. I recalled how, coming home from school and laying our report cards on the table, far from being abashed by the contrast between my good marks and his bad ones, he would have us all laughing by saying, 'Ah well, Jennie has the brains of the family but I have the good looks.' Often neighbours would say to Mother, 'What a nice lad your Tommy is. A proper gentleman.' Comment on me, though unspoken, was obvious. I was 'stuck-up'. He would never pass a friend or neighbour without a jovial word. I would not so much as look their way. I was not at all 'stuck-up'. I was far more in sympathy especially with the poorest in that mining community than my brother who, if the truth be told, was a bit of a snob. But I would be making for the library, or off on a country walk, my head in the clouds, living in my own bookish world and just not noticing anyone.

There is a lot of talk and research about how far we are made by our environment and how far by inherited characteristics. I don't know the answer and, as far as I can gather, neither does anyone else. But you had only to look at my brother and myself to see that I had inherited some of the toughness of Great-Grannie Jennie Pollock and her formidable daughter, my Grandmother Greig, while my brother had inherited some of the charm, the fecklessness and the fey Highland qualities of Grandfather Greig. My grandfather was a companionable man who loved his fiddle and his dram and was easy-going with his children, who all loved him. He earned his living as a mason and there were many days in the harsh Scottish climate when he and his workmates had to abandon outside work and foregather in the warmth of the back-room of a pub. They would pass the time with a dram and a song and the scrape of the fiddle. Their Scotland had changed little from the eighteenth-century Scottish village life that Robert Burns knew. No radio, wireless, cinema, disco-thèques, or brain-washing from the mass media. They had to make their own songs, their own music, their own talk, and talk they did about everything under the sun.

Grandfather Greig became so fond of his dram and his free-dom that he ended his days in lodging houses. He was the ne'er-do-well of the family, but my mother would not hear a word said against him. 'He had nae bad in him; he was an enemy only to himself,' she would say, then her face would light up as she told how when they were children he would make his fiddle say 'ma-ma, pa-pa', and lots of other delight-ful sounds his children enjoyed. By the time I was growing up he had become a wanderer. I saw a lot of Grandfather Lee, but nothing of Grandfather Greig. The only early memory I have of him is feeling very proud when someone pointed out to me stone figures adorning a building in Cowdenbeath High Street which were his work.

Maybe if my brother had not gone to Australia, had re-mained under the influence of his parents, and under my in-fluence, he could have been steadied into living a normal responsible life. I am not at all sure, but anyhow there was no holding him. He was determined to be off, not to the real Australia, but to a fantasy world of his own imagination. He expected quick and spectacular success. When this did not come he sheltered from reality first by heavy drinking, after having been brought up in a teetotal home, then by drugs. When I met him in Liverpool, jauntily walking down the gangway from the ship, I half knew something was far wrong, but all the memories of our young years together came flooding back. This was my brother. He had been ill. I would see he had the best possible medical attention. He would be his old self again.

There was no hope. For the next sixteen years as an Australian ex-Serviceman he had every care taken of him in Australian hospitals, then again and again, running away to London he had every possible treatment in our hospitals. Our home was also our parent's home. We could not turn him away. I was afraid for Nye. Harbouring a junkie! Although I seldom kept letters, I carefully hoarded every one my brother sent us. They set out the whole tragic story of his deterioration, and would be there to protect Nye if my brother involved us during one of his insane periods in a public scandal or court proceedings. Just how close I was to a complete collapse at that time is shown in a letter I wrote to Nye. But thank God I did not send it to him. Throughout my life some of the letters I wrote to one or two intimate friends or diary notes written in times of stress no doubt helped me. In this letter, dated 3 June 1957, I wrote:

I stand amazed when I watch you respond so ably to problems put to you and jobs imposed on you, against the desolation and nihilism of your spirit. I am left naked and lame. I don't have your virtuosity. I have to have something to sustain me. Every human being can be helped to be their best self or reduced by discouragement to a breakdown of the whole organism, physical and emotional . . . I have given more time to your problems, when you are under heavy strain, than to my own, for I have not seen them as separate . . . But every human being must have *some* living room. The spirit has to be fed as well as the body . . . We are all queer creatures. In the end the spirit dominates. I do not know what 'spirit' means precisely, neither do you. My poor sick mother could tell both of us better than any professor, but I do know that my spirit is not strong enough to take all the punishment it has had to take in recent times.

I am tormented by the thought that in writing to you at all, I am being abominably selfish. I am not sure about anything except that through all the pain and frustration of these days you remain very precious to me. I don't want you hurt. I don't know quite what to do for the best. Shut up, and take the consequences, sit tight on the safety valve, ease things a little by small squeals that humiliate me more than they annoy you, or pretend I am being 'unselfish' by not asking for your co-operation, by deceiving you into believing that all is well, that a sick woman needs only a few more vitamin pills and she will cease bothering about anything except the weeds in her garden.

I say again, thank God I held on to enough sanity not to send that letter. I thought it had been destroyed long ago, but along with so much else it has survived among my private papers. When I talk of Nye's 'desolation and nihilism of spirit' I am talking of myself, not of Nye. He had dark moods in that summer of 1957 as the problems presented to all of us by nuclear weapons pressed in on our consciousness, but he was more hopeful than despairing. He was looking forward to the parliamentary recess when we could escape together to Asheridge, to the privacy of our home and the pleasures of country life that meant so much to him.

In my sick state I thought I was deceiving him about my troubles, while the truth was he was all too aware of what I was going through, and his unfailing tenderness sustained me more than I was capable of realizing. At the very time I wrote that mad letter that I was not quite mad enough to address and post, he was staying with our Mackie friends in Scotland and in a letter to me he wrote:

Darling Jennie,

You sounded very depressed last night on the phone, and you left me very anxious about you. I do hope nothing more serious upset you than a passing mood. I went to bed full of worries and conjectures about you. I realize your vitality is low now, particularly when you need it most ... Darling, I love you very much and am always upset when I think you are worried or unwell. So please buck up and remember we have a whole summer ahead of us to spend at the farm. You must hug the thought of our secret happiness and not let public duties weigh on you too heavily.

In a situation where Mother and Nye had both come to a time in their lives when they needed a great deal of tender care, what should I have done? Resigned from Parliament?

That is how some women would have eased matters. The reason why there are so few women MPş is not just because of prejudice on the part of the selection committees. That still exists although personally I never met with it. That kind of obstacle will lessen as more women by upbringing and temperament free themselves from age-old assumptions that we are all alike and all must be confined to the domestic sphere. Some women can be completely happy caring for their home and family. My mother would say rather complacently to our unfailing delight, 'I never had to work.' She, who was first up, often last to go to bed, who would have thought it immoral to lie down in the middle of the day? What she meant was that she had never had to go out to work. She was the most hard-working of her mother's daughters in the old hotel days, fretted when her life became too easy after my brother and I left home, and was 'in her glory', to use her own words, once she came south to look after Nye and me as well as my father. She was a superb 'professional'. Everything got done without fuss or bother. I think of her when I hear a woman say apologetically, when asked what she does, 'I am only a housewife.' That is what social conditioning has done: the work of the cook, cleaner, nurse, gardener and the hundred and one other skills which go to the making of a good home down-graded in comparison with the relatively simple business of pounding a typewriter, working in a shop or a factory, or for that matter in a lawyer's office or in Parliament.

But there are other women, and I am one of them, who are not suited to a life confined to the home, however much we may love a good home as the background to our lives. It would have made matters worse, not better, if I had given up my political work. As soon as I could walk I was trotting behind my father, enthralled by his songs, his stories, all he was doing. That was where my interest lay. I was incapable of cooking and a hopeless blunderer in other domestic tasks. I had never been interested to learn those skills and had never had need of them. I was as helpless as an old-fashioned male. My parents helped me to do the work I wanted to do, but not many women are so fortunate. The tug of domestic ties can be a greater barrier to women entering Parliament than the prejudices of selection conferences. How many women can leave husbands or children or maybe an invalid or ageing parent for days, sometimes weeks at a time while they are engaged in public work? There is also the expense of paying for someone else to keep the home fires burning while the politically orientated woman is absent from home. Women with a well-to-do family background have an obvious advantage. That is one more reason why there are so few working-class women in Parliament.

There was not much I could hide from Nye. Then and always he knew more about me than I knew myself. Never once did his concern give place to irritation while I was going through this difficult time in our lives. For myself, I can say just this. He never saw my diary notes or the despairing letter I wrote to him when I was struggling against pressures and frustrations that had become too much for me. Later in the summer, travelling together or at home together in the parliamentary recess enabled me to regain my balance, but at times it was still hard going. On 13 February 1958 I made a list in my diary of all the things I had to attend to. I wrote:

Arrived at Gosfield Street off night sleeper from Cannock. Ni's shoulder and neck very bad. Jack in to massage him. Ni in despondent mood about party affairs. Must get into a reasonable flat before the end of the income tax year. Earnings from journalism here and abroad and broadcasts and rise in parliamentary salary have drastically changed our position, so must spend more on elementary comfort and machinery. Not possible before financially. Now the irony is, physical difficulties in the way. Every flat-hunting project hopeless. Rents anywhere near the House of Commons fantastic. We shall end up underspending because anything in the least suitable far too dear. The West End property prices don't belong to this world. No use having a flat unless in walking distance to the House. Traffic congestions would make it impossible to reach. Vexed that last night Ni, very tired, came back to this cheerless place and no food or anything for him. He hates restaurants. Ni hopelessly dependent on having me around.

Will be glad when we can get into a more reasonable design for living and working – or does that never come? Ma at eighty needs constant care and attention. Bab Wilson leaves for Dundee on Monday, Jenny, Duncan, Elsie and young Duncan arrive Saturday, Katherine our housekeeper in hospital having a baby so it is going to be one more of those weekends when Ni and I have to look after everyone else when we so badly need to be looked after. Have cancelled Alfred Hecht and Howard. Hard on Ni that for the first time in his life he has a home where he cannot with safety so much as ask a friend to a meal. The top priority is that Ma is kept as happy as possible but what other man would give so much?

Have cancelled spring visit to Kashmir. Cannot possibly go so far with Ma and Ni so much in need of a great deal more care than they would then have. This period hopelessly tangled and wearing. Housekeeper ill, daily woman ill, farm manager ill and useless, holding the place together with emergency help, paid, and services from friends. But friends, however loving, have their own lives and commitments, not available often when most needed. Peggy [secretary] back this week after being off ill since end of December. Joyce Wheeler a charming emergency aid. If free I would have asked her to be a resident secretary when we get a suitable flat but she is better off in her present civil service job. Bank statement lost or mislaid. Have asked Peggy to telephone Cheshire and we shall search this weekend. But it is really going to the verge of insanity to carry the mounting responsibilities of these days without more help.

Priorities for both of us always our public work and for me Ni's needs before my own. This puzzles some people. What they do not understand is that it has nothing to do with husband and wife relationship, but that Ni does the things I want done better than I can do them myself, so is worth sustaining. But we have now reached a point when private chores must be carried for us a great deal more, both on the domestic side and political side or our effectiveness is bound to be seriously impeded. That has already happened to me and has been going on too long. Now I must stop and think and get some order out of improvisation. I might have said chaos but it is chaos only about small things. There is nothing chaotic about how Ni does his public work Worried though to see him look so tired. Sixty is a watershed. Neither of us can take the present situation much longer...

Just had Rochdale election result. All jubilant except Ni. He says it will turn out to be a disaster for the Labour Party. A revival in the Liberal Party will enable it once more at a critical moment to sell out to the Tories. Looks as if critical moments will be plentiful. Added to hydrogen war fears there is now the American slump. Five million unemployed by next month. Britain's problems by the autumn can be desperate. But prophesy is no good. The unexpected usually happens.

The first thing I had to do once I began to be well again was to look at our bank account. What could we afford? The irony of the situation was that we now had a better income than at any previous time but had been too busy to spend it sensibly. Until *L'Express* began syndicating Nye's weekly article he wrote and spoke for socialist causes unpaid. I did too, except for my American lecture tours. Any addition to our income from an occasional article in the non-socialist press was negligible. Now our parliamentary salaries had been increased and were augmented by payments for the syndicated articles.

In London we had rented an appallingly furnished two-roomed flat that did not even have a bath. It was simply a camp where we could sleep those mid-week evenings when Parliament sat until midnight or later, and we were unable to drive home. I decided I must make a further effort to find and furnish a small flat near the House of Commons that would give us a civilized base in London. I was good on the furnishing front. I knew where to look for old pieces; no more modern stuff, thank you. My most cherished possession is a chair that I got Nye to carry back on his head from the Caledonian market. It cost five shillings. All this time, the disciplines of a lifetime ensured that neither of us neglected our constituency and parliamentary work. I came close to doing so, but was now slowly climbing back up the slippery slope from the depths of nervous exhaustion that had almost destroyed me. Once our housekeeper and farm manager were well enough to be back at work, I began to cope with the changes in our home life now that we had to do much that formerly my mother had done for us.

My one real sacrifice was having to refuse an invitation from the University of Jammu and Kashmir to deliver some extension lectures there. I was fascinated by the beauty of so much of India as well as by the complexity of its social and economic problems. Other invitations that would have meant spending time away from home I also declined. There could be no neglect of constituency and parliamentary duties, but the rest of my time and strength was needed at Asheridge. I like getting my own way. I have a strong ego. But my love for Nye and for my mother was stronger still. It was that more than anything else that helped to free me from the crushed, strangled feeling that had driven me close to madness.

23. Confusion and Strife over Nuclear Disarmament

During the summer of 1957 an awareness of all the horrendous consequences that nuclear power could let loose on all of us took possession of the minds and imagination of the active members of the Labour Party as they met to prepare their resolutions for the Annual Party Conference in the autumn. All else was dwarfed by comparison.

When not travelling abroad Nye and I spent every moment we could in the seclusion of our Asheridge home. But just as the peace of our first country cottage was shadowed by the news from Europe of what was happening to Hitler's victims in the period immediately before the Second World War, we were now obsessed by the horror and magnitude of the new threat to mankind. What to do? How best to act? I must not give the impression that we thought of nothing else. Nye had the great gift of knowing how to change gear; I mean by that how to set aside political preoccupations for a time while we entertained friends who came and went, or while he tried to teach me to share his capacity for total absorption in the music he loved so much, or as we went off on voyages of discovery in the surrounding fields and woodlands. Then he loved to pester Ma in the kitchen as he enjoyed an experimental kind of cooking. They concocted between them all kinds of dishes, I taking not the slightest interest beyond maybe setting a table worthy of their expertise. I seldom helped in the kitchen. This was not just laziness or selfishness. It was that my mother had always been so quick and skilled that she preferred to have the kitchen to herself. This suited both of us, for I had had to make my way by winning scholarships, and that kind of work I did well because I enjoyed it. We were each experts in our own way and had a perfect understanding.

Another favourite recreation with Nye was visiting the local fishmonger, butcher and wine merchant. Again I was uninterested and a complete ignoramus, but he knew his way about and was on cordial terms with the shop assistants. He was quite at home wandering into the rear of the shops and making his own discerning selections. Nor did he forget to parade his own expertise, for had he not learned all the secrets of the butchery business as a butcher's assistant in Tredegar while still a schoolboy? On one occasion when I was shopping with him I wondered a little uneasily what a leading Conservative businessman could make of us. We were buying wellingtons for Nigel, a small boy who was holidaying with us. When he was duly fitted he said, 'Thank you, Uncle Nye. I shall take those home with me.' 'Oh no, you will not,' Nye sternly replied. 'These remain at Asheridge. They are part of the farm capital.'

Later on, anyone listening to Nye and Nigel bargaining about wage rates would also have heard some surprising exchanges. The two farm men we employed good-naturedly allowed the child to work with them. This was his first job. He was earning his pay by the sweat of his brow. But he did

I Nigel Samuel accept
the sum of 32/- in full discharge
of any claim I may have
on Mr Aneurin Bevan for the work
done by me on Asheridge Farm
the year of our Lord 1957.

Signed Nigel Samuel
Countersigned Nye Bevan

not think sixpence an hour was an adequate wage. The men, having a bit of fun, told him he must insist on a higher rate, a shilling if possible, but no settling for less than ninepence. So battle was joined. At the end of a happy but exhausting day the youngster had had his bath and come to join us in pyjamas and dressing-gown, I thought he would be glad to slip off to bed immediately after supper. But not a bit of it. Nye had a labour dispute on his hands. As we sat round the fire I was amused listening to the two of them. At point one I heard Nye saying, 'Then of course there is your keep.' A scandalized child's voice piped up, 'But, Uncle Nye, I am your guest.' They were having a good time pitting their wits against one another. Finally, Nye drew up a contract which they both formally signed.

When looking through old papers I found that it had somehow survived, which is why I recall so vividly this particular romp among so many others. Ours was a good home for children, that is, when we were living in the country. They could have lots of freedom, Ma to cook for them, Nye to entertain them, and myself keeping a watchful eye to see that all was well. I have always been fond of children, but have never had any urge to produce my own. 'None or a litter,' Nye would say. I was quite content so long as we had one another, were able to look after my parents, help to maintain a home for Nye's widowed mother in Tredegar, enjoy the companionship of friends and meet conscientiously the strenuous demands of our public responsibilities. I could not have carried out my political duties and at the same time have reared a family, so it is just as well that I had no urge to do so. There was also the forward thrust of fascism over Europe with little evidence that our Tory Establishment had any real will to resist. What a world in which to bring children! Of course none of that would have counted if I had had what so many women have, that is a deep need for motherhood.

When Nye was thinking aloud or talking with friends, one theme that began to appear more and more was whether we had not forfeited for good the place we might have occupied in the world. Had our failure to strike out on an independent course, friendly to all but subservient to none, done us irreparable harm? Did we matter any more on the wider world stage? But these gloomy thoughts would pass, and never more so than in the days leading up to the 1957 Conference of the Labour Party. The line taken by the Socialist International that summer buoyed up his hopes. Our visit to Khrushchev strengthened his belief that all was by no means lost. We must strike out for disengagement in Europe, oppose the rearming of Germany, create an anti-nuclear club of the nations that did not yet have nuclear weapons. We ourselves should be ready to give up testing and making the bomb, even though we had the know-how, and in this way strengthen and inspire the non-aligned nations.

These were Nye's views. Now as always he sought the most effective way of transforming abstract guidelines into action. It was this that brought about the violent revulsion against him during that Brighton Conference. The vote in favour of unilateral nuclear disarmament was 781,000: the vote against 5,836,000. But these figures do not give the true picture of the divisions among wounded, highly emotional Conference delegates. Nye had spoken from the platform for the Executive, and the block votes of the big unions were massed on the side of official party policy. But among the great majority of activists in the local Labour Parties, feeling was passionately and rigidly on the side of a declaration in favour of immediate unilateral nuclear disarmament. Year after year at our Annual Conferences we abolish public schools, the House of Lords, health charges, and much else besides, the resolutions ranging from what we could hopefully look forward to achieving in the future to others that belonged to cloud-cuckoo-land. They set out the yearnings of idealistic men and women, most of whom worked hard during the year at constituency level to bring about a democratic socialist Britain.

Nye's dilemma at Brighton that year was that as Shadow Foreign Secretary he had either to resign from that position or accept the majority view of the NEC. If the vote in the NEC had gone in favour of unilateral nuclear disarmament he would have explained to the Conference that they had now to give their minds to the problem of how best to make their good intentions a reality. Obviously one essential was to get rid of the Tory Government and establish a Labour Government with a substantial working majority. Only then could we get down to business. But nothing could have done more to damage the prospects of winning the General Election we then thought was due very soon than Nye going off once more into the wilderness, and on what he thought was a distinction without a difference. It was not a question of wanting or not wanting to lessen the danger of nuclear war. It was how this could best be done. Nye was ardently concerned to win the coming General Election. The stakes were too dangerously high for any personal considerations to matter, although he dreaded the struggles that would confront him with Hugh Gaitskell as Prime Minister and himself as Foreign Secretary. But this was one more challenge, and the hardest of all he had had to meet in his long life of fighting against impossible odds. He could not run away from it.

There were those in the Parliamentary Labour Party and on the NEC who would have been all too happy if he had refused to accept the majority decision of the NEC, but although not a romantic, in the sense of imagining that one man could change the course of history if the currents were too strongly against him, he did believe that as Foreign Secretary at that particular time he could capitalize on his relations with the non-aligned countries, with Khrushchev and with some powerful American friends, in ways that might make a worthwhile contribution to reducing world tensions. That was his objective. Nye knew he would be hotly opposed by many of the conference delegates, but what took him by surprise and threw him off his balance was the venomous nature of much of that opposition. Were these his friends? Were these the comrades he had fought for over so many years? Could they really believe that he was a small-time career politician prepared to sacrifice his principles in order to become second-in-command to the right-wing leader of the Party?

The night before the crucial debate Sam Watson, and some other trade union leaders who were personally well disposed towards Nye, urged him not to divide the party at the very time when if we held together we could win the coming Election. Later in the evening Hugh Gaitskell knocked at our bedroom door and handed Nye a typewritten copy of the speech he intended to deliver the following day. It lay on the dressing-table unread. Neither of us felt any urge to read it, we knew what Hugh intended to say. Nye was giving all his thoughts to what he himself would say.

He did not have even me on his side. I did not argue with him that evening, he had to be left in peace to work things out for himself, but he was in no doubt that I would have preferred him to take the easy way. I dreaded the violence of the Conference atmosphere which I knew would be generated by the dedicated advocates of immediate unilateral nuclear disarmament, but, like Nye, I did not foresee the bitterness of the personal attacks made by some delegates who ought to have known him well enough not to have doubted his motives. Disagreement was one thing: character assassination quite another. The Tory press gleefully announced 'Bevan into Bevin'. The right wing of the Party, to use latter-day jargon, kept a low profile. It was the left wing who were in full voice. We were all engulfed in a tidal wave of uncontrollable emotion. Anyone reading Nye's speech to the Conference, now that time makes it possible for us to do so without our eyes blinded by the hysteria of the atmosphere then, will see that he asked the delegates to play for higher stakes than they had in mind. 'Give me a chance,' he pleaded, 'to see what a Labour Government can do. If we fail to influence other nations, we can always fall back on unilateral action.' Considering that Nye had not even convinced me before he made his speech it is not to be wondered at that he took so many of the delegates completely by surprise. We were comfortably on the tram-lines. Why could he not just go along with us?

The Annual Conference takes place in the autumn. We had been abroad or at home most of the summer months, which meant that no educational campaign had been carried out with opportunities for Nye to explain how he had been influenced by his contacts with leaders of the Socialist International and with Khrushchev. It was part of his hopefulness at that time that he believed Britain could influence world opinion substantially. He wanted to tackle the job in what he considered to be the most effective way. Even now, after more than twenty years, I can hardly bear to recall that Conference and its aftermath. Nye had flourished on hard-fought political battles with Conservatives and with the right wing of the Labour Party. He was used to fighting hard for what he believed in and expected others to fight just as hard. 'This is my truth, now tell me yours,' was, as I have already said, one of his favourite quotations. But this was something new. We both believed in keeping our armour on in public. If you are in a fight you must expect to be hurt, but you must not rejoice your enemies and distress your friends by allowing the extent of your hurt to be known. Now we were both being guarded with one another in private. Nye tried to hide from me just how mortal the wounds were that had been inflicted on him by many of those he had been closely associated with over the years. It was not their disagreement that had darkened his life. It was the sheer malignity of some of the remarks hurled at him and the poison pen letters sent to him.

When he said to me as we sat quietly by our fireside, 'I can just about save this Party, but I shall destroy myself in doing so,' I turned his thoughts to the immediate sensuous world around us and did not ask him to explain. Long-winded explanations were never our way. To Hugh and Margaret Delargy and other friends I learned later he had used those same words. Destroy himself? I was not alarmed about his health at that time. The only thing that worried me in that respect was when he had a heavy chest cold. The wheezing roused all my fears that it might be the beginning of something worse – the dreaded miners' disease, pneumoconiosis. Otherwise he had great strength and resilience, much more than I had. The knowledge that after the election, if we won, he would have to fight for what he considered Britain's rightful place in the councils of the world, with Gaitskell continually trying to interfere, was not a cheerful prospect, but he had braced himself for this stage in the struggle.

Following the Brighton Conference a number of lectures were arranged for him in America so that he could begin to undo the bogy-man image of him depicted in their press as well as our own. Afterwards Adlai Stevenson wrote to him saying, 'I can report with fair accuracy that your visit was an unqualified success. I gather it may even have been helpful in Washington.' Leading banking and business associations he had addressed wrote letters of thanks to him which went beyond the demands of mere politeness. He was still lampooned in the popular press, but many of the people at the centre of things in America had discovered that, however much they might disagree with him, he was not the crude lout they had been led to expect.

Throughout 1958 the Campaign for Nuclear Disarmament went from strength to strength and Michael Foot, who was editing *Tribune*, gave front-page prominence to the slogan: 'The paper that leads the anti-H-bomb Campaign.' When I had time to reflect seriously about it all, I had come round to accepting Nye's point of view. I was furious with Michael. Besides being editor, he was one of *Tribune*'s three directors, the other two being Howard Samuel and myself. Michael had richly earned the right to have his point of view forcefully stated. But what about Nye? Had he no rights? Were only letters and comments traducing his point of view to be published? Michael is of the breed who will go to the stake for their convictions. He passionately disagreed with Nye and refused to give equal prominence to their differing views. The more sensitive and imaginative the mind, the fiercer the impact of that first realization of the yawning hell opened up at our feet by all that nuclear warfare could mean. No two men had a greater share of sensitivity and imagination than Michael and Nye. But at one time, so tense was the strain on their relationship that they almost came to blows. Michael's gifted wife, Jill Craigie, was the peacemaker. She also helped me to understand that however harsh the strains on Nye and myself, Michael and she were also almost at breaking-point.

Since 1945 Michael had had to carry the main burden of seeing that *Tribune* came out each of the fifty-two weeks of the year. In addition to the editorial burden he had worried himself sleepless over circulation, financial and general business matters. Every time someone came along, from Woodrow Wyatt to Bob Edwards, who lightened his burden, the relief was only transitory. More attractive offers were made to them and accepted. As Jill put it, that made Michael a kind of permanent schoolmaster, bringing on the bright pupils, then losing them and finding the basic grind once more on his shoulders. Howard Samuel and Jack Hylton gave financial support to *Tribune* in order to help Nye, whose political views they shared. It did not seem to me nor to them to make any sense for them to continue to do so in that 1958 atmosphere. Michael wanted it all his own way. He would not permit either of his two fellow directors to have any say in the running of the paper. That made me bloody-minded, but Nye persuaded his friends to continue to support *Tribune*. No doubt that was sound liberal doctrine, but I was not by temperament as good a liberal as all that.

By the autumn Conference of 1958 once more the political climate was changing. There was no protest when Nye made a long detailed speech on foreign affairs. He was given an ovation. I was elected a member of the Women's Section of the NEC. In the Shadow Cabinet elections, instead of coming last in the poll, Nye came first. We believed that the long-delayed General Election could not be postponed much longer. Right, left and centre, we had all at least one thing in common: we were all anxious to win it and therefore this was no time to highlight our differences. But there was no joy, none of the old elan as Nye went about his duties. There was no easy comradeship with many of his former friends, and he had never been in close social contact with the right of the party. There were exceptions of course in both wings, but it was friends from abroad who best understood and sustained him. In the spring of 1959 *L'Express* arranged a conference in Paris, inviting among others Mendès-France, Nenni and Nye. It took place instead at Asheridge, as Nye was not well enough to travel to Paris. He was convalescing after his usual weakness – a severe chest cold. Mendès-France was accompanied by Jean-Jacques Servan-Schreiber, Karol Kewes, and other members of the *L'Express* staff. Nenni brought his friend and patron, Dino Gentili, with him. There was just room round our dining-table for the principal guests, including Cartier-Bresson. It was a strict rule with us not to allow press photographers into our home, but our Parisian friends did not know this. I was quite unaware that photographs were being taken by the unobtrusive man in the background. I am glad of this exception, for the work of this superb artist-photographer brings back a hopeful and memorable get-together.

Our good fortune was that 'The Blue Ball', a pub within five minutes walk of the farm, had as its landlord a friendly north-countryman who shared our political views. His lively wife, Ann, was equally friendly. They did not do catering, but as a favour to us provided lunch for the accompanying secretaries and drivers. This was the least of the favours they did us. Every time there was a real or manufactured political crisis, a swarm of journalists would drive out from London and alight at 'The Blue Ball'. Besides quenching their thirst, they were hunting for news, and news meant unearthing any bit of dirt or scandal they could take back to an approving editor to be used against Nye. What they did not know was that as soon as they appeared either Ann or her husband went quietly to their back-room and telephoned us. We then closed all doors and windows and all farm and garden gates. In the pub the locals as well as the managers – it was a tied house – had nothing to say to the gentlemen of the press.

One summer day when Nye and I sauntered down to the 'The Blue Ball' in the cool of the evening when the Fleet Street boys had departed, we were greeted with boisterous laughter. Our friends had become bored with being prodded by journalists, so decided to give them a belly-full. They retailed such outrageous tales about Nye that the press men realized they were being taken for a ride. After that press tactics changed. They came right up the narrow lane leading to the farmhouse and planted an enormous contraption immediately outside the garden gate. It beamed lights on to the farmhouse and took photographs. If we had been trapped there it would have been impossible for us to get through to our home. They would have had us cornered. But again the press boys were outwitted. As we were driving home late at night, a light flashed in front of us from the side of the road below 'The Blue Ball'. It was our farm manager, who had been alerted by Ann, as had my mother, who was cheerfully and calmly waiting for us behind drawn curtains and locked doors. As she had said to Margaret Delargy on the occasion when the hall carpet of our London home had been set on fire, she was never a coward. We had been to a party that evening. I was wearing a long dress and high-heeled shoes. Scrambling round muddy fields and over hedges with my shoes repeatedly sticking in the mud so that I had to be half-carried, was not exactly fun. But at last we were able to steal like thieves into our back kitchen.

While Mendès-France and Nenni were with us at Asheridge, Nye was vibrantly alert and showed no sign of fatigue. Yet I recall that at one moment when he was perched on the window-sill talking to Mendès-France I looked at him, and for the first time I wondered if there might be something seriously wrong with him. That was in the spring of 1959. But Nye's resilience asserted itself once again. Besides carrying on his normal parliamentary and constituency duties he went off to

Russia in September as a member of an official Labour Party delegation. Hugh Gaitskell had been tactless as usual. Nye had made every possible effort to hold the Party together, including telling the delegates to the 1958 Conference that the leadership issue was settled. We had one and all to concentrate on defeating the Tories. He was indignant therefore when as Deputy Leader he was not consulted, but simply informed that the delegation to Russia would consist of Gaitskell, Denis Healey, himself and wives. Nye did not look forward to this trip but had to go; as Shadow Foreign Secretary he could not refuse, especially as he had been urging more direct contacts with the Russian leaders. But I had not the slightest wish to return to Russia in such circumstances. Karol Kewes took my place. The Russian authorities were helpful in arranging a last-minute visa for Karol. As he spoke Russian he was not only a congenial companion for Nye, but was also most helpful. On his return Nye enjoyed telling of the fun he had had reciting a love poem by Joseph Dietzgen, author of *The Positive Outcome of Philosophy*, to the solemn Russians who apparently knew only his Marxist writings.

This kind of official jamboree involved a continual round of rich meals and endless toasts. Before returning to London, Hugh Gaitskell was due to address a gathering of international journalists, but he was too unwell to do so – the copious toasts he was obliged to drink on the last evening of their visit had been too much for him. Nye covered up for Hugh. He took the Conference, and not the slightest hint was given of the cause of Hugh's indisposition. That was only common decency. Some of the journalists were quite well aware of why Hugh was under the weather, but not a word appeared in the press. That too was only common decency. But, oh boy, just think what some of those journalists would have made of it if it had been the other way round! There would have been no reticence then. 'Bevan too drunk to carry out his duties' would have screamed at us from the headlines.

Nye throughout his whole public life put up with a great deal of abuse and blatant misrepresentation without resorting to so much as a threat of legal action. His attitude was, 'They say, let them say. Let us get on with it.' Then he would be vaulting ahead to the next job that had to be done. Mischievous elements in Fleet Street would have been delighted to make replying to misrepresentations a full-time occupation for him. Once set on that course you have to keep it up, for when you fail to reply there is a good second story for the agile newspaper man. Aha! No denial! So the reader is left to infer that the press have reported truly. But Nye, like the rest of us, was not all of a piece. He could be tolerant and philosophical up to a point, but one thing he was not prepared to put up with was any suggestion that when sent abroad, in a representative capacity, instead of doing his job in a responsible manner, he was lurching around in a drunken condition. When the *Spectator* published an account of a Socialist International Conference in Venice which gave that kind of impression, an apology was all Nye asked for. It was only when this was refused that he began legal proceedings.

There was another element in the situation that counted heavily with Nye. He was no puritanical kill-joy. In his leisure hours when in holiday mood he enjoyed good wine and good company. But he was in Venice in a representative capacity on serious Party business, his expenses paid for by the hard-earned money of Party workers, including his own people in South Wales. They must not be allowed to believe that he had let them down. Anyhow, altogether, I can tell you he was blazingly angry. He was not going to have the disciplines he had imposed upon himself on public occasions all through the years made light of. Also his pride was hurt. This time, a venomously hostile Tory journal had gone too far and had to take the consequences.

24. Nye's Fight for Life

The long delayed date of the General Election – 8 October 1959 – was announced while the British delegation was still in Russia. Nye hurried home to Asheridge and prepared for his usual strenuous speaking tour. He had returned from Moscow in what I thought was fairly good shape. Throughout the campaign he was careful to guard his every word because he could not afford to have some chance aside blown up out of context as had happened to him so often before. He was desperately concerned that Labour should win. There was nothing personal in this; on the contrary he often talked of how much he longed for a sabbatical year. He did not grudge this privilege to his friend Yigal Allon, but when Yigal visited Asheridge on his way to St Antony's College, Oxford, he told him how much he would like to get the halter off his neck for a time. Yigal was a member of the Knesset, a joint editor of his party's paper, yet he could leave it all to study in Oxford with the knowledge that his seat in the Knesset and all his other political posts would be waiting for him when he returned to Israel. There could be no immunity from the daily grind for Nye. Our constitution did not permit a Member of Parliament to absent himself in order to devote a year to quiet study and reflection.

During the campaign all my recurrent fears for Nye's health returned when I switched on the television one evening. His appearance panicked me. His last meeting before the final weekend in his own constituency ought to have been in Michael Foot's constituency. By then he was too ill to reach Devonport. As soon as my own election was over I could not wait even for the following day to reach home. A friend drove me to Asheridge during the night. But once again Nye rallied.

Michael Foot had lost the Election. In his own words, when Jill and he visited Asheridge, 'Nye took special care to bind up the particular fresh wounds which I had received at Devonport. No prodigal son was ever welcomed with such a feast as my wife and I had at Asheridge that gloomy weekend.'

There was no coming together of the so-called Bevanites, but immediately following the Election Hugh Gaitskell gathered his ring-wing friends around him in his Hampstead home. They decided the party should change its name, abandon further measures of nationalization and much more of a profoundly reactionary nature. Having been routed, they were planning not to rally the Party and once more advance, but to make a headlong retreat. When Parliament resumed and again when a disconsolate Party met for a two-day conference in Blackpool, far from sharing this defeatist attitude, Nye again argued robustly for faith in our own distinctive socialist policies and philosophy:

I have enough faith in my fellow creatures in Britain to believe that ... when they realize that their new homes that they have been put into are mortgaged to the hilt, when they realize that the money lender has been elevated to the highest position in the land, when they realize that the refinements for which they should look are not there, that it is a vulgar society of which no decent person could be proud ... when the years go by and they see the challenge of modern society not being met by the Tories ... who are unable to exploit the resources of their scientists because they are prevented by the greed of their capitalism from doing so, when they realize that the flower of youth goes abroad today because they are not being given opportunities to use their skill and their knowledge properly at home, when they realize that all the tides of history are flowing in our direction, that we are not beaten, that we represent the future: then, when we say it and mean it, then we shall lead our people to where they deserve to be led.

This was Nye's conference. Delegates turned to him for the assurance that they had not fought and believed in vain. Even among traditionally right-wing delegates there was little enthusiasm for the timid call to retreat sounded by Hugh

Gaitskell and his friends. Now, as always at such times, Nye lavished all his wit and eloquence on binding the Party together. This was no time to maximize differences. Barbara Castle was Conference chairman that year and made a brilliant rousing speech on the opening day. Nye got everyone in a good mood when he said:

Yesterday Barbara quoted from a speech which I made some years ago and she said that I believed that Socialism in the context of modern society meant the conquest of the commanding heights of the economy. Hugh Gaitskell quoted the same thing. So Barbara and Hugh quoted me. I used to be taught as a boy, not at a university, but even in the board school, one of Euclid's deductions: if two things are equal to a third thing, they are equal to one another. If Euclid's deduction is correct, Barbara and Hugh are both equal to me, and therefore must be equal to one another. So we have a kind of Trinity. I am not going to lay myself open to a charge of blasphemy by trying to describe our different roles. I am not certain in which capacity I am speaking, whether as the father, the son or the holy ghost. But you will have seen that, despite the attempts which are made to exploit our differences of opinion, those differences are not really fundamental differences of a character that should divide this movement permanently.

So, in playful terms, but with his serious purpose understood by all, Nye raised the spirits of the delegates. Then he thrust home the essence of his creed:

I am not a Communist. I am a social democrat. I believe that it is possible for a modern intelligent community to organize its economic life rationally, with decent orders of priority, and it is not necessary to resort to dictatorship to do so. If I did not believe that, I would be a Communist; I would not be a capitalist. I believe that this country of ours and this movement of ours, despite our setbacks, nevertheless is being looked upon by the rest of the world as the custodian of democratic representative government.

He said a great deal more and was greeted with heartfelt cheers. There was nothing fake – and every delegate knew it – about his patriotism, his burning faith in his country and its people, and the contribution he believed we could and should make to the building of a better world. As we drove home to Asheridge, he said, 'One more Conference behind us.' There was an undercurrent of buoyancy in his tone. He had relished the affection and trust wafted to him from the body of the hall as much as he had suffered from the withdrawal of affection and trust by many of those same delegates two years before.

It was now time to begin to think about arrangements for Christmas. It always followed the same ritual. Sometime before Nye would pace up and down our sitting-room floor, damning and blasting its vulgar commercialism, and vowing he would have nothing to do with it. Mother paid not the slightest attention. She enjoyed herself assembling Christmas cards and presents for family children and children of friends who had any reason to expect what she called a 'minding' from us. By Christmas Eve the house was festooned with the cards friends had sent, and a large Christmas tree complete with glitter and lights and baubles, with an angel on top, delighted Ma as much as it did any child.

It was then that the depths of Nye's hypocrisy were exposed. He would turn to Mother in alarm to ask what about Johnnie or Jane or some other child who would be expecting a present. All was well. All had been remembered. When we called on friends during the Christmas season where there were children in the home, we took with us the traditional 'minding'. It was Nye who handed the gifts to the children, beaming down on them like a good old-fashioned Santa Claus. That was Nye. His head off in one direction, his heart in another. It was his pride and joy to rear choice, well-fattened capons to present to his friends at Christmas-time. If only they could have called to collect their bird that would have been all right with everyone. But on top of all the other preparations, to have to package and post the capons was just a bit much. We swore under our breath, but did not utter one word of complaint as we loved Nye too much to spoil his pleasure in spreading bounty all around.

This Christmas Vladimir Dedijer, his beautiful wife, Vera, and their three children were going to be with us. At that time

Vlado occupied a position in Yugoslav politics half-way between his friend Milovan Djilas and his leader, Marshal Tito. He had defended Djilas's right to express his views without necessarily agreeing with all of them.

After the Blackpool Conference, Nye had taken the advice of his doctor friend, Sir Daniel Davies, and agreed to go into the Royal Free Hospital on 27 December for treatment of a stomach ulcer. I was thankful to have friends and children with us that Christmas as it helped to keep the coming operation in the background. We did not talk about it and, whatever Nye may have thought, I was certainly anxious but not unduly alarmed. It would be a relief to get the operation over, as Nye for some time had been eating badly and losing weight.

On the day of the operation I waited, resting for most of the time in the top-floor bedroom of a friend's London home for news of how it was going. Hour after hour passed. I was sick with apprehension. This long time must mean that Nye's life was in danger. Then came the message that the operation was safely over and I could see him the following day. Those who have visited anyone immediately after a major operation will know the shock of that first reunion. Nye had just enough strength to turn his head towards me. All I said was, 'Darling, be on my side.' His wonderful eyes, expressive at all times and reflecting his every mood, signalled that he understood. He would fight to be well again. He was not going to leave me. He was not going to leave all he treasured so much in life in spite of the bad times. At that moment I did not know what I was asking. If I had known the full gravity of Nye's illness, would I have wanted him to go through the hell on earth he had to endure those next few months? I don't think so. It would not have made sense for either of us.

It was only the day before he had recovered sufficiently to be ready to come home that his doctor, Dan Davies, invited me to his home for lunch and told me for the first time that Nye had cancer. Why, why, I asked, did you not tell me this sooner? Because, Dan replied, if I had, Nye would have seen it in your eyes and we could not have pulled him through. At one point Nye insisted on knowing the prognosis. Meeting me in the corridor Dan handed me a sheet of paper with typewritten notes which he said were the laboratory findings. Would I give it to Nye? I did. He was satisfied. It set out clearly the full extent of the surgery that had taken place. Most of the stomach had been removed. But there was no mention of cancer.

There was a close bond of friendship between those two highly emotional Welshmen. Why did Dan act as he did? Was it because he could not bear to pronounce the death sentence on his friend? How can any of us ever know just how and why we behave as we do in times of uncertainty and stress? All I do know is that his only concern from first to last was to help his friend in every way he could.

The next day, when I called to take Nye home, he was fully dressed and sitting in a comfortable armchair that Dan had brought over from his home to soften the austerity of the small amenity ward in which Nye was being nursed. Nye had insisted of course on no special favours. He was a Health Service patient, not a private patient. But no one can prevent the avalanche of flowers that flow in to anyone who has been as much in the news as Nye was, nor the special care that anyone in his critical condition receives from devoted nurses and doctors. Nye's eyes were sparkling, he was cracking jokes with the barber who was trimming his hair and simply could not wait to get home. How was the farm? How was everything and everyone? He was as excited as a schoolboy released from the restraints of a boarding school, and savouring the joys of freedom to come.

I had made a pact with Nye's doctor and with Mr George Quist, the distinguished surgeon who had carried out the operation. There must be no disclosure to Nye of the most deadly part of his illness. He might live only six months, maybe a year, maybe several years. That was what I was told. And of course I was hoping for a miracle. I wanted him to have every scrap of happiness in the time that remained to him. If the recovery he was making one day failed to continue, if it became clear that he would have to be told the whole truth, then I must tell him, no one else. Not even Archie Lush, his closest friend, shared my knowledge. Everyone around Nye must help him enjoy life, not depress him. One wonderful June morning after Nye had been home for some time, he was up and dressed and had walked to the bottom of the valley before I was awake. He gathered roses from the garden, still wet with dew, and threw them on to my bed. Not being a romantic Welshman, I was aware of a number of small crawly creatures that had come in along with the roses, but of course I was not dull enough to mention them. 'Going in the right direction,' Nye said, mimicking me, for every time I saw any sign of improvement I was apt to say that.

As Nye's strength revived I had to deal as best I could with an endless stream of requests from friends and from the press to be allowed to call on him. It was early days. 'Don't force the pace, Nye,' I counselled him. But we decided it was time to allow a few of the more responsible newspaper correspondents to interview him. On 29 March the *Guardian* published the following:

Mr Bevan, who was speaking at his farm at Asheridge, Buckingham, with his wife, Miss Jennie Lee, beside him, said that his chief wish was to take this first opportunity of expressing publicly his deep gratitude for the treatment he received in hospital and for the letters of sympathy sent to him by people from all over the world.

'I cannot be more grateful than I am for the care and sustained attention I received at the Royal Free Hospital, both from my doctors and surgeons and the staff. I realize that they were under very considerable strain at the time, particularly because of the publicity they had to undergo. Only those who are acquainted with hospital administration will realize the ordeal they had to go through.'

Expressing his 'very warm thanks' for letters received, Mr Bevan said that many were 'very moving indeed'. It had been physically impossible for him to reply individually, and he hoped that the writers would 'take this acknowledgement, inadequate though it is, as an expression of my very grateful thanks for their thoughtfulness'. As well as letters of goodwill, offers to lend Mr Bevan country homes for his convalescence have come from all types of people. The homes offered 'range from caravans to castles', said Miss Lee.

Although still in an early stage of convalescence from his operation at the end of last year, Mr Bevan is not confined to bed. His present routine is to 'get up a little later than I used to do before the illness' and go to bed about ten or eleven o'clock.

Mr Bevan disclosed that since his return from hospital he had been doing a lot of reading. One of the books that had deeply impressed him had been J. B. Priestley's latest work on English literature, but he had not been reading political biographies.

'I understand that Mr Macmillan reads political biographies. I have never been able to achieve that degree of credulity. My experience of public life has taught me to know that most of them are entirely unreliable. I would rather take my fiction straight.'

He also denied that he had started writing his memoirs. There was 'no basis at all' in this rumour. 'I strongly disapprove of people in active public life writing their memoirs. They do nothing but mischief. If they tell the truth it is hurtful, but usually they don't tell the truth.' He had been reading newspapers avidly – 'it is my one form of continuous fiction' – and had been watching television much more than previously, without becoming in any sense an addict to the screen.

'I am depressed and horrified by the low standards of most of the programmes. There are one or two items that seem to be excellent. Hancock, for instance, is quite superb – in the best music-hall tradition. Most of the rest I find awful. The attempt to convey the theatre to television is really too dreary for words.'

Mr Bevan said that he had made his decision not to stand for reelection as Party Treasurer even before his illness. 'I do not think it is right to continue with both jobs. There is no foundation at all for the report that I am thinking of giving up the deputy leadership and retaining my position as Treasurer.'

Throughout the interview Mr Bevan was smiling and cheerful and evidently keen to get back to work. But his wife made it clear that she is determined to let him take no chances by a premature return to full activity. She would, she said, 'fight hard' to see that he gets a long enough break. 'He ought to have the fullest time in order to get back into fighting form.'

Nye meant every word of what he said in that interview. He

had no thought of retiring from active political involvement. He was spoiling to be back in the fight.

Among all the invitations from complete strangers as well as from personal friends offering us the hospitality of their homes while Nye was convalescing, we decided it would be pleasant to accept two – first, a short stay in Brighton, then later a more ambitious journey to the south of France. In France we would stay with Kathleen and Graham Sutherland. Alfred Hecht had commissioned Graham to paint Nye, and this Graham was keen to do. The plan was that Graham would work on the portrait while we were his guests.

I bought two summer dresses for this holiday we were both looking forward to so much, and while parading in front of Nye, showing them off, I began to laugh. He wanted to know what the joke was. I reminded him of the first time I had asked his judgement on something I was wearing. We were then living in Guilford Street and had not long been together. I had bought myself a leopard-skin coat. Nye was still in bed when I returned from shopping. He half-opened one sleepy eye, took one look at me and said, 'I don't mind you being a tart, but not at that price.' I fled back to the shop. It was a cheap, nasty imitation fur, not the sort of thing I would normally have fallen for, but an importunate salesman in a small shop off Shaftesbury Avenue had been too much for me. We all make mistakes!

All was going well. I kept my secret knowledge as far from my thoughts as I could and lived from day to day.

Incidentally, although Nye and Graham Sutherland enjoyed one another's company, the idea that got around that Nye, for malicious reasons, had persuaded Graham to do an unattractive portrait of Churchill is total nonsense. Nye knew nothing about this proposal until after the decision was taken by an all-party committee of Members of Parliament, who thought it would be a good idea to give Winston a present from his parliamentary colleagues on his eightieth birthday. But what to give? One more piece of silver? Winston had been deluged with gifts from every corner of the world, some of them of great value. He would soon be eighty. He was well provided with worldly goods – and you can't take it with you.

I was a member of this all-party committee. Mr Frank McLeavy, another Labour Member, later Lord McLeavy, suggested, 'What about a good likeness?' We all agreed this was worth thinking about. Why not a portrait of Winston painted by one of our most distinguished artists, a portrait of Churchill as a House of Commons man, a great Commoner, that could later find its permanent home in a suitable corner of the Palace of Westminster? Without a single dissenting voice we made this our choice. Various artists were suggested. I proposed Graham Sutherland. This was warmly received and our decision was unanimous.

Graham was commissioned by us to paint Churchill, the House of Commons man. The first hurdle was coping with Winston's desire to be painted in flowing ceremonial robes, but when he gave in on this point, the painting went ahead. Who could have foreseen the sequel? No gift was ever conceived with more good will and in complete good faith. I regret the public repudiation, the ill will and ultimate destruction of the painting. It has done Graham Sutherland's reputation no harm, but the whole affair has highlighted the less enlightened, indeed the childish side, of the great man whom, irrespective of party, we were seeking to honour.

Our friend, Lewis Cohen, had written to us to say that he was going to Israel in May and that if we cared to use his Brighton home we would find that his housekeeper would give us a warm welcome and would look after us well. I counted on Brighton air speeding Nye's recovery, and we had several friends in the vicinity so we would not be in any sense isolated. All was well for the first few days, then the bad time began. Nye was racked with pain. It was essential to get him home. Our friend's car and chauffeur were put at his disposal for the return journey.

Nye once again rallied and enjoyed being up and around the garden and the farm, but this did not last. He developed thrombosis, a swelling of his right leg and was again housebound. I was fast losing hope of any long period of recovery, but I must not on any account show what I was feeling. His doctor wanted him to return to the Royal Free. That he would not do, so we worked out a plan that ensured careful but unobtrusive nursing twenty-four hours of the day. A young nurse was sent out from London, but although she was more than helpful, Nye rebelled against her presence: he found it uncongenial to have a uniformed nurse fussing over him. Jack Buchan was a skilled physiotherapist, as well as a friend. Nye was used to having him around and his doctors knew that Jack could be trusted to give the injection each night needed to ensure pain-free sleep, and to do all the rest of the tasks that could only be done by a trained nurse. Trude was staying with us at the time as she was between jobs. No one could look less like a regular nurse than this young Austrian, but she was totally reliable.

Jack and she teamed up as Nye's day-time nurses and I was his night nurse. One morning he woke earlier than usual, and asked for one of his pain-killing tablets. I said he could have one if he wished, but that Jack wanted him to have it a bit later. He turned over on his side, went to sleep again, muttering, not wrathfully, but just sleepily, 'That bloody Nazi.' When I went to Jack's bedroom and tapped him on the shoulder to wake him, I reported faithfully how the night had gone. Jack had the gift of being sound asleep one moment and wide awake the next. When I told him Nye's remark, his face lit up as if he had been given some wondrous award. Only Nye, we agreed, could make a curse sound like a caress.

Every other forenoon either Sir Dan or Mr George Quist drove out from London and sometimes they came together. We would carry up coffee with brandy or tea with whisky, and hear laughter coming from the bedroom. They were talking about everything under the sun except Nye's illness. He quizzed them sharply at times for Nye had quite a lot of medical knowledge, but they kept their promise to me. These two distinguished medical men who were giving so much of their time driving out to Asheridge, knew they were not nursing a future Foreign Secretary or Prime Minister. They had no thought of reward. They knew Nye had not long to live. So too with Jack Buchan. Other friends were fervently anxious to help in any way they could.

We could not save Nye. All we could do was try to keep him as free as possible from pain. It helped to keep a cheerful atmosphere that Jack, who had gone through an agonizing time a few years before when his young wife had died of lung cancer and who had lived alone since then, had fallen in love with Trude. But she was not yet sure. You can imagine the teasing they had to put up with from Nye's impish tongue. Then there were the tidal waves of good wishes that came to him from every point of the political compass and from all over the world. This all helped. Spiritually he recovered from the wounds inflicted by the unilateral disarmers in 1957 and 1958, but they had done their deadly work. Until their attacks began, he never had so much as a stomach ache. Severe colds and congested shoulder muscles which often had to be massaged were his health problems. It was my stomach he worried about, not his own. Until almost the last days of his life Nye would sit up in bed or in an armchair by the window planning ahead. The legend that he died a broken, defeated man is just one more of the lies that were told about him. He expected to be well again and the overwhelming assurances he received that so many people were anxious to see him back in public life helped to restore his old eagerness.

In an introduction to a new edition of his book *In Place of Fear* published in 1961, the year after his death, I wrote:

I am grateful to the wide world of friends whose loving, urgent, passionate words came breaking around us in one tidal wave after another, during his last long illness. I know how much they helped. Ni was thinking and planning ahead, taking an almost sensuous pleasure in using his beautiful mind, to his last moment of consciousness. He never knew defeat.

That is how it was. In the end he went quietly to sleep. The gentle, unpretentious husband of Nye's younger sister was

with him during the last moments of his life as well as Jack.
We thought it prudent to have a member of Nye's family present at this late stage. I had been with Nye all the previous
night and was at once awakened and taken to his bedside.
Grief came after. My first emotion was thankfulness that there
had been no last-minute awareness that we had deceived him.
That was what I had so much dreaded. Nye's doctors had
entrusted Jack with the drugs needed to hold back pain and
ensure sleep. For days before the end, I did not say anything,
I just looked at Jack imploringly. He knew what was in my
mind. I need not have feared. No man was ever nursed with
greater love or greater skill.

If I had to live through that time again would I have behaved differently? No. I could not save his life, but at least
after all he had suffered he was given time to recover from the
emotional scars that shortened his life. He was looking forward to that visit to France, talking even about the next
Annual Conference of the Party. 'You always wanted a sabbatical year,' I reminded him, 'so forget about the Conference.
You have often said that public life is as much a test of vitality
as of anything else. No one will grudge you all the time you
need to get your strength back.'

The stomach ulcer that killed Nye was brought on by tension and repression. He was too proud to show his wounds in
public, and in private what he most cared about was hiding
from me as much as he could of the abuse that was being
heaped upon him. I do not have Nye's charity or breadth of
vision. Even now the old bitterness wells up inside me when I
recall the depth of his sadness during the hysterical attacks on
him by some anti-bomb warriors who ought to have known
better. Of course they were not all like that. Michael Foot and
Nye, for instance, quarrelled violently. But there was no
poison in the blows they rained on one another for neither
doubted the other's integrity.

I telephoned Michael the day before Nye's operation and
told him to go to the hospital, take several books with him,
have a good rough argument, make Nye feel everything was

normal. In his life of Nye, Michael records that Nye was in a teasing mood, in the best of good spirits. The nearest they came to an argument was when Nye rebuked Michael for his 'quixotry' in standing again for his native Devonport although Nye had warned him he could not possibly win there. 'Now you must look properly for another seat,' Nye went on, adding, 'Perhaps you need not look further than Ebbw Vale.' Michael told him not to talk rubbish and they went on to speak of other things. 'All was back to normal between us,' Michael concluded.

It was to Michael I turned in the first terrible days after Nye's death. I could not rest. There was so much that had still to be done. I had listened to a BBC broadcast, allegedly about Nye, that was a complete travesty. Hardly a single friend who had known him back through the long years and had understood him and shared his views, was included in that programme. I wrote off to Michael in spluttering indignation. He replied:

I agree we must watch most carefully what is written and said about Nye and of course I agree with you that a great deal will have to be said by those who really knew him. I know it is too early to think of such matters, but I think you should decide to write Nye's full political biography. Nobody else knows the full truth in anything like the same sense. The whole movement requires to be re-educated. I believe that if you decided to do it, it would be a political act of the first importance.

I had neither the strength nor the skill at that time to be able to write coherently about Nye, even if I had wished to do so. Instead I continued to lean on Michael. On 6 July, the day after Nye died, I had written to him:

Dear Michael,
Ni is asleep next door. Later today he will be taken home to Wales. Tomorrow he will be cremated in keeping with his known views. It will be near Tredegar, a small family gathering. Later in the week, a memorial service will be held in Tredegar to give a chance to his own

people to ease their sore hearts. Later still a suitable memorial and place in the hills will be found.

I wrote to Donald Soper and to Mervyn Stockwood two days ago. Donald may show you the letter as I wish for accuracy. I have no copy. But here is essentially what I said to him: Ni was never a hypocrite. No falseness must touch him once he is no longer able to defend his views. He was not a cold-blooded rationalist. He was no calculating machine. He was a great humanist whose religion lay in loving his fellow-men and trying to serve them. He could kneel reverently in chapel, synagogue, Eastern mosque, Catholic cathedral on occasions when friends called him there for marriage or dedication or burial services. He knelt reverently in respect to a friend and a friend's faith, but he never pretended to be other than he was, a great humanist. Often, especially in these last few years, he talked of 'the mystery that lies at the heart of life', nothing more definite than that.

I have asked Donald and Mervyn to help me in their respective worlds to see that only true things are attributed to Ni.

25. Worlds Apart

So what was it all about? What were we striving for all those years? Did it really matter? Or has it all now passed into the limbo of history, leaving hardly a trace behind? The answer has still to be given, nor will it be finally given in the near future for the stakes are too high and the protagonists show little sign of any will to compromise. I am leaving aside for the moment the supreme issue of how the world will deal with nuclear power. That dwarfs all else, but each country has its own internal problems to solve. Ours is whether peaceful, constitutional, parliamentary government will be the main instrument carrying us forward to a more urbane, civilized society, or whether Parliament will deteriorate into a mere charade, outward forms remaining, but real power residing elsewhere.

Nye was never a lazy thinker. He knew what he wanted, but he never deceived himself into believing that the struggle to establish democratic participation in industry, with Parliament the final arbiter in settling social and economic priorities, was going to be won easily. He never underestimated the stubborn, cynical technique of the Tory Establishment in fighting every reform leading to better conditions for working people, and then, if forced to give ground, claiming as their own the very proposals they had done all in their power to thwart.

I am appalled by the cruelty, or if you prefer, the crass ignorance of those who talk about the 'good old days'. Good old days for whom? Most certainly not for the great majority of mankind. Nye's most violent outbursts, his 'vermin' speech, for instance, was triggered off by his early memories.

It was his own flesh and blood, his own friends and neighbours, the children who had been his playmates in his school years, who were humiliated, thrown on the scrap heap, subjected to the vicious Means Test. He identified completely with the victims of capitalist muddle and greed, but he had also imagination enough to understand those brought up to affluence and their assumption that they were intrinsically superior. That is why, though he hated the system, he did not hate individual human beings. He knew that they were fashioned by their environment, just as much as he was himself. It was this gift of empathy that explains his attitude to Winston Churchill. When asked if he disliked Churchill, his reply was:

> It was hard for even his political opponents – in the House of Commons at any rate – to *dislike* him. I say in the House of Commons because people who remember the vigour with which he set about organizing the armed forces to be able, if necessary, to smash the strikers in 1926, regarded him as a monster. In the House of Commons, however, in spite of the brutality with which he sometimes laid about him, it was impossible systematically to dislike him. His sulkiness and morose ill-temper were frequently almost forgivable, so childish were they, but nearly always his sulks would explode in a fit of rage, and after that he would forgive and forget with as much generosity as public life allows.

As Nye was the younger man, it was assumed that he would outlive Churchill. The above is a quotation from the memorial article he wrote about Churchill for the *Observer* while they were still both very much alive. Still more revealing is an article by Nye published in *Tribune* in February 1944. He prophesied that Churchill's personal ascendancy was a wasting asset, that victory would puff it into a brief blaze, that 'no doubt he and the Tories associated with him would try to use it to light their way to victory at the polls before it died down in diminishing smoulderings. But those who do not belong to his political and personal entourage would be foolish to imagine they can warm themselves at the fire for long.' Then he went on to say:

This is merely the immortal tragedy of all public life. The *hero's* need of the people outlasts *their* need of him. *They* obey the pressures of contemporary conditions whilst *he* strives to perpetuate the situation where he stood supreme. *He* is therefore overwhelmed by a nostalgia for past glory whereas *they* are pushed on by new needs, impelled by other hopes and led by other nascent heroes.

Nye was making, as was his custom, an objective, philo-

POLITICAL PRE-VIEW

sophical appraisement of the political situation. Later events proved just how right he was.

When I joined combat with Churchill on first entering Parliament in 1929, no doubt he regarded my blows as no more than the flick of a butterfly's wing. I was not a serious challenge to him, so he could treat me with old-world courtesy. With Nye it was different. During and after the Second World War Churchill heartily detested Nye, called him a Minister of Disease, a squalid nuisance, and much else of a similar kind. Of course Nye gave blow for blow, and no doubt those that hurt most were when Nye enjoyed himself by reducing the House of Commons to helpless laughter at Churchill's expense. Even some of Churchill's most fervent admirers were unable to keep a straight face when, during a debate on the conduct of the Italian Campaign, Nye accused the Allied High Command of approaching the Italian mainland like 'an old man approaching a young bride, fascinated, sluggish and apprehensive'.

There was not the same molten anger in Nye's disagreements with the wartime leader as there was in his disagreements with the right wing of the Labour Party. The reason for this was quite simply that he expected a Tory to behave like a Tory, but he did not lightly accept leading members of the Labour and trade union movement behaving like Tories. At the crucial moment in 1940 when Churchill became Prime Minister, we were both more than thankful. Recalling that time in the same *Observer* article, Nye wrote:

When the people of this country might have been depressed by the brute facts of Dunkirk, Churchill was persuading them to think about Queen Elizabeth and the defeat of the Armada. His contribution was to fling a Union Jack over five tanks and get people to behave as though they had become fifteen.

They were fighting the same enemy, but there the common ground between them ended. There are different ways of winning a war as well as of losing one. Military strategy is inescapably bound up with the kind of post-war world we hope to win through to. Nye, more than anyone else, was responsible for Churchill's political downfall in 1945. Churchill could have pulled Attlee and Bevin behind his chariot wheels. But the returning soldiers, who were as benevolent as Nye towards Churchill when they thought of his 1940 heroic, romantic summons to all of us to fight on the beaches and all that, were not prepared to be at the mercy of Churchill, leader of the Tory Party, when it came to rebuilding our lives after the war.

One revealing incident, the sort of thing that was of the very essence of Winston, occurred shortly after Nye's resignation from the Labour Government in 1951. He and I were sitting together in the Smoking Room of the House of Commons, having a quiet cup of tea. Winston came in, walked to the bar, ordered a whisky, then before leaving, went out of his way to pass the table where we were sitting. He did not look at Nye, nor address a single word to him. What he did do was say to me: 'I shee you are shtanding by your hushband.' 'Yes,' I said jokingly, 'someone must put a bit of backbone into him.' Quick as a flash came Winston's next remark: 'Do not undereshtimate your hushband.' With that he walked stolidly out of the room. It was his way of greeting a foe at the moment when his old adversary was down and out. Both men fought for what they believed in; but their memories of the past and their hopes for the future were irreconcilable. In the war years all the big battalions were on Churchill's side: it was a David and Goliath affair. But no matter the odds against him, Nye was certain that history was on his side. It was this that gave him his superb self-confidence.

26. Conclusion

It was Michael Foot, not Archie Lush, Nye's oldest and closest friend, who was my safety valve in the years immediately following Nye's death. Archie and I seldom met. We agreed that it was better for us not to do so, we could only increase the pain for one another. But we never entirely lost touch. Writing to him in the early months of 1963 I ask:

Would you say Ni had an unhappy life in the years you were most closely associated with him? Or did his vitality, his love of a fight, the feeling that the world was all before him, make up for unsatisfactory living conditions? Certainly the home from home that Ada and you gave him was one of the bright spots all those years. Later on, with the help of Ma and Dad, I was able to give him at least some of the sweets of life. And again, he was vividly responsive. Often I scolded him when he came home driving through the night from Wales or the North, as I felt he was overtaxing his strength. But nothing would stop him. He was just anxious to be back in his own home.

Like you, if my concern for all the values of my life died, I would not be able to support what remains to me of physical existence. Also, it would make a mockery of ALL our lives. There it is, Arch. For you, as well as for me, the real triumph would be to learn to be happy, preoccupied with pleasant or worthwhile things, not just keeping up appearances so that old enemies cannot see how raw the wounds remain. Also, in your case, it is not fair to Ada that you should not make a heroic effort. My guess is that once you finish at County Hall you will be more relaxed, gather your physical strength together and generally be much better placed. Your incorrigible curiosity will take you on all kinds of excursions, intellectual as well as physical. And what a countryside you have! Michael told me that it was you who gave him the phrase – 'Ni loved the brave things of Wales.'

Remember that included you as well as the mountains.

With love to you both,

J

While Archie and I were struggling to win back some kind of peace of mind and often not succeeding, Michael was giving his time and talent to assembling the material for a study of Nye's life. The only help I could give him was a chaotic jumble of letters, documents and recollections. On 17 October 1965, in reply to some of his questions, I wrote:

Dear Michael,

I have not got over the impulse to run away from the very mention of Ni's name. Strangers of all kinds come up to me to say kind, admiring things and I am at best abrupt with them instead of taking their remarks in the spirit they are offered. Afterwards I am displeased with myself for being so self-indulgent. Explanation? So far as I understand myself, it is unbearable pain, resentment and wrath when I recall much that Ni had to suffer. He had a great capacity for suffering, for self-torment, as well as for taking both intellectual and sensual delight in being alive. In my bitter moments, I have said to myself a thousand times – he did not die, he was murdered. That great frame and brilliant mind would have carried him through another ten years on top form, maybe longer, if the tensions imposed on him had not been more than any sensitive, responsive human being could possibly stand.

He was beset, misjudged, maligned, on every side. He was caught in an impasse from which there was no way out. For anyone with Ni's temperament, to have to work in double harness with Hugh Gaitskell was plain hell. They were not only poles apart in their political thinking. They were totally different kinds of animals. But refusal to do so would once more split the movement at a time when, rightly or wrongly, he deeply believed mankind was again and again within a hair's-breadth of nuclear war. He had sufficient confidence in his Party, and in himself, to believe it was urgently necessary to get the Tories out. As Foreign Secretary, with Gaitskell as PM, he would have had a monstrous burden to carry. But he was willing to face up to this.

Could he have behaved differently? Could he have been more tactful? Instead of resigning in 1951, for instance, should he have bowed his head and waited his time? There can be no absolute answer to that kind of conundrum but Ni gave the answer in part when he repeated on different, difficult occasions: 'In public life, those who would change things must shout to be heard.' You have heard him often on that theme. Being Ni, with his temperament, gifts and circumstances, he could do no other. He did not know he was mortally ill. He guessed it sometimes. He questioned and cross-questioned his doctors, John Buchan and me, but we managed to deceive him and I am proud of that and take what comfort I can from it. He was spared at least the final sorrow of knowing that he would never complete his job, that he was beaten by illness, that I would somehow have to go on without him.

He was optimistic, he enjoyed the praise and love that encircled him, he was ready to start all over again.

Of all that was said or written about Nye in the following years the tribute Israel Sieff paid to his friend was the most sensitively discerning. In his *Memoirs*, published in 1970, ten years after Nye's death, he wrote:

I look back with gratitude on my friendship with Aneurin Bevan. It seems hardly credible to me that he died nearly ten years ago – his presence still abounds in my everyday life. Unlike Churchill, Bevan did not have the long-delayed chance to become a great man. He died before his time. A universal tragedy: had he lived he could have done much for his country; and, he could have realized the potential in himself. I am prejudiced: he was my friend. For many years I lived in a house I bought from him. In some respects I found myself more sympathetic to the beatings of his heart and mind than to any other man's. Simon's [Simon Marks] mind I found complementary: Nye's supplementary. I owe him a great deal.

I did not believe in Nye's politics, or at any rate, in those nostrums of the hustings, that uneasy electoral combination of prospectuses and shibboleths to which he nominally subscribed. I am not sure how much he believed in them himself. He was profoundly committed in his attitude to human beings and society, he was empirical about arrangements and institutions. This, I think, would have shown if he had become Prime Minister. What a voice and vision would then have dominated the life of Britain! How many dark places would have been illuminated, how many doubts and dangers would have been dispelled. Our problems would not have been waved away by a magician's wand overnight; but the attempt to solve them would have been rendered meaningful and more exciting. And I believe they would have been solved. Wherever our proper, realistic level in the modern world lies, Nye would have seen it, and could have led us there. We would have gone there eyes open, tail up, ready to make it not a retreat but a triumph. Men must be led by men who above all can speak to them. They are the prophets, whose reason for being is to point a way ahead and make man able and willing to tread it. What makes an Isaiah is an unconquerable faith that good is not only morally better than evil, but that it is socially stronger too, the ability to get ordinary men to think the same and act accordingly. The first task of political leadership is to get men to lift up their hearts. Churchill did it in 1940. Weizmann did it time and time again, Nye would have done it for Britain today.

As well as admiring Nye's powers, my heart warmed to his nature. Like all great men he was a simple man, and like them fundamentally a philosopher and a poet. (His wife, Jennie, also my friend of many years' standing, I have always thought of as dedicated to political action as her mode of being.) One day Nye and I were talking together in his house after lunch and I mentioned Spinoza. 'Why do you think so highly of Spinoza?' Nye asked. 'Because he so perfectly expresses the connection between freedom and morality; because he explains God, eternity, and the life here and now in a way that makes sense to me: man's "highest good" is "knowledge of his union with Nature" in the "intellectual love of God" by which, in and through the practising of virtue, he may enter into "blessedness", enjoying it continuously, that state of mind being the part of eternal life which is knowable here, what else there is, if any, remaining unknown.'

Nye sat in silence for a moment or two looking not so much as a man pondering what he has heard as a man pondering what he will do. Then he left the room and came back with a sheaf of papers. 'Did you know I wrote poetry?' he asked. 'No,' I said, 'I certainly did not.' I knew he read it: he could recite Shakespeare, Keats, Shelley and Wordsworth endlessly. 'Well, I do,' he said, 'and I want to read you some.' So, rather shyly, especially for a man who was so uninhibited, and so used to hearing the sound of his own voice, he began to read. He read several poems to me. 'So you see, Isreal, I too know something about philosophy,' he said, when he had finished, as though something I had said had given him the impression that I thought philosophy was above or below him, or at any rate alien to his way of life. 'Why don't you publish those poems?' I asked. 'Oh, I couldn't,' he said. 'I'm too shy. What would my friends say? There's hardly anybody I'd dare read the stuff to.' And he collected his papers and left the room, taking his poems back to where he had got them from. Neither he nor I mentioned them again, nor to this day do I know any more about them.

Voluble and irrepressible as he was, Nye, like many other men who resemble him, had the gift of silent companionship. Sometimes, after we had been pottering in the garden together, or strolling around my grounds or the fields around his house, we would sit down in his or my sitting-room. Each of us would pick up a book, or a magazine, or a newspaper, and we would read. If one of us came on something that impressed him, he would read it out to the other. Then we would resume our silence. Sometimes we would read to each other in this way for an hour or two. He was not much good at games, but he and I loved playing bowls together. 'If there's one thing I have learned to master,' he said, stooping to deliver a wood shining in the late summer sun, 'it is *bias*. But having mastered it I would not want to live without it.' We both loved good simple food and claret, and talk aimed not at complicating but at simplifying life.

Nye belongs in that gallery of the dwelling-place of my mind in which I keep my private collection of great men, those I think great whether I knew them or not, and whenever or wherever they lived. Nye did not believe that the everyday life that surrounded him was the best that could be. On the contrary, he believed it fell far short of what was possible, that it ought to be better, and that it could be made so – here, now, in our lifetime, this very day. He believed that, and he fought for his belief to the end. His greatness was in his humanity, his essential humility, his sense of the all-human predicament, and his passionate fight to lift his fellow-men out of it. The power of his vision was his conviction that it was simply bound to come to pass.

That same year I wrote in my diary:

Glad to have Archie in London with me for a week but wounded when he told me that Tredegar people, hungry for knowledge about Ni, have thought that because I have not given interviews, written articles, a book, or had a book ghosted for me, there was something wrong between us.

Slowly, with difficulty, I found myself forced to the conclusion that it was wrong of me to be so reserved, so unready to talk about him to friends who had loved him, and that it was irresponsible of me to leave future students of the history of those years at the mercy of what was written about him in journals owned and controlled by his political opponents. He insisted all his life that his private world remain private. If we had allowed our home to be invaded and vulgarized, if we had paraded together on public platforms, I don't think we could have survived. Or rather, if we had been capable of that kind of behaviour, we would have been different kinds of people. But, in the end I have to face the fact that privacy is a luxury not allowed to people in public life in the kind of world we now live in. If the truth about Nye is not told, there will be those with little or no knowledge of the real man who will weave every kind of fiction around him, not all of it, of course, unfriendly.

As Michael Foot has chronicled Nye's public life with meticulous care and a wealth of detail, it would have been a nonsense for me to do less well what Michael has done superbly well. So there is much I short-circuit in discussing public events. But there was still much to tell about the private Nye, who was as great a delight to his family and friends as he was a scourge to those he believed were responsible for inflicting unnecessary poverty on their fellow men and for driving a demented world to the brink of nuclear war. It has taken me a long time to make up my mind to write as candidly as I have done. I hope I have made the right decision.

Index

Perspectives on the Left in Penguins

ARGUMENTS FOR SOCIALISM
Tony Benn
Edited by Chris Mullin

Tony Benn, the most controversial figure in British politics, outlines a strong democratic-socialist approach to the most crucial issues in our political life over the next decade.

'Benn's faith in the capacity of ordinary people to govern themselves emerges here as the most attractive feature of the politics of a man so often caricatured by the popular press as the Labour Party's major threat to democracy and freedom' – *Literary Review*

'Of importance not only to the Labour movement but also to the country as a whole' – *Tribune*

POLITICS IS FOR PEOPLE
Shirley Williams

Politicians everywhere must change their thinking if we are to move forward the achievements of the post-war years.

Shirley Williams represents a major influence on political thinking on the Left. In this book she throws the debate open, blueprinting for us what she sees as acceptable and workable solutions for the future of our country. Industrialism is at crisis point and we must be ready to face the challenge.

Stimulating, caring, honest and backed up by carefully marshalled facts, her book bears out her deeply held conviction – politics is, and *must be*, for people.

Penguins on Politics

THE LEFT IN BRITAIN 1956 – 1968
David Widgery

In Hungary in 1956 Stalin's tanks blew apart the Left in the rest of the world. Old complacences were shattered, while new parties, new ideas and events brought a new militancy. The ferment continued for a decade and burst out in 1968 in Paris and across much of the world.

This book tells the story of those years in Britain, The New Left, CND, student politics, civil rights and a transformed trade union movement can all be seen springing up from that initial catastrophic break-up. David Widgery has written a lucid and exciting narrative of a time when the Left seemed invincible on the streets and impotent everywhere else. Each of his chapters is extensively illustrated by documents, pamphlets and articles showing how working-class movements combined with middle-class writers to bring about a completely changed understanding of what it now means to be 'on the Left'.

THE MEANING OF CONSERVATISM
Roger Scruton

Roger Scruton challenges those who would regard themselves as conservatives, and their opponents. Locating the system of beliefs that make up the conservative outlook, he argues that these have little in common with the creed of liberalism and are only tenuously related to the doctrine of 'market economy'. The evils of socialism, he maintains, lie precisely where its supporters find its strengths, and he goes on to reject the political vision that has made the conservative position seem outmoded and irrational.

His book presents a new and striking challenge to Marxism, pointing out that the Marxist conceptions can be used to formulate conclusions diametrically opposed to socialist dogmas, and offers new perspectives on the prevailing liberal theories of law, citizenship and the state.

MEMORIES OF A CATHOLIC GIRLHOOD
Mary McCarthy

'There is an element of *tour de force* in this brilliant book' – *Observer*
Blending memories and family myths, Mary McCarthy takes us back
to the twenties, when she was orphaned into a world of relations as
colourful, potent and mysterious as the Catholic religion. From her black
veiled Jewish grandmother to her wicked Uncle Myers who beat her for
the good of her soul, here are the people who inspired her devastating
sense of the sublime and ridiculous, and her witty, novelist's
imagination.

ABOUT TIME
Penelope Mortimer
Winner of the Whitbread Award

Her ironic and delightful autobiography of girlhood between the wars.
After leaving her fifth school, Penelope Mortimer was sent to train as a
secretary, but soon moved on, via London University and Bloomsbury,
to marriage and the birth of her first daugher in Hitler's Vienna. On the
outbreak of war, she celebrated her twenty-first birthday in the Café de
Paris – 'we drank champagne to the present and future, but not to the
past that I have tried to celebrate here.'
'It goes down not so much like a madeleine as like a lemon water-ice on a
hot day, sharp and gritty as well as smooth and sweet . . . leaving a taste
for more' – *Listener*

Published in Pelicans

THE HIDDEN PERSUADERS
Vance Packard

In a new epilogue to his classic study of the American advertising machine, Vance Packard reveals that, far from losing ground as the innocent Fifties grew into the sophisticated Seventies, its power has grown accordingly: an $8 billion business has turned into a $40 billion industry. Their technologists now include brain specialists, neurophysiologists, hypnotechnicians, voice-pitch analysts. Their victims are the new stereotypes; the liberated woman, the independent man, the militant mother, the chic suburbanite, the swinging New Waver.

Whether or not we fall into such categories, we are all to some extent persuadable – Vance Packard definitively and entertainingly explains why and how.

WHO'S WATCHING YOU?
BRITAIN'S SECURITY SERVICES AND THE OFFICIAL SECRETS ACT
Crispin Aubrey

The security services, invisible, unaccountable, surrounded by a mystique of dark glasses and turned-up collars, have grown steadily in size; so too has their expenditure on the most sophisticated techniques of mass surveillance.

Their net falls on trade unionists, students, anti-nuclear protesters, Welsh Nationalists, investigative journalists and a host of possible 'subversives'; Crispin Aubrey stumbled into this web one dark and rainy night in 1977, was arrested by the Special Branch and charged under the Official Secrets Act. His subsequent trial, the 'ABC trial', attained a legal significance and had political repercussions far beyond the facts of the case.

CLEMENTINE CHURCHILL
Mary Soames

Lady Soames describes her book as 'a labour of love – but I trust not of blind love', others have acclaimed it as one of the outstanding biographies of the decade:

'Perceptive and affectionate, shrewd and tender . . . a joy to read' – Elizabeth Longford
'Lady Soames has carried out the extremely delicate and difficult task of writing the real story of her mother. I found it particularly moving because I had a very deep affection for her father and mother' – Harold Macmillan
'A triumph . . . her subject, unknown yet well-known, is enthralling' – Eric James in *The Times*

BLOOMSBURY: A HOUSE OF LIONS
Leon Edel

Pulitzer prize-winner and world renowned for his biography of Henry James, Leon Edel has brought his enormous talents to bear in this elegant, vivid and beautifully written introduction to such figures as Virginia Woolf, Maynard Keynes, Duncan Grant, Roger Fry and Vanessa Bell.

'[I am] overwhelmed by the beauty of this book . . . an artist of the first rank dealing with artists of the first rank' – Nigel Nicolson